THE MINISTERS' WAR

THE MINISTERS' WAR

JOHN W. MEARS,
THE ONEIDA COMMUNITY,
AND THE CRUSADE
FOR PUBLIC MORALITY

MICHAEL DOYLE

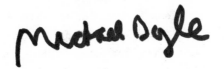

Syracuse University Press

For a listing of books published and distributed by Syracuse University Press,
visit www.SyracuseUniversityPress.syr.edu.

ISBN: 978-0-8156-3576-5 (hardcover)   978-0-8156-1098-4 (paperback)
978-0-8156-5441-4 (e-book)

Library of Congress Cataloging-in-Publication Data
Names: Doyle, Michael, 1956– author.
Title: The ministers' war : John W. Mears, the Oneida Community, and the
    crusade for public morality / Michael Doyle.
Description: 1st [edition]. | Syracuse, NY : Syracuse University Press, 2018. |
    Includes bibliographical references and index.
Identifiers: LCCN 2017056043 (print) | LCCN 2018001312 (ebook) |
    ISBN 9780815654414 (e-book) | ISBN 9780815635765 (hardcover : alk. paper) |
    ISBN 9780815610984 (pbk. : alk. paper)
Subjects: LCSH: Mears, John W. (John William), 1825–1881. | Presbyterian
    Church—New York (State)—Clergy—Biography. | Oneida Community. |
    Collective settlements—New York (State)—History—19th century.
Classification: LCC BX9225.M3973 (ebook) | LCC BX9225.M3973 D69 2018
    (print) | DDC 974.7/64041—dc23
LC record available at https://lccn.loc.gov/2017056043

Manufactured in the United States of America

To my children—Matthew, Brendan, and Margaret

CONTENTS

ILLUSTRATIONS

ACKNOWLEDGMENTS

I MUST START WITH MY DAD, William Curtis Doyle. Now deceased, he was an Oneida County native. But for him, I would have remained characteristically clueless. We once were on an Upstate New York escapade related to my first book, *The Forestport Breaks*, when he suggested that we take a detour to see the Mansion House. That, he told me, was the Oneida Community—a place, he added, that was infamous for its peculiar social practices. His voice hinted at mystery and fascination.

The seed was planted.

Once I moved from dalliance to dedicated research, gracious librarians and archivists helped me pick up the trail. Hamilton College archivist Katherine Collett cheerfully answered every question and steered me toward crucial documents. The staff at the Syracuse University Libraries Department of Special Collections, keepers of the Oneida Community Collection, provided invaluable assistance. They also deserve kudos for making many documents available online, which made research much easier. The Oneida Community Mansion House remains a living reminder of the place's history, and the nonprofit organization that sustains it deserves both thanks and tangible support.

The partners who maintain the HathiTrust Digital Library have done everyone a great service, turning every connected computer into a world-class library. When it comes to New York–related publications, nothing beats Tom Tryniski's remarkable website, Old Fulton NY Post Cards. The Utica College, Syracuse University, Union College, Hamilton College, Cornell University, and University of Virginia libraries all yielded useful information, and the Library of Congress is a national treasure to which I often returned. The Presbyterian Historical Society provided unique materials, as did the Oneida County Courthouse and the Oneida County Historical Society.

This work builds on the research done by others. Of particular note, Constance Noyes Robertson's *Oneida Community: The Breakup, 1876–1881* included invaluable materials not readily found elsewhere, and there's a treasure trove in the documents compiled by George Wallingford Noyes and edited by Lawrence Foster in *Free Love in Utopia: John Humphrey Noyes and the Origin of the Oneida Community*. I also want to commend the scholarly work of Ellen Wayland-Smith, who kindly agreed to take a look at my manuscript, as well as the work done by Robert S. Fogarty, Spencer Klaw, Mark J. Dunkelman, Nancy F. Cott, Donna Dennis, Helen Lefkowitz Horowitz, and Chris Jennings. Not least, I tip my hat to the innumerable nineteenth-century journalists whose first drafts of history laid a foundation upon which I could build.

Several anonymous reviewers scrutinized early drafts of the manuscript and provided candid critiques that were both sharp-eyed and sympathetic enough to sustain hope. Whoever these reviewers are, I owe them a lot.

Many people at Syracuse University Press have helped shepherd this project along. Acquisitions editor Alison M. Shay has been stalwart throughout, and a true partner. Mona Hamlin, Suzanne Guiod, and Alice Randel Pfeiffer all offered early guidance and support, and copyeditor Jessica LeTourneur Bax polished and repaired the manuscript.

My wife, Beth, has steadied me, from before the start to beyond the finish.

THE MINISTERS' WAR

PROLOGUE

JOHN W. MEARS laid into every nineteenth-century filth and frailty.

The all-purpose crusader condemned drinkers, pornographers, and free lovers. He denounced Mormons, Sabbath breakers, and Roman Catholics. He shushed college rowdies and derided Philadelphia's clamorous streetcars. He ridiculed the evolutionary claims of Charles Darwin and Thomas Huxley. He lashed corporations, infidels, and foreigners. He warned against operas and called for cleaning Pennsylvania's polluted rivers—not a metaphor, but the actual Schuylkill.

His very title flew as a banner, stiffening the brigades before battle: Reverend John W. Mears, D. D., the Albert Barnes Professor of Intellectual and Moral Philosophy at Hamilton College. No sin escaped his whip, but two, in particular, drove him on. One was the Oneida Community. The other was alcohol.

"It has become," Mears wrote, "THE curse of our time, the demon to be cast out of modern society."[1]

Mears sermonized and he wrote and he ran against liquor, the intoxicant that sapped the will and tainted the soul. Nor was he mere cheerleader or scribe, a pennant waver—Mears entered the lists. Mears ran for Congress in New York as Oneida County's Prohibition Party candidate in 1878. Utica's groggeries won that round, but the loss only whet his appetite. Mears returned as the Prohibition candidate for New York governor the next year. He did not intend to stop there. He kept pressing—he could never stop.

"We must enter upon a lifelong course of self-denial," Mears wrote. "Do not jeopardize the souls for whom Christ died for the sake of a little tickling of the palate or glow of the nerves."[2]

Mears, like others of his time, preached the necessity of constant vigilance over both self and society. Everywhere, throughout Mears's career prime in the 1870s, hazards arose. Immigrants diluted the American character. Roman Catholics unsettled the Protestant faithful. Scientific inquisition challenged biblical certainty. Wheeler-dealers corrupted the body politic. Birth control freed sexual behavior from its God-given consequence. Labor unions revolted against business owners. Liquor rotted the American work ethic and weakened family bonds. Sordid literature incited lust. Rampant speculation crashed the market. Mormons threatened monogamous marriage. All in all, radical ideas disrupted good order.

"Social theories the most startling [are] striking at the prevailing opinions of civilized society," Cephus Brainerd of New York's Young Men's Christian Association warned in 1872.[3]

Alarms sounded from every corner. Thomas Nast's cartoons in *Harper's Weekly* during the 1870s, historian Benjamin Justice observed, seemed "an exercise in paranoia [where] conspiracies, violence and threats to the American way of life" abounded.[4] Nast's popularity showed that he reflected public sentiment. The dark fear of conspiracies that helped the anti-Masonry movement grow from its New York State roots through the 1830s still pulsed through the populace in the 1870s.

However, the most pressing threat to man was himself. The nineteenth-century imagery was consistently vivid; unregulated passions would overwhelm a man. Without constant self-control, Sylvester Graham warned in 1838, "our systems will continue to be living volcanoes of bad feelings and bad passions, which however correct our abstract principles of morality may be, will continually break out in immoral actions."[5] The passions were hydraulic, powerful enough to turn pistons. Or, the passions were an animal, safe only when caged. As Illinois congressman Shelby M. Cullom put it, while championing an anti-polygamy bill in 1870, "the lustful and unbridled passions of men, devised by Satan himself to destroy purity and authorize whoredom" had erupted in the Mormon marriage system.[6]

"Repress the premature development of the passions," author W. S. Chipley warned fathers, teachers, and young men in 1861.[7]

Left unbridled, passions and sundry other threats pooled up into dank pockets of disease. Again, the rhetorical imagery was consistent. Chinese immigrants, a California congressman warned in 1875, represented a "deadly blight."[8] Another congressman, urging in 1873 the passage of anti-obscenity legislation, railed against "pestilential literature," while anti-vice majordomo Anthony Comstock called obscene materials the "deadly poison, cast into the fountain of moral purity."[9] Comstock's fellow anti-smut lobbyist, the Philadelphia-based Joseph Leeds, diagnosed in 1875 the "germs of licentiousness."[10] Anti-Mormon writer Alfred Trumble warned in 1882 that "the shameful, deep, devouring, sloughing spot of corruption . . . from its stronghold in Utah is eating its way beyond the borders into the neighboring communities."[11] Even masturbation was, an author warned in 1860, a "polluting stream [that] flows through all grades of society."[12] The characterizations of moral threat as infection were more than just a fervid rhetorical device; they were, as historian Catherine Lee said of the 1870s fear of syphilis-ridden Chinese prostitutes, associated "with a newly developing germ theory that explained disease and health."[13]

Against these vividly realized dangers of infection, disease, and corruption, crusaders inevitably arose. The Woman's Christian Temperance Union formed in 1874, following organization of the Prohibition Party in 1869. The New York Society for the Suppression of Vice formed in 1873, and Congress passed the Act for the Suppression of Trade in, and Circulation of, Obscene Literature and Articles of Immoral Use—more commonly known as the Comstock Act—that same year. Responding to the perceived influx of Chinese prostitutes and polygamous wives, in 1875 Congress passed the country's first restrictive immigration statute. It was a bill, its chief author explained, to "place a dividing line between vice and virtue," and Rep. Howard Page of California was explicit about the sexual threat, with his claim that 90 percent of Chinese women in the United States were prostitutes.[14] The American Committee for the Prevention of Legalizing

Prostitution convened in 1877. In 1879 the Supreme Court upheld the Mormon-targeting Morrill Act for the Suppression of Polygamy.

Of all passions, the most virulent was sexual passion. It was the root passion, and it was expressed most unapologetically in the Oneida Community, the New York State–based experiment in Bible-based Communism that Mears called "one of the most revolting and disgraceful evils of our state."[15]

The Oneida Community, established west of Utica by John Humphrey Noyes and about thirty pioneering followers in 1848, was a radical social experiment conceived on the notion that Jesus Christ's Second Coming had already occurred. Its members, who numbered two hundred-plus adults by the 1870s, followed what they saw as the lead of the primitive Christian church. They held everything and everyone in common. They lived together under one roof. They ate, worked, and shared their carnal selves together. Though it was not precisely a free-love community, as its detractors portrayed it, the Oneida Community, through its system of "complex marriage," followed looser sexual practices than did traditional society. Eschewing monogamy, men and women were polyamorous, albeit in a regulated fashion. Exclusive relationships were actively discouraged. Through the practice of "male continence," Oneida Community members were meant to enjoy sexual intercourse as an act of connectedness. Through the principle of "ascending fellowship," Noyes taught that the young would benefit spiritually through sexual association with their elders.

"He argued from the Bible that in the kingdom of Heaven there is no marriage, since marriage is like slavery; a form of selfish personal ownership," anthropologist Anita Newcomb McGee summed up in 1891. "And to overcome this selfishness among Perfectionists, Noyes devised an extraordinary system of regulated promiscuity, beginning at earliest puberty, and by a method of his own invention, he separated the amative from the propagative functions."[16]

Naturally, the Oneida Community had its detractors. Oneida, one Union College crusader said in the early 1870s, was a foul, pestilential plague spot that required cleansing and disinfection. That was hardly the worst—even as it won the respect of its neighbors and business partners, the Oneida Community always inspired critical rhetoric.

Mears, then, was shadowing others when he took up his various causes. He was not unique in his exhortations. Rather, he embodied the forces of nineteenth-century morality at work. His career is illustrative, a case study in zeal. While much has been written of John Humphrey Noyes and the Oneida Community, Mears in particular and other opponents in general have received scant attention. They deserve more, for they are a lively lot, from high-minded clergymen and philosophy professors to scandal-seeking journalists and downright fabulists. Fascinating in their own right, they provide, as well, a distinctive view of Noyes and Oneida, conveyed often through the sermons, essays, and newspaper accounts of their time.

Mears merits special consideration, both because he led the final campaign against the Oneida Community and because he spread himself so broadly across the landscape of morality. His congressional and gubernatorial aspirations revealed the role of temperance in nineteenth-century political campaigns. His collection of documents conveyed the fascination and dread incited by obscene mailings, and his anti-Mormon discourse summed up the feelings of many. His position as a Hamilton College professor helped mold the school during its formative years. He fortified the library, strengthened the curriculum, and straightened the school's Presbyterian spine. Through his constant campaigns, he expanded the school's reputation as well as his own. He gained public recognition not just for himself, but for the men's college that was still finding its way.

Moreover, Mears's position at Hamilton College gave him a fortress from which he could lob charges and accumulate grievances against the Oneida Community, located only thirteen miles away. Some of New York State's most prominent church leaders were close by in Syracuse, adding organizational support and a chorus of influential voices, while the proximity to Oneida provided constant incentive. It was the dragon he had been training to slay. The Oneida Community was, Mears said, a "den of shameful immoralities." It was a place of "corrupt concubinage," poisoned by "moral defilement" and "vile passion." It was, he said, an "Epicurean sty."

One blow after another, Mears built his case against the Oneida Community. He wrote, lectured, lobbied, and rallied. Mears gathered forces, up until his signature achievement, when in 1879 he helped summon the New York State clergy for a Syracuse convention that would, once and for all, cleanse the Oneida Community.

Mears was by no means Oneida's sole opponent, but he was especially persistent, articulate, and, in a way, fortunate, when it came to his defining crusade. When the smoke cleared, many thought Mears had won. After John Humphrey Noyes abruptly left Oneida in June 1879, fearing persecution, and then two months later when the Oneida Community abandoned its signature complex marriage scheme, it was Mears proclaimed as the prevailing party. In the moment, it was true. The law might not, in fact, have been chasing Noyes, but Mears helped convince him it was. Attorney Frank D. Budlong conveyed the conventional acclaim when he wrote to Mears that Oneida's surrender showed "God and morality shall finally triumph, and that the way to uproot an evil is to stir up a moral sentiment so strong against it that it cannot exist."[17]

So, yes, Mears triumphed when the Oneida Community abandoned complex marriage, shed its sinful raiment, and donned modest garb. People paired off into couples. The commune became a corporation. Mears was heralded for it and was prompted to seek his next campaign.

"I am now entering upon a new decade in my life," Mears wrote his mother, about the time of his 1879 Oneida triumph. "I wonder what the Lord has in store for me for the next 10 years."[18]

In a hilltop cemetery in Clinton, New York, his squared headstone provides the answer: John W. Mears died in 1881 at the age of fifty-six.

Mears's accomplishments quickly slipped into shade. Nothing lasted. His movements dissipated. College students remain rowdy. Mormonism prospers. Prohibition was repealed. The material world is more polluted than ever. And as to Mears's signature fight—combatting the Oneida Community—it's Noyes, the bête noire, whose reputation prevails. The established view was expressed by early Noyes biographer Robert Allerton Parker, whose *A Yankee Saint: John Humphrey Noyes and the Oneida Community* (1935) cast Mears as a zealot ablaze with "fury" who did not reason but rather "trumpeted" and "insisted" and "shouted" and "seemed incapable of believing" anything but the worst about Noyes.[19]

So why spend time with him? Mears does not appear, by the brief and conventional rendering that is his customary historical fate, to be particularly inviting company. He seems, in fact, to have been a scold and a priggish and long-winded lecturer. However, there was one particular observation from an Oneida Community account several days after the 1879 Syracuse convention of his fellow morality promoters:

"Professor Mears," the Oneida periodical reported, "was dodging about with a black patch over one eye, presenting a very comical appearance."[20]

I have since examined the contemporary portraitures. None show Mears with a patch. His obituary does not mention one, nor do the Hamilton student periodicals. Neither his correspondence nor other newspaper accounts provide confirmation. Yet there Mears was, according to the *O. C. Journal*, wearing a black patch at the 1879 Syracuse convention, the peak of his public life. The singular image fixated me:

John W. Mears: The one-eyed reverend who fought free love.

His infirmity surely spoke volumes. Only, it was in code, the message conveyed through metaphor. Could its meaning be found in the fact that Mears saw sin everywhere? He saw it in rowdyism, in whiskey, and he saw it climactically—or, perhaps better said, anti-climactically—at the Oneida Community. Eventually, the sight of it blinded him. The virtuous man could not turn away from the evil that seared his sight. As Nietzsche said, "for when you gaze long into the abyss, the abyss also gazes into you." Mears might have appreciated that, German philosophy being one of his fascinations.

Noyes himself, strangely enough, knew the danger of gazing too long. He might have been thinking of Mears, or his reverential ilk, when he warned that "insanity generally comes from too long gazing at some one subject that is absorbing enough to hold and compel thought til the brain gets sore."[21] So maybe Mears paid a price for obsessively seeing the devil's work and gazing too fixedly at a subject that was, as Noyes warned, "hot with interest."

Or maybe Mears was always half-blind. He was just born that way, or he was rendered in some ghastly, early accident so he could never see the world in its entirety. He was single-minded in his fight against sin because he was single-eyed in how he saw life. One permanently closed eye rendered the world two-dimensional instead of three. The disability perhaps explained him. Maybe Mears, bluntly put, was crippled, and could not see Oneida's other dimensions.

"The fruition of Professor Mears' theology was blindness to everything that was good in a system that had been productive of nothing but good," Oneida Community member Allan Estlake wrote.[22]

Certainly, Mears wouldn't be the only lame one entangled with Oneida. A Union College professor who preceded him as an anti-Oneida crusader was profoundly deaf: a castigator, who could not hear. Noyes himself often spoke in little more than a whisper: a preacher, who could not speak. Then there was Mears: the moralist who could not fully see. Perhaps these were all heavenly admonishments, divine twists on an obsession.

There is no written evidence of such a lasting injury, which surely there would have to be. So maybe Mears had but a mote in his eye, a passing inconvenience that was patched over. Of all the possibilities, that seems most likely.

Or, of course, the Oneida Community account could simply be wrong, as so many other newspaper reports have been. Both Noyes and Mears knew that; it was one truth they shared. Mears and Noyes both loathed the press, though both used it for their own purposes. Noyes said it made his "spiritual eyes ache to look over the popular newspapers. With their murders and their hangings and shipwrecks and car-smashings and man-roastings, they may be said to be all the time in the white heat of hell fire."[23] Mears, seeing eye to eye with Noyes on this one point, said it was "a matter of profound regret that this ubiquitous agency is so generally unscrupulous as to the character of the news which it reports, that it so often panders to depraved tastes."[24] Even the Oneida Community's own reporters, Noyes said, were "always anxious for news that is sharp and racy and will produce a sensation."[25] Errors, too, come with the turf. It's like Mears said of the press coverage of the 1879 Syracuse conference; it was, he said, "garbled, incorrect, injurious and absurd."[26]

Whatever the meaning, John Mears was reported at least once to have worn a black patch. True or not, the image captivated me. The questions gripped me: What did Mears see that drove him, and to what was he blind? Who, exactly, was he?

• • •

John Mears, it turns out, was a Yale Divinity School graduate, just like John Humphrey Noyes. He was rigorously trained; like Noyes, he graduated from college at nineteen. He was a diligent translator. He loved the dense cogitations of Immanuel Kant. Mears was a leader, such as of organizations like the New York State Teachers Association. His peers esteemed him. He also knew failure firsthand. He struggled at his first church. An orphanage he helped found following the Civil War closed amid scandal.

And, like Noyes, he could write, often and well. In 1867, he completed a 477-page book about the Reformation in the Netherlands. He wrote a 475-page book about Jews. He wrote a 147-page encomium to the slain Protestants of France, in which Mears, this agitator against a religious commune, observed without a smidgeon of self-consciousness that history can judge zealots harshly. "The very flower of mankind," Mears wrote, "while their persecutors have blotted their names with ignominy."[27]

Mears erupted with words, about everything and anything at all. In 1879, amid his culminating Oneida battle, Mears finished a 350-page book about fourteenth-century Bohemia. When he first started in on the Oneida Community, in 1873, Mears had finished a 313-page book about Madagascar. Of all strange territories, Mears chose that island to explore. Though, perhaps, his interest was more than scholarly. Like Oneida, Madagascar was a morally foreign and (perceived) dangerous place; and, it seems, all the more fascinating for it.

"Polygamy was universally practiced," Mears wrote, "and the morals of the people were of the worst description."[28]

Something in Madagascar drew John Mears. He had to explore the place, far from his own home. Some of this story, he might have simply surmised. His sourcing is vague. We are, apparently, simply meant to trust him. He probably got some things wrong; he may even have missed the point altogether. Still, credit him for trying. Mistakes and all, Mears made his own path.

The past is like that for me. It is my Madagascar, the place that wants mapping. I must go there, after Mears. I must see where his eye went.

1   SOUNDING THE ALARM

SAINT VALENTINE'S DAY 1879 lit passions beneath a wintry chill.

The morning temperature barely cracked fourteen degrees above zero in Syracuse, New York, a city of some fifty-four thousand residents. It was bundling weather, an incitement to warm. Newspapers circulating along the Erie Canal recommended frostbite remedies that involved gunpowder and lard. Several days earlier, a drunkard fell asleep on nearby railroad tracks, addled beyond recognition. He was an object lesson for members of the sixteen anti-alcohol organizations quartered in Syracuse, from the Sons of Temperance to the Father Matthew Total Abstinence Benevolent Association: the half-frozen man who couldn't recall his own name embodied intemperance, appetite unchecked.

Below the surface, heat gathered. Even Saint Valentine's Day risked its incontinent release. The holiday dedicated to love had been uncelebrated in the United States until the 1840s, when, the *Philadelphia Public Ledger* reported in 1845, "the fashion of half-serious, half-comic love-making, and humbug amorous declarations made on paper through the Post" took root in cities.[1] In the several decades since, romantic declarations had become a mass-produced commodity, divided between the elevated and the earthy. Courtly sentiments were conveyed through, as the *Tri-States Union* in New York's Port Jervis put it on February 14, 1879, "decorated lace paper, fine bits of poetry and other tokens." But these innocent decorations also had a shadow, conveyed in ribald verse and saucy illustrations. Some satirical valentines of the era showed men looking up women's skirts, or firemen manhandling their provocatively charged hoses.[2] Love, it seemed, had two sides—an ethereal heart and a carnal bottom.

Romantic expressions, like the underlying passions themselves, consequently required restraint. On February 13, 1879, the *Utica Morning Herald* urged everyone to "have all the fun out of the old custom that you can, but be decent about it." On the same day, the *Brockport Republic* likewise admonished readers that "as St. Valentine was a good man, the valentines should be good." This meant euphemism and sentiment, the abstracting of sex into romance. Otherwise, given too much of an outlet, passions might erupt, stronger than any lace could hold. The signs were everywhere. In Watertown, seventy miles north of Syracuse, an extra postal clerk had been hired in anticipation of heavy Saint Valentine's Day mail volumes. On Friday, February 14, some five thousand Saint Valentine's Day cards swamped the Utica Post Office.

Early that afternoon, John W. Mears walked uphill toward Syracuse University's Hall of Languages, located about a mile from the city's downtown. The fifty-three-year-old Hamilton College professor admired solidity, physical and metaphysical assertions made to last, and he could be reassured by the Hall of Languages that commanded an otherwise undeveloped fifty-acre campus site. Though only opened six years before, the three-and-a-half-story limestone edifice conveyed the heft of an ancient castle. One of its two towers held a six-hundred-pound iron bell for ringing out in celebration or in warning.

Mears was a bell ringer in his own way, a man who summoned others to action. Endowed with unflagging energy that had powered him from obscure Presbyterian pulpits to his current post as Hamilton's Albert Barnes Professor of Moral and Intellectual Philosophy, Mears existed in a constant state of alarm.

"He aimed at righteousness rather than popularity," a eulogist said, calling Mears one who "most fully possessed the courage of his convictions, and who did not hesitate to grapple manfully with the most difficult problems of society."[3]

Mears looked the part of the crusader, stern and abstemious. His goatee was streaked with gray, and his high forehead had been rising by the year. One former student described him as conscientious to a fault, a man who "might severely rebuke the fun-loving spirit of

1. The Hall of Languages. Photograph Collection, University Archives, Special Collections Research Center, Syracuse University Libraries.

the students" but who was still respected for his own "truth-loving spirit."[4] He was not one for taking the easy way out. Truth warranted struggle. Intellectually and morally aggressive, a fomenter of clash, Mears was, many agreed, an able controversialist.

"This was partly due to his love of right," a former student named Gilbert Reid recalled, "and partly due to his love of agitation. He hated deadness."[5]

From his parents, Mears had inherited his Presbyterian ardor and intellectual pugnacity, a willingness to stand apart. His father had been spiritually saved, and turned against his Pennsylvania hometown's potent liquor purveyors, during a revival led half a century before by the electrifying Reverend Charles Grandison Finney. His mother had taught Sunday school in a church that was vastly outnumbered by other denominations. Together, his mother and father set the tone. By the time he was twelve, while his peers were out horsing around, young John Mears was committing to memory the 107 questions and answers of the Westminster Shorter Catechism. Peer resistance only spurred him on. He devoted his adult years to a series of struggles that had helped make him, by Saint Valentine's Day 1879, a public figure known beyond the Hamilton College campus.

With the Oneida Community, Mears knew he would confront his toughest challenge yet. The Oneida Community had withstood all prior assaults, from prosecutors, professors, and clergymen. Newspaper reporters had exposed it. Book authors had written volumes about it. Mears himself had tried once before to attack it. Nothing stuck. As the *Utica Morning Herald* noted that Saint Valentine's Day, "inquiry has been started more than once with an eye to the indictment of the members" of the Oneida Community. These earlier campaigns had failed, one after another.

Still, Mears's mid-February 1879 timing seemed opportune. Just a few weeks before, the US Supreme Court had blessed conventional marriage by upholding a law banning Mormon polygamy. Polygamy, Chief Justice Morrison R. Waite explained in words that Mears found congenial, "has always been odious among the northern and western nations of Europe, and until the establishment of the Mormon Church, was almost exclusively a feature of the life of Asiatic and African people."[6] The ruling swelled anti-Mormon public opinion, of the kind Mears and his allies hoped to summon against the Oneida Community. Chief Justice Waite's decision aligned law and conventional morality, emboldening the Community's opponents.

Mears arrived at the Hall of Languages before the 2:30 p.m. scheduled start of the conference convened to launch the new fight against Oneida. Anticipating the moment to come, he ascended the stairs to the parlor. The four dozen or so men gathering there were a well-ordered lot. The host was Erastus O. Haven, Syracuse University's chancellor, fatigued from his struggles to keep the new school afloat. Bishop Frederic Dan Huntington, the top Episcopalian in central New York, sat nearby, stately and self-consciously erect.

Reverend Jesse Peck, a ponderous, sixty-seven-year-old bishop of the Methodist Episcopal Church and one of the original incorporators of Syracuse University, loomed over most men. Peck was gargantuan, described by one admirer as having the "formidable proportions of a giant; tall, broad-shouldered and stout of limb, big round head totally bald at the dome, sad, sympathetic eyes, with heavy shaggy eyebrows."[7] In a way, Peck had grown too big for his britches (so to speak), as he faced both financial and physical strain, but his massive presence contributed to the overall impression that this latest anti-Oneida crusade was a substantial effort.

"Here," one Syracuse newspaperman would sum up, "were venerable bishops, more or less venerable doctors of divinity, a college president, several college professors, clergymen, ordinary and extraordinary, doctors of medicine and councilors-at-law, two editors and a sprinkling of common people."[8]

Half a dozen or more far-flung reporters sauntered into the parlor. They had not been invited, but the Oneida Community had always been big news, its complex marriage scheme the subject of endless fascination. The crusaders who periodically rose against Oneida, too, were accustomed to newspaper coverage. Typically, they tried to turn publicity against Oneida like penicillin against mold. On this day, though, Mears wanted the reporters out.

"This meeting," Mears said, "was not intended to be made public. It was, that is to say, intended for private distribution. Not that there is anything unworthy of public knowledge. We have nothing to hide.

"What I mean to say," Mears continued, "is that these are meant to be only preliminary discussions. A preamble, as it were. It is, perhaps, desirable that we confine the discussion to those who were invited."[9]

Mears was adamant. At his insistence, the meeting was suspended until the intruders departed. They didn't leave the Hall of Languages, though. The men who had traveled to Syracuse midwinter would not simply be brushed off like snow from an overcoat. Somehow, they would piece together versions of the story, not unlike historians eavesdropping on the past.

Inside the parlor, following Bishop Peck's prayer for heavenly guidance, Mears offered a brief history of the Oneida Community. Then, the foundation set, Mears began his passionate denunciation of the plague spot, the carnal corruption, the Epicurean sty once conceived by John Humphrey Noyes as the kingdom come.

2   LOVE THY NEIGHBOR

JOHN HUMPHREY NOYES loved shamelessly.

Once, with a favored sexual partner named Tirzah Miller, Noyes mused about sexual intercourse as performance art.

"He said he would have a man and woman go up upon the stage, unprepared from among the audience, whence a couch being furnished, they should disrobe themselves and dance or perform other evolutions, until the man is prepared," Tirzah recounted.[1]

The ensuing action, Noyes maintained, would edify spectators and provide, he added, "pleasure to a great many of the older people who now have nothing to do with the matter." A public sexual performance would, as well, demonstrate the dropping of shame and thus furnish proof, Noyes told Tirzah, that heaven on earth had been attained.

The public performance remained an unconsummated plot. In many other ways, though, Noyes staged a revolution as he actively flouted conventions governing sexual conduct. He started by lifting the veil covering sexual organs and the act for which they were divinely designed. Shame was the mark of separation, and sexual congress reenacted the essential unity of man and woman. As an exercise in reclaiming the swamp, Noyes once suggested enumerating all the "savory, clean, wholesome objects" to which human sexual organs might be compared. Taking point, he offered the image of "the telescope with which he penetrates her heavens, and seeks the star of her heart."[2] Sexual performance, too, was to be perfected as well as its metaphoric expression.

"With this strange people," observed Dr. Ely Van de Warker, a nineteenth-century Syracuse University professor and gynecologist who studied the Oneida Community's women, "the sexual relation was made to realize, in a certain sense, an artistic fulfillment."[3]

The liberated sexual expression flowed naturally from Noyes's distinctive theological construct. Love connected neighbor to neighbor; not as abstraction or metaphor, but physically, the word made flesh. As Ellen Wayland-Smith put it, for Noyes, "sexual union was a practical way for souls to bind themselves to one another in the common medium of Christ's body."[4] Sex was about more than pleasure, then; it dissolved the barrier separating men and women.

Boundaries correspondingly fell, one after another. Even incest, Noyes mused, might be tolerated. If the risk of propagation could be eliminated, Noyes said, "the only plausible objection to amative intercourse between near relatives . . . is removed."[5] This was not mere theory. Noyes practiced, after a fashion, what he preached. Tirzah Miller, with whom he had intercourse, was his niece, the daughter of his younger sister. By the time Tirzah was fifteen, in 1868, Noyes was praising her for her sexual warmth, confiding in her that "there is as much difference between women in respect to ability to make social music as there is between a grand piano and a tenpenny whistle."[6]

Age differences, too, meant nothing. Or, put another way, they meant everything. A concept called *ascending fellowship* underlay the sexual administration of the Oneida Community. Put bluntly, it amounted to pairing younger men with older women, and vice versa.

"It is regarded as better for the young of both sexes to associate in love with persons older than themselves, and if possible with those who are spiritual and have been some time in school of self-control, and who are thus able to make love safe and edifying," the *Oneida Circular* explained on August 23, 1856.

The young had much to learn, and the old longed to teach them. It was an argument useful to Noyes and the other middle-aged men of the Community. Ascending fellowship, for the elders of the Oneida Community, licensed access to a flock of younger women. Theory and self-interest aligned in perfect harmony.

"The girls were taught that, as their first impressions of sexual experience were naturally the most momentous, it was of the greater importance that they should receive those impressions through those members who would be most likely to elevate them with the consciousness of having innocently exercised a pure and natural function on the spiritual plane," Community member Allan Estlake explained.[7]

Not everyone felt so elevated by the experience. Ascending fellowship kept young couples apart. Teenage boys, their libidos ablaze, were bound to older women who were safe from propagative consequences.

"I was hardly more than 12 when I was initiated into the immoral practices of Noyes," one embittered Oneida Community veteran recounted in the *New York Herald* on January 18, 1882. "I was put to sleep with first one old woman and then another, all of them older than 60 years of age. As I became older and larger, I was allowed the society of younger women of 35 and 40."

Sex, Noyes preached, was the vital center of society, the soul of the fine arts; without it, we are dead and barren. With it, Noyes said, we are electric.

Men and women alike listened closely when Noyes spoke. He was, even his critics conceded, a compelling character. While not especially tall, standing about five feet, ten inches, he was a full-bodied presence. By the time John Mears crossed his path, a chronic bronchial affliction and throat condition had rendered Noyes all but speechless, and he was growing progressively deafer, but his blue eyes still pierced and his mind still searched, like a telescope turned toward distant stars.

John Humphrey Noyes was born in Brattleboro, Vermont, on September 3, 1811. His father, also John, was a Dartmouth College graduate who returned to Vermont and moved from business into politics, serving two years in the Vermont state legislature and one term in Congress. A late bloomer, the elder Noyes was forty when he married a woman sixteen years his junior named Polly Hayes.

John Humphrey Noyes's father was both distant and demanding, absent during stretches of young John's childhood. He was hardheaded, a brusque businessman who drank too much. Polly was devout, praying that young John, her fourth child and first son, would enter the ministry. When it came time for college, his father hoped for Yale, but Polly wanted him closer. Dartmouth, she reasoned, would

2. John Humphrey Noyes.
Oneida Community Col-
lection, Special Collections
Research Center, Syracuse
University Libraries.

better protect her son's morals. In 1826, at the age of fifteen, Noyes
enrolled at his father's alma mater.

Noyes was a diligent student but a painfully shy young man. To
his journal, a constant companion, he could confess his own shame
at bashfulness with the ladies. "Oh, for a brazen front and nerves of
steel," he wrote. "I swear by Jove, I will be impudent!"[8] Eventually,
he would be that, and more, but he was still painfully self-conscious
when he graduated with Phi Beta Kappa honors in 1830 at the age of
nineteen.

Noyes initially apprenticed law with a relative, but that did not
take. Other forces moved him. By 1831, subsequently dubbed the
"year of revivals," protracted soul-saving, life-changing meetings
were the order of the day. Evangelical preachers roamed New England, summoning the masses to recommit themselves to the Lord. A
four-day revival meeting in his hometown of Putney that September
brought Noyes to the brink. He resisted, at first, discomfited by the

sight of people losing control of themselves while under the hand of the spirit. Self-control was important to Noyes. Finally, though, he submitted.

"The Millennium was supposed to be very near," Noyes recounted. "I fully entered into the enthusiasm of the time."[9]

A mere four weeks following his conversion, Noyes enrolled in the Andover Theological Seminary. It soon disappointed him. Book learning was prized above spirituality, and Noyes said he found in the seminary "at least as much levity, bickering, jealousy, intrigue and sensuality" as he ever found among any other gathering of young men.[10] Temptations, too, assailed Noyes—in particular, the love for food, the will-eroding appetite Noyes termed "alimentiveness."

Still, Noyes took from Andover at least one lasting lesson. Weekly, he would gather along with other students preparing for overseas service with the American Board of Missions. The outward-bound seminarians would then psychologically dismember one another, fault by fault. "This exercise," Noyes recalled, "sometimes cruelly crucified self-complacency, but it was contrary to the regulations of the society for anyone to be provoked or to complain."[11] Years later, Noyes would drive his Oneida Community followers through similar emotional sweat baths called *mutual criticism*.

Overall, though, Andover frustrated Noyes's spiritual requirements. Noyes then set out for Yale Divinity School shortly after his twenty-first birthday in the fall of 1832. Yale, he had concluded, offered him greater freedom to conduct his own spiritual explorations. In New Haven, he could learn from Nathaniel William Taylor, the school's Professor of Didactic Theology. Then in his mid-forties, Taylor rejected grim Calvinist notions that man was innately depraved and incapable of saving one's self. It just might be possible, he thought, to be made more perfect. Taylor, moreover, urged students to think for themselves.[12] That, Noyes did. He subjected himself to a cleansing regime of temperance, exercise, and prayer. He took pride in the punishing self-discipline that enabled him to study the Bible twelve to sixteen hours a day.[13]

Noyes carefully read the works of John Wesley, who taught that a diligent Christian might live without sin. This was a heretical thought to those who believed with John Calvin that man was immutably sinful. Nonetheless, the idea seized Noyes, who received his license to preach in August 1833. By that November he was broaching the notion of perfectionism. Revelation reached Noyes: faith perfects.

Noyes came to believe the Lord had returned in the year AD 70 with the destruction of Jerusalem. With this Second Advent, Noyes concluded, the final kingdom of God began in heaven, and was made manifest in the physical world. Noyes articulated this version of Perfectionism at an evening sermon on February 20, 1834, at the New Haven Free Church, a splinter group spun off in reaction to rigid mainstream Calvinism. Even for these liberated souls, Noyes's sermon went awfully far. "He that committeth sin is of the devil," Noyes proclaimed, conveying that it was possible to avoid both the sin and the devil—to be, in a word, perfect.

The word spread. Noyes relished the attention and elaborated on his vision. He likened the perfected human state to that of a book, correct in every crucial respect even if marred by an occasional typo. Discomfited, the New Haven Free Church expelled Noyes, the Congregational Church regional elders stripped him of his license to preach, and Yale bid him farewell.

"My good name in the great world was gone," Noyes confessed. "My friends were fast falling away. I was indeed becoming an outcast. Yet I rejoiced and leaped for joy."[14]

Persecution was part of the visionary's job description. A sinful world was bound to persecute the godly, but some persecution, Noyes learned, arose from his own mind, loudest when he was alone. Emotionally distressed, in May 1834 Noyes traveled to New York City, where he hoped to meet with leading religious figures, including the famed evangelist Charles Grandison Finney. Instead, the elders rebuffed him. Noyes fell into an emotional pit that would forge his character. He felt all around him the spirit of Satan. He dared not sleep, for fear of what would become of him. For three weeks, he indulged his appetites—exactly how much became later disputed. Formerly abstemious, Noyes began to drink. Once diet conscious, he savored the spiciest meals. In the words of William Hepworth Dixon, a vivid but unreliable chronicler, Noyes had "drunk, and gorged, and wantoned with the flesh."[15]

Noyes spent his time in New York City much differently. He drank, but only just enough to show himself above temptation. He sojourned among the Green Street harlots, but only to deliver unto the fallen women free Bibles and the word of the Lord. One way or another, Noyes was testing his own mettle. He declared himself the victor after three weeks, save for the temporary loss of his hat to a drunken sailor. Other reports to the contrary, he swore that he never violated the laws of man or God. His innocence, he said, was carried safely through the storm.

Back in New Haven, financially supported by his parents, Noyes began publishing in August 1834 his newly evolving beliefs in a monthly newspaper called the *Perfectionist*. He then wandered, enduring the pangs of an unrequited passion for Abigail Merwin, a pious early convert who was eight years older than he. Distraught upon hearing that she had married another, Noyes expressed his feelings in a letter in January 1837. The letter finally put Noyes on the map.

Denied Abigail, Noyes raised his sights higher. He rejected the worldly marriage she had submitted herself to. "In a holy community," Noyes wrote, "there is no more reason why sexual intercourse should be restrained by law, than why eating and drinking should be."[16] He might call a certain woman his wife, but she does not belong to him, she belongs to all and to none. She is dear, Noyes said, in the hands of a stranger.

"When the will of God is done on earth as it is in heaven, there will be no marriage," Noyes declaimed. "The marriage-supper of the Lamb is a feast at which every dish is free to every guest."

Abigail could be his, after all; she could be everybody's. With his musings, Noyes fashioned a key to unlock the marriage chains that bound his beloved to another. It was still all theory, for the sexually innocent Noyes. If anything, he was trying to convince himself that he had no need of the possessive feelings that so pained him. But whatever the motivations, Noyes's musings caused a sensation. His letter circulated among Perfectionists and was eventually published without his permission in August 1837 in a Philadelphia-based periodical called the *Battle-Axe; or, Weapons of War*. Dedicated, as writer Ellen Wayland-Smith noted, to "the ideal of Christian free love,"[17] and managed by an editor who "believed marriage a curse and apostasy," the *Battle-Axe* was a suitable venue. Though originally attributed to an anonymous author, what became known as the Battle-Axe Letter was, in time, owned up to by Noyes.

Noyes was now impudent, notorious. An anti-prostitution journal called the *Advocate of Moral Reform* articulated the conventional reaction that would shadow Noyes, warning that "unbridled license stalks among the ruins, smiling at the havoc she has made."[18] Noyes was also, for all that, still single. Noyes did, though, have other followers. One of them was a slightly older Vermont native named Harriet A. Holton.

Plain looking, self-conscious, and sincere, Harriet had been engaged once but otherwise had been unlucky in love. She first got to know Noyes from afar, as a follower of his writings starting in about 1834. She heard Noyes preach the first time in the winter of 1836, finding "there was spiritual power in his words which communicated light and peace to my soul."[19] By the winter of 1837, Harriet had collected all available editions of his periodical, the *Witness*, and she began sending him money to keep it going.[20]

Harriet saw in Noyes a man she could follow. Their epistolary relationship accelerated when Noyes sent a letter on June 11, 1838, asking for her hand in a peculiar way. Noyes advised Harriet that he would not call their partnership a marriage until he had, as he put it, "defined it." Noyes then declared that "we can enter into no engagements with each other, which shall limit the range of our affections, as they are limited in matrimonial engagements by the fashion of this world."[21] Harriet accepted Noyes's offer, not objecting to his assessment that "there was no particular love of the sentimental kind between us."

Less than three weeks after the peculiar proposal, they married. Noyes was twenty-seven, Harriet was thirty. Their honeymoon was a coming together of innocents.

"The truth that will come out in the judgment is, that I never knew woman sexually until I was married," Noyes later testified.[22]

With his new wife's money, Noyes resumed promoting Perfectionism. Harriet became pregnant but lost the child, the first of four stillbirths she would endure over six years. While Harriet gave birth to a son named Theodore in 1841, her pregnancy travails proved to Noyes the dangers of unfettered conception.

"After our last disappointment," Noyes recounted, "I told my wife I would never again expose her to such fruitless suffering."[23]

Noyes cogitated on sexual intercourse. The act, he reasoned, served both a propagative and a social function. Socially, Noyes reasoned, intercourse allowed the communion of spirits. For women, though, the consequences could be severe, from the agonies of childbirth to the traumatic loss of a baby. Even a successful birth made a wife a propagative drudge. During the early decades of the nineteenth century, the average white American woman had between six and eight live births. These were the fortunate ones. As late as 1850, the white US infant mortality rate surpassed 216 deaths per 1,000 births.

Others had reflected on the same heavy toll, and conceived their own solutions.

Ann Lee, born in England in 1736, was married to a blacksmith as a teenager. She became pregnant eight times. Four of the pregnancies ended in stillbirth. None of her four other children lived past the age of six. From this horror, Lee concluded that sex was not just a grievance—it was a sin to be subjugated. While her husband felt otherwise, and eventually skipped town with a prostitute, Lee emigrated to the United States with a small circle of disciples in 1774. They established the first community of Shakers near Albany, in time adopting an excruciating code of conduct designed to suppress carnal desires.

Lee's horrific personal experiences shaped her interpretation of Matthew 22:23–30, where Jesus instructed that "in the resurrection they neither marry, nor are given in marriage." The verse was crucial to both the Shakers and the Oneidans, though they interpreted the end of marriage in radically different ways. While Noyes envisioned sexual behavior continuing in the new state of complex marriage, Lee saw the end of marriage as coincident with the end of sex.

Private conversations between Shaker men and women were prohibited. They could not hug, kiss, or shake hands with one another. They ate at separate tables. Shakers were directed to shun "lewd conversation, pictures, postures and literature having a tendency to stimulate the amative passion."[24] When that failed to keep desire at bay, they were to "withdraw immediately from each other's presence, and war against that filthy spirit." The suppressed sexual energies were alleviated or at least expressed only by the rigidly formalized dancing that gave the Shakers their name.

The Shakers' enforced celibacy eliminated the expense of sexual intercourse, but also its reward. Noyes, who studied the Shakers closely and respectfully, said this was like cutting the knot instead of untying it. The trick, he reasoned, was how to extend the benefits of sex without paying the price. Noyes experimented. In 1844, he unveiled his solution. He called it *male continence.*

Male continence was not coitus interruptus, the risky pre-climax withdrawal. A near-contemporary of Noyes, Robert Dale Owen had proposed male withdrawal as the solution to the problematic consequences of sexual intercourse in his 1830s-era treatise *Moral Physiology.* Owen, like Noyes, appreciated sexual intercourse both for its propagative and its pleasurable purposes. It makes man, he said, a "happier and better being." Like Noyes, Owen recognized self-control as essential to prolonging the experience and avoiding the costs. Withdrawal requires, Owen acknowledged, "a mental effort and a partial sacrifice." But, like Noyes, Owen was confident in man's power to cultivate the necessary willpower. And, as would Noyes, Owen insisted his physical prescription was intended with the purest of motives.

"Libertines and debauchees! Cast my book aside!" Owen implored. "You will find nothing in it to satisfy a licentious curiosity."[25]

Noyes would later deny being influenced by Owen. Male continence, Noyes insisted, differed altogether from withdrawal. Withdrawal followed by climax wasted the life force. It was casting the seed by the side of the road, the sin of Onan. Continence prevented male climax altogether. It was the way, Noyes said, to secure the profits of amativeness without the expense of propagation or the spiritual waste of onanism. Certainly, continence taxed the man, especially one still serving his sexual apprenticeship, but Noyes preached the power of the will to regulate the deeper self. After all, Noyes reasoned, men stopped short all the time. They might glance at a beautiful woman, and then move on. They might savor a kiss, and take no more.

"The propagative crisis," Noyes insisted, "far from being an involuntary part of sexual intercourse, is a matter clearly within the province of the will, subject to enlightened voluntary control."[26]

An alternative might have been the use of prophylactics. Technological advances in the 1830s and 1840s made possible by the 1850s the mass production of inexpensive rubber condoms and, by the end of the decade, the flexible vaginal diaphragm.[27] Prophylactic use would have allowed men to engage in sexual intercourse while still preventing the unwanted consequences. It, too, would allow amativeness without propagation. Easing the self-discipline required by male continence, though, also deprived the man of salutary spiritual benefits. A condom licensed the man to indulge his base lust. A male orgasm was selfish, anti-social, and draining. It was masturbatory. Instead, retaining semen enabled the man to retain the vital life force.

Noyes, in any event, explained his understanding of sexual intercourse as having a beginning, middle, and end. Its beginning is the entering. A series of reciprocal motions followed. Finally, climax. Male continence confined sex to the first two phases, avoiding the final climax. With his knack for metaphor, Noyes likened intercourse to a stream in three conditions: a fall, the rapids above the fall, and the still water above the rapids. A man willing to learn, Noyes counseled, could confine his excursions to the "region of easy rowing."

Conventional minds thought it bad enough that Noyes sought to separate intercourse from its God-given propagative purpose, allowing pleasure for pleasure's sake. Physical dangers accompanied the moral harm. Incomplete intercourse, one critic warned, caused a "breaking-down of the nervous system, derangements of the circulation, of the organs of respiration and of the digestive system,"[28] not to mention uterine cancer, mammary congestion, sterility, and fibrous tumors.

Endlessly metaphorical, Noyes countered that "it is as foolish and cruel to expend one's seed on a wife merely for the sake of getting rid of it as it would be to fire a gun at one's best friend merely for the sake of unloading it."[29] Male continence, Oneida Community members would proclaim, protected men from exhaustion and women from misery, while rewarding them abundantly. The self-discipline required of the properly continent male did take some getting used to and, perhaps, some divine help along the way. One man, while testifying to the benefits of withholding from orgasm, allowed that "my experience has also been that the theory was utterly impractical without the presence of Christ."[30]

• • •

Noyes had gathered his family about him in Putney, starting what became known as the Society of Inquiry. The extended family members spent several hours a day reading, discussing or cogitating in silence. They ate a common breakfast, worked on the farm midday, and in the evening gathered for song or lessons. By 1843, there were some twenty-eight adults and nine children enrolled in the Putney community.

The roundelay heated up in 1846, when Noyes was attracted to a woman named Mary Cragin. Mary's husband, George, in turn, drew nearer to Harriet Noyes. After heartfelt conversations, the couples, along with Noyes's two sisters and brothers-in-law, agreed to open up their relationships. In November 1846, the four couples signed a statement proclaiming that "all individual proprietorship either of persons or things is surrendered, and absolute community of interests takes the place of the laws and fashions which preside over property and family relations in the world."[31] Slowly, the veil was lifted. By the summer of 1847, the Putney community's *Spiritual Magazine* was making it known that separate households and property exclusiveness had come to an end.

"The possessive feeling," Noyes maintained, "is the same, in essence, when it relates to women as when it relates to money, or any other property."[32]

The Putney neighbors were already distressed over claims about faith healing. One, a Methodist clergyman then in his late forties named Hubbard Eastman, condemned Noyes as a "hydra-headed monster of iniquity,"[33] a charge elaborated upon in Eastman's 432-plus-page denunciation published in May 1849 under the title *Noyesism Unveiled: A History of the Sect Self-Styled Perfectionists*. Eastman's was the first of the book-length denunciations to arise against Noyes, and it set the distempered tone for others.

Noyes and his followers, Eastman declared, espoused beliefs that "aim a deadly blow at the foundations of the civil and social fabric," and were "fatal to the moral principles" of all who inhaled them.[34] And, like other crusaders to come, Eastman apologized in advance for airing the foul corruptions associated with the evil Noyes. "The subject, we are aware, is naturally uninviting, and actually quite repulsive," Eastman wrote, "but however irksome or unpleasant the task imposed, exposure is necessary in order to afford timely warning to the unwary."[35]

Noyes was arrested in late October 1847 on charges of adultery and fornication. Rather than fight the case or face, as he feared, mob action, in late November 1847 Noyes left Vermont. His case came to trial months later. With Noyes absent, the only question was how much of a $2,000 bond Noyes would forfeit. Summoning the rhetorical excess that would become commonplace, the prosecutor declared the alleged adulterer had been indicted for "two of the worst crimes known to the law."[36] The judge, only partially convinced, reduced the bond to $1,000.

With that, Noyes's Vermont venture was done. He would begin again in New York State, where he would find a region of easier rowing.

3 THE ONEIDA COMMUNITY

NOYES REPLANTED HIMSELF in the rich soil of New York's "burned-over district."

It felt like home.

Stretching roughly between Utica in the east to Rochester in the west, and bisected by the Erie Canal, the region had been tilled over the years by a cavalcade of spiritual searchers, zealots, and the occasional charlatan. Evangelist Charles Grandison Finney, whose influence touched Noyes as well as John W. Mears's father, had been educated at the Hamilton-Oneida Academy, the precursor to Hamilton College. Finney's subsequent success leading Presbyterian revivals likewise began in Oneida County in 1825, and religiously inflected temperance and anti-slavery crusades crested throughout the burned-over district, historian Whitney Cross recounted. A decades-long Presbyterian schism, in which Mears and his mentor Albert Barnes would emphatically take sides, "developed from quarrels bred primarily in this region," Cross noted.[1]

It was also, historian Chris Jennings observed, a "hotbed of Perfectionism," with some 40 percent of the subscribers to Noyes's *Witness* living in the burned-over district.[2]

In January 1848, Noyes traveled to Madison County, located in the heart of this region, at the invitation of a fellow Perfectionist named Jonathan Burt. There, on land along Oneida Creek, Noyes found a sawmill, a farmhouse, a hut, and a few scattered buildings on 160 acres. The residents were congenial, although, Burt acknowledged, the women were "somewhat disconcerted" at Noyes's exposition of male continence.[3]

By the summer of 1848, seventeen members of the original Putney community had reunited at Oneida. "Thus the Putney Association died and rose again," the *First Annual Report of Oneida Association* recounted the following January.[4] The report was a thorough piece of work—too thorough, for some. Back in Vermont, a charge of circulating copies of the document would be brought and settled for a fine of $15 and court costs of $33.99.[5]

The frank report included a forthright history, acknowledging the "public excitement" that had arisen in Vermont. The report spelled out Noyes's theory of property, predicated upon the notion that God retains ownership of all, even as man kept on grabbing. Let go, Noyes urged. The acquisitive feeling expressed by the possessive pronoun "mine" was the same, whether referring to money, or real estate, or women. New members of Oneida Community would sell their property and surrender the proceeds to the common good; so, too, they would surrender their unique carnal claims.

"The secret history of the human heart," Noyes wrote, "will bear out the assertion that it is capable of loving any number of times and any number of persons."[6]

Noyes believed in varying the routine. Monogamy, he complained, "gives to sexual appetite only scanty and monotonous allowance."[7] Moreover, sexual activity put a glow on the cheeks, a spring in the step. A conventionally married man grows lazy. A courting man keeps grooming himself. Never one for modestly concealing his abilities, Noyes circulated the *First Annual Report* among a wide circle of prominent men that included *New York Tribune* editor Horace Greeley and utopian dabbler Henry James Senior. By January 1849, the core of followers had grown at Oneida to 87. A year later, the Oneida Community claimed 172 members, and a year after that there were 205.

Noyes's followers were not alone in exploring new social frontiers. By the 1850s, northeastern and midwestern states were dotted with upwards of seventy intentional communities founded upon socialist principles that necessitated a rethinking of the property implications of monogamous marriage.[8] Each of these communities had to work through a solution to the conjoined issues of ownership, jealousy, propagation, and desire. At Oneida, members embraced universal love but it was not, strictly speaking, free love.

As a rule, men and women slept apart. Sleep, Noyes preached, was a solo act. Men and women should come together, awake, to edify one another. Certain other protocols regulated sexual conduct. The man would usually initiate the invitation but a Community leader would review the requests. By going through a third party, Noyes believed, modesty and wisdom would both be served. A request might be refused without face-to-face embarrassment, while the dangers of selfish privacy would be avoided. Women could refuse a sexual invitation but rejection was subtly discouraged. Energy was to be shared, not stored. If accepted, the man would typically visit the woman's room for the "interview session," as it was modestly called. Excessive talking was discouraged.

"The tongue has its field to itself all day," Noyes counseled. "Why should not the other members have their turn?"[9]

Sexual intercourse typically occurred with couples on their sides, the woman pulling one leg up, and the man entering her from behind. Entry mattered. Noyes believed "the sweetest and noblest period of intercourse with woman is . . . that first moment of simple presence and spiritual effusion before the muscular exercise begins."[10] The exercise might proceed leisurely; Community member George Cragin recalled that "the sexual interviews lasted generally an hour and a half."

"We do not mean there would be continuous intercourse for that length of time," Cragin clarified. "But that the pair would be together for that period. The actual intercourse might be limited to several sessions of but a few minutes at a time."[11]

Male fortitude was prized, allowing women to reach, as Cragin put it, the point of "sexual crisis," perhaps multiple times. This frank recognition of female sexual desire was a radical thought, at least in some circles. One 1858 textbook entitled *Functions and Disorders of the Reproductive Organs* framed a more conventional, though not universally held view, that "the majority of women (happily for them) are not very much troubled with sexual feelings of any kind."[12] Oneida's women felt otherwise. Following the conclusion of sexual intercourse, the man would withdraw to his own room. With masturbation discouraged, nocturnal emissions typically brought relief for the otherwise continent man.

By funneling requests through the Community's administrators, Noyes exercised control, rewarding the dutiful and disciplining the derelict. Young men or others incapable of restraining themselves were partnered with older women beyond childbearing age until, as Noyes put it, they learned to restrain themselves from "the crisis which they are so eager for."[13] The truly recalcitrant were denied sexual access altogether. The system, Noyes said, ensured good order and good health. It was the very opposite of licentiousness, and though many Community members adapted themselves to management's dictates, some chafed. One unhappy writer reported in 1871 that "no 'social freedom' is permitted without Noyes' consent . . . and if one is lazy and discontented, 'social freedom' is withheld."[14] Noyes's own son, Theodore, underscored the point after the Community broke up, observing that "the power of regulating the sexual relations of the members . . . by common consent delegated to Father and his subordinates, constituted by far the most effectual means of government."[15]

The principle of ascending fellowship channeled sexual energy. Ascending fellowship meant associating with those of greater experience and higher spiritual and carnal control. It meant the young and old would come together. This was not always an easy sale for the young. Ascending fellowship was, anti-Oneida author John Ellis cynically believed, designed by middle-aged men with the cunning of old roués for their own satisfaction. "They are failing in bodily vigor," Ellis observed, "but their salacious appetites are still strong."[16] Ellis saw in ascending fellowship a corrupt bargain, with older women acquiescing so they might also secure the embrace of younger partners.

Well-ordered freedom went beyond sexual partnering. Noyes wanted to liberate women from certain strictures. Excessive attention to adornment confined the soul as well as the flesh. Instead of restrictive bustles and dresses that swept the ground, Oneida women developed a distinctive ankle-length set of trousers called pantalets. They cut their hair short, freeing themselves from unnecessary entanglements. Mutual criticism, meanwhile, kept the Community honest, as Noyes refined the art of the personal critique he had learned at Andover. The Community tried several modifications of the form, but Noyes consistently maintained the high ground, critiquing others while remaining largely immune himself.

Criticism could get quite pointed. John Ellis cited a member named Sydney Jocelyn, slapped with the observation that he "had no great fondness for the caresses of the ancient ladies."[17] Ellis cannot be fully trusted as a reporter, but it was certainly the case that young men and women would face public criticism for falling into the trap of exclusive, romantic love. On another, more typical evening, a Mr. Hazelton was chastised for having a spirit that was "hard and disobedient and full of unbelief."[18] Another Community member, a young woman, was praised for her "vital temperament," but criticized for disrespect and inattentiveness. "She will fly through a room, on some impulsive errand of generosity, perhaps," it was said, and "leave both doors open, and half-knock down anybody in her way."[19] Another Community resident was told he had a "rather rude way of talking to associates," although this gentleman did have some offsetting virtues.

"He has a good spirit about music," his fellow Community members allowed, "and is obedient to Mr. Noyes' suggestions about the band."[20]

4   A VORTEX OF IMPURITY

SAMUEL B. GARVIN could be a hard man.

He had run a tough campaign for Oneida County district attorney in 1850, challenging incumbent Roscoe Conkling. Conkling, the son of a well-connected man, was a Whig who had been appointed at the improbably young age of twenty by New York governor Hamilton Fish.[1] The thirty-nine-year-old Garvin and his allies effectively cast him as too young for the job, and the charges stuck. The Democrat Garvin won with 52 percent of the vote, though Conkling would not stay down long. In time, he would be elected to the US Senate.

But in 1851, while Conkling was still nursing his wounds, Garvin consolidated his position as lead prosecutor for the county of about one hundred thousand residents. Garvin was inclined toward action, and he stirred when he first heard reports that an Oneida Community member named Henry Seymour was beating his young wife. Garvin's subsequent foray against the Oneida Community, and his ultimate failure to dislodge it, foreshadowed other fights to come.

An early Oneida convert, Seymour's wife, Tryphena, had testified in the Oneida Community's *First Annual Report* how the Community's principles would restore man to the original purity of the Garden of Eden. She sounded smitten, enthusing how her hidden selfishness had been consumed by the Holy Spirit pervading the Community. But by December 1850, she began to seem insubordinate and unsettled at times, prompting her husband Henry to discipline her. The chastisement didn't stick. By mid-September 1851, Tryphena appeared hysterical. She cried at nights; she wandered about and ranted.[2] Henry tried reasoning with her, and when she did not

change he beat her. Seymour confessed, the *Oneida Journal* reported
on October 2, 1851, that he had "whipped Tryphena with a rawhide
every day for three weeks, that her back was in consequence as black
as his pantaloons, and that one of her eyes was so badly injured that
he was doubtful whether she would ever see out of it again."[3] Supposedly, Seymour thought he might knock some sense back into his
young wife.

Tryphena's father, Mr. Hubbard, was already ill-disposed toward
the Oneida Community for luring away his daughter, and her whip-
ping revived his ire. Garvin, in neighboring Oneida County, learned
of the allegations of domestic violence and summoned Oneida Community members to testify before a grand jury. They did not include
Noyes, who since 1849 had been spending much of his time at an
outpost in Brooklyn. The morning of October 7, 1851, an Oneida
County constable, Lucius Hubbard, escorted nine Community residents to Utica. Constable Hubbard was not entirely neutral in the
affair—he was Tryphena's brother.

For Garvin, the assault and battery allegations against Henry Seymour provided an opening. The Oneida Community was still only
several years old, and its exotic social practices were murky to outsiders. Once Garvin had its members on the stand, he could plumb
Oneida's depths. Community resident J. L. Skinner was questioned
about the Community's "social principles and arrangements," the
Oneida Journal reported.[4] For half an hour, Fanny M. Leonard was
interrogated about intimate matters ranging from her marriage to the
Community's sleeping arrangements. Similar questions were pressed
upon the wife of Community member Jonathan Burt.

Garvin was fishing, and though his full intentions were unclear,
the nine Community members left Utica under a dark cloud. They
knew how Noyes had been run out of Putney. A week later, one Community member visited with Timothy Jenkins, a wealthy attorney
residing nearby. Jenkins was a former Oneida County district attorney
who had subsequently served two terms in Congress. Turned out by
the voters in 1848, Jenkins had won his House seat back in 1850,
running, as it happened, on the same Democratic ticket as Garvin.[5]

Jenkins was not known as a particularly warm character, but the fifty-two-year-old lawyer and Vernon resident knew the local legal system and he knew Oneida. The previous year, he had met with Burt and another Community member to discuss the tense relations with the Hubbard family.[6] On Burt's return visit in 1851, Jenkins said that Garvin, his fellow Democrat, had also been to see him concerning Oneida. Jenkins had assured Garvin that the Community had a good reputation for regularity. While not condoning Seymour's violence against Tryphena, Jenkins said he told Garvin that no indictment should turn simply upon the Community's peculiar views about marriage.[7]

Jenkins's endorsement, while it did not end the matter, exemplified the kind of neighborly support that would sustain the Oneida Community for the next several decades. With Oneida, familiarity bred respect. The Community's radical internal practices were strange, but Noyes and his followers did not proselytize. That, combined with the mutually beneficial commercial relationships established over time, encouraged a tolerant attitude that frustrated more than one crusader over the years.

The morning of October 21, Oneida County High Sheriff John R. Jones nonetheless arrived bearing a warrant for ten Community residents. A businessman and politician, Jones had been sheriff for only a year and he had no personal feelings against the Community. He was simply carrying out his orders.[8]

The Community men appeared in Utica before Judge P. Sheldon Root. Root set a bond of $200 for each of the Community members, with an extra $200 for Seymour because of the added assault and battery charge. The Community leaders knew definitive action was needed. A defensive petition was prepared, addressed to the district attorney, in which the signatories characterized the Community members as honorable business men and good neighbors. The petition was circulated for the first few weeks of November among the Oneida Community's neighbors, a number of whom signed without hesitation.

By the end of November 1851, Garvin told Jenkins that he would agree to whatever settlement could be reached. A subsequent conversation with Tryphena's family led to a deal in which the Community would pay for her care at the Utica Insane Asylum. Once she was released, moreover, the Community would pay her a stipend. Garvin relented, for a time, but others did not. The *New York Observer* opined in January 1852 that the Community was a "foul body" whose members lived "in a state of vile concupiscence and even worse." Foreshadowing future attacks by Mears and others, the paper said the Community's *First Annual Report* propounded a "theory of promiscuous intercourse" that was "so loathsome in its details [and] so shocking to all the sensibilities even of the coarsest of decent people that we cannot defile the columns of our paper with their recital." Even the "foulest days and darkest places of Roman Catholic iniquity" could hardly compare with Oneida's evils, the *Observer* warned.[9]

The Oneida Community residents declared in March 1852 that they were temporarily discontinuing complex marriage. Community leader John R. Miller, a businessman who was married to Noyes's sister Charlotte, even assured Garvin on April 29 that "we have decided to break up our Association, if that is what you want, and if you will give us time to do so quietly."[10] The assault and battery case against Seymour was dropped, and there was to be no further prosecution against the other Community members.

The tactical talk of disassociation, though, did not go very far. From Washington, DC, Timothy Jenkins wrote to urge Community members not to abandon their property. By being reasonably prudent, the congressman counseled, the Oneida Community would soon get along with its neighbors. Legally speaking, Jenkins said, Oneida seemed safe. In another tactical move, the Community threw itself open to the public with a grand strawberry festival in June that drew about eighty families from nearby towns. Even the Hubbard family showed up for the start of what would become a strawberry feasting tradition at Oneida.

Community leaders sought whatever other influence they could find. A lawyer from Vernon named Josiah Whipple Jenkins drafted another petition in late July. Generally known as Whipple, Jenkins was Timothy Jenkins's cousin and, for a time, his law partner. He had a diverse clientele, which once included abolitionist John Brown.[11] While Whipple helped rally public support for Oneida, the brother-in-law of a Community member, an influential Universalist minister from Utica, privately urged Garvin to ease up.

In September 1852, after considerable back and forth, John Miller, on behalf of the Community, paid $20 for court costs, and Garvin affirmed there would be no prosecution. The Oneida Community was off the hook—saved, Noyes declared, "by the manifest and sublime movements of the armies of Heaven in our favor."[12] In truth, the Community's own adroit maneuvering had been reinforced by the kind of strong neighborly relationships that would sustain it for years to come. And the heat having died down, Oneida resumed its merry ways. In late August, the *Oneida Circular* proclaimed the resurrection of the radical doctrines, with the "abandonment of the entire fashion of this world, especially marriage and involuntary propagation."[13]

• • •

The next battles came like waves, cresting every few years.

A 1797 Yale College graduate, Reverend Israel Brainerd had been a longtime minister in Verona, about six miles from the Oneida Community. He was in his early seventies when Noyes transplanted his community from Putney to Upstate New York. Though Brainerd had formally resigned his position at the First Church of Verona by then, he had continued preaching. As Brainerd learned of the new Oneida Community's practices, he had, his daughter Elizabeth Thompson later recounted to Mears, "rode from town to town, exposing its loathsome doctrine to clergymen, lawyers, judges and other men of influence, and implored them to join him in efforts to break up the concern."[14] Unfortunately, Elizabeth told Mears, her father could not rally the forces. The failure unsettled a man accustomed to leading Christian followers onward.

"I have had great enjoyment in the things of religion, particularly in revivals," Reverend Brainerd acknowledged, but "I have also had seasons of distressing darkness."[15]

One of the men unconvinced by Reverend Brainerd's campaign and others like it was a onetime US attorney for the northern district of New York, Joshua A. Spencer. A Whig who once lived in a small town about four miles from Oneida, Spencer served as the region's chief federal prosecutor from 1841 to 1845, before being elected as a state senator and, in 1848, as mayor of Utica. Spencer was not particularly scholarly as a lawyer, but he had a knack for handling juries and cross-examining witnesses.[16] He could tell a strong case from a weak one, and from his political experience he could assess public sentiment. A defense attorney named Abram Wakeman later recalled how Spencer supposedly declined an invitation to aid in suppressing the Community.

"He declared that they had just as much right to their views, however mistaken they were, as the gentlemen who complained had to theirs," Wakeman recalled.[17]

Another kind of crusade came in 1870, when Dr. John B. Ellis published *Free Love and Its Votaries: Or, American Socialism Unmasked*, a lengthy but fanciful denunciation. Ellis had dug into the dreaded subject and emerged with a 502-page behemoth. Ellis warned that the "evil principle of Free Love" had been spreading through many circles. Among them, he enumerated, were the "Oneida Communists . . . Spiritualists, Advocates of Woman Suffrage [and] Friends of Free Divorce."[18]

"This book is not a work of fiction," Ellis assured readers, "but a simple record of terrible facts."[19] He then went on to excoriate the "hideous immorality" of the Oneida Community, calling it "an outrage that a community such as the Oneida Saints should be permitted to exist."[20] Stirring up outrage, of course, could also profit a publisher angling for a quick buck. The work was billed as "the most startling book of modern times," in one notice in the September 7, 1870, issue of the *Lewis County Democrat*. A run of other small ads in New York State newspapers, like one in the *Sag Harbor Express* on December 22, 1870, sought "agents" to peddle the book, promising "large sales, immense profits, stupendous revelations and startling disclosures."

The author John B. Ellis was, the New York City–based United States Publishing Co. proclaimed, both well-known and well-respected.

Much of Ellis's book, though, appeared to be lifted straight from English writer William Hepworth Dixon, whose 1867 study, *Spiritual Wives*, explored the lives of Mormons, Shakers, and Oneida Community residents, among others. Dixon's account had been challenged by Noyes as unreliable, but there was no question about Dixon's identity. He had, in fact, arrived at the Oneida Community with a letter of introduction from publisher Horace Greeley, an acquaintance of Noyes's. When *Free Love and Its Votaries* was published, Noyes and Oneida Community leaders tried to find out more about Ellis, its putative author. The New York City–based publishing company, at least, had a track record of producing such volumes as the lavishly illustrated *Wonders of the World*. No one, though, seemed to have heard of Dr. John B. Ellis. He was, it seemed, fictional, much like the book published under his name.

"The actual author of this 'brave' book is a literary gentleman living in the upper part of the city, who does not wish to have his name mentioned in connection with it," Noyes revealed. "He was employed to get it up by a publishing house that got the idea of it some years ago from a sensational story about the O. C. [Oneida Community] in a Philadelphia paper, and that confessedly had no object in view but to make money by it."[21]

Free Love and Its Votaries, whatever its origins, epitomized the blend of teasing insinuations, draped-over details, and emphatic condemnations that a certain class of writers customarily applied to Oneida. Two years before Ellis, an even more alarming work of fiction entitled *Poor Ellen Stuart's Fate; Or, Victim of the Free Love Institute in Oneida, N.Y.: A True and Thrilling Account of Miss Ellen Stuart's Captivity in a Free Love Institute, and Her Tragic Escape and Sufferings* had likewise aroused the public. Writer Charles Wesley Alexander imbued his forty-eight-page work with all the tricks of the trade.

Poor Ellen, as recounted by Alexander, is beset by an evil stepmother and some stepsisters straight out of Cinderella's nightmares. Driven from her home, Ellen finds herself in a remote house deep in Oneida County, where a sinister seducer named Mr. Hertzler explains himself.

"This is a Free Love Institute," Mr. Hertzler tells Ellen. "Here, we all love each other, and enjoy each other's society without the trammels which bigoted religions throw around the intercourse of the sexes."[22]

When Ellen resists Mr. Hertzler, several corrupted women spit in her face, beat her with their fists and, the final straw, call her Miss Prude. Poor Ellen weeps. The fiendish Mr. Hertzler tries a gentler technique, offering Ellen a glass of wine.

"We call it," Mr. Hertzler says, "the nectar of Venus and Cupid."[23]

Ellen does not allow the wine to pass her lips and finally manages to flee the place, finding brief respite before, alas, she succumbs, fatally done in by her ordeal.

"I can tell you one thing," one man sums up following Ellen's demise, speaking for all those outraged by the Free Love Institute. "If the people up in Oneida County could only find out where the place is exactly, it wouldn't be there long."[24]

The fantastical, near-pornographic claims about Poor Ellen's capture by the Oneida Free Love Institute matched the similarly outraged accounting of other nineteenth-century religions or sects. Sexual energy dominated all other passions, pulsing dangerously close to the surface. Suppression could not stop it for long; the pressure was hydraulic. It required proper channeling. Deny the passion altogether, and it would pervert into nightmare. Animus against Roman Catholics, which Mears shared, heated up over fears that passions unnaturally chained by celibacy would turn deviant. As George Bourne warned in his 1847 work, *The American Text-Book of Popery*, "at length the laboring desire bursts forth, and glows with volcanic heat and fury."[25]

But hacks and bigots were not the only ones fanning the flames. The learned, too, led some Oneida fights.

A Schenectady resident named E. P. Freeman, unhappy over his son's seduction into the Oneida Community, railed against it for a while after the Civil War before drawing the attention of Tayler Lewis, a professor of Greek at Union College. Freeman would bring Lewis literature from the Community, and the outraged professor soon adopted Freeman's cause as his own.[26]

Lewis was no John Ellis—he was a tangible man. He had graduated from Union College in 1820 and worked as a lawyer, studying Greek, Hebrew, and Latin in his spare time until he left the practice of law altogether. He took up teaching, first in New York City and then, in 1849, back at his alma mater. Like Mears, Lewis was prolific, authoring books on topics ranging from a defense of capital punishment to an exploration of the African continent. A layman in the Dutch Reformed Church, he could converse easily in Greek, and sometimes conducted his reflections in that language. His copy of the Hebrew Bible was thumb-worn and note-filled, as was his Koran.[27]

Lewis believed in discipline, rigorously applied. In one presentation, a critic said, Lewis had "maintained the manly character of flogging as a mode of punishing prison offenses."[28] Evil required a forceful response, and Lewis was quick to march against moral error. His many causes included temperance, opposition to women's suffrage, and support for amending the Constitution to acknowledge God as the source of all law.

"He was so essentially by nature a controversialist that if some luckless opponent haply quoted bad Latin or worse Greek, he would take him up in an instant and impale him on Latin syntax or Greek prosody," the *Methodist Quarterly Review* recounted.[29]

Lewis felt for old man Freeman, whose son, Lewis wrote, "had been drawn into this vortex of impurity." The professor already knew what it meant to lose a loved one, as one of his sons had died in the Civil War. The shock was said to have destroyed his hearing. For a time, Lewis employed an ear trumpet, until he had to resort to written conversation. Sciatica crippled him. Still, Lewis mobilized, writing in the November 30, 1871, edition of the *New York Independent* an article entitled "The Mormons and the Oneida Community." The headline conveyed guilt by association, for Mormons were commonly reviled. But even Mormonism, Lewis warned, could not compare to Oneida. While he acknowledged the "pleasant buildings, gardens abounding in fruit, grounds beautifully laid out," Lewis saw through to a "foul, pestilential plague-spot that calls aloud not only for cleansing and disinfection, but for an utter blotting out from the face of the earth."

"It is," Lewis wrote, "nothing more nor less than an open brothel. It is a place where is practiced, justified and unblushingly proclaimed the most unrestrained license of sexual intercourse.

"We can only allude to their writings," Lewis went on. "They are too vile for reference or citation. The county of Oneida has courts, grand juries, district attorneys. Why are they not performing their duties?"

The *New York Independent* balanced Lewis's diatribe with an editorial praising the Oneida Community members as a peaceful, industrious people with sincere religious motives. Even so, the Community could not ignore Lewis's attacks. In the May 20, 1872, *Oneida Circular*, a Community writer stated that "from certain allusions in it, and from its general tone and language," it was inferred that the real author was "an old gentleman in Schenectady." E. P. Freeman's grievous mutterings, it was clear, had propelled Lewis. Lewis followed up, again in the *New York Independent*, with a plea for national legislation regulating marriage.

The fulminations seemed futile, as the Community remained intact when the shouting was done. In the several decades since Noyes had moved his commune to Upstate New York, the roots had deepened.

"It had been criticized, analyzed, condemned and denounced," one nineteenth-century observer noted, "but all without any sensible impression."[30]

John W. Mears vowed that he would, by God, change that.

5 THE VIRTUOUS MAN

JOHN W. MEARS was born into a good, Christian family.

The future crusader was born on August 10, 1825, in Reading, Pennsylvania, the oldest of Henry Haller and Anna Birkenbine Mears's seven children.[1] His father was an "eminently sociable and amiable" character who was "thrown into dangers" when young, Mears reported, but who managed to escape unscathed. No "taint of dissipation was upon his character or his constitution," Mears was relieved to say.[2]

For that, Mears's father could thank his deeply pious wife as well as the charismatic preacher Charles Grandison Finney. Finney's extended revival in Reading during the winter of 1829–30, though reportedly resisted by local beer-loving Germans and intemperate newspaper editors, rescued men from the brink of hell. One of the saved, Finney later recalled, was a Reading merchant who had recently equipped his distillery with the latest sin-tinged equipment.

"But as soon as he was converted," Finney wrote, "he gave up all thought of going any farther with that business."[3]

Mears's mother had already "made public profession of her faith in Christ" at the age of fifteen, a eulogist recalled.[4] Anna began teaching Sunday school at the Reading church, where she would later immerse her children. Lutherans abounded in the greater Berks County region and the Presbyterian church attended by the Mears family was greatly outnumbered. The year Mears was born, when the city's population had reached about five thousand residents, Reading's sole Presbyterian church claimed only sixty-eight congregants.[5] This early experience of being doctrinally outnumbered may have toughened Mears's hide, enabling him to stand apart and hold firm.

One of the area's leading Presbyterians, Judge William Darling, changed Mears's life at least as much as Finney had changed his father's. Darling was a man of many parts—imposing in church, courthouse, and commerce alike. He served as a Berks County judge, helped managed the Reading Foundry, and led the American Sunday School Union. He was a temperance man. Judge Darling was also a father—his son, Henry, was a slightly older friend of Mears.[6] Many years later, the two boys would be reunited as colleagues at Hamilton College.

One memorable Sunday in Reading, when the regular minister was absent, Judge Darling stepped in as a substitute. Something clicked, and his sermon moved young John to tears. Mears talked at length with his mother about what he had heard, and met with Judge Darling himself. Mears knew, henceforth, whose path he would follow. Moreover, Darling offered fortuitous connections that would later aid Mears. In particular, the judge was an ally of Albert Barnes, a prominent Presbyterian minister and fellow temperance advocate. Mears would eventually be guided by Barnes, from his first church pulpit to his eventual appointment as Hamilton College's Albert Barnes Professor of Intellectual and Moral Philosophy.

Judge Darling's words landed, like providential seeds, in the right soil at the right time. Mears's home, though laced with virtue, was a little unsettled. His father, twenty-eight years old in the year Mears was born, had what his son called a roving disposition. The senior Mears took on various jobs; including, apparently, a brief turn running a family distillery. The temperance spirit, his son explained, eventually became such that Henry was moved "to give up the business, lucrative as it was, first on Sunday, and then altogether."[7]

Forsaking drink, whether as solace or source of income, Mears's father was "smitten with a desire to try his fortune in the new states" out west. At one point leaving his wife and children home in Reading, Henry "penetrated the almost unbroken wilderness" and tried his hand at the "great rivers of the West, in arks and flatboats," reaching at least as far as New Orleans.[8] His father's departure on one western trip when John was about twelve stirred particularly intense emotions.

Left behind, Anna Mears and her children coped as best they could. They would need an anchor to steady them amid uncertain seas.

Henry finally returned and moved his family to Philadelphia in 1836, where he sought more opportunities. Eventually, he would find success, founding, with his son George, a profitable grain merchant firm. Unexpectedly, their commercial gain would in time make John Mears's academic career possible. John himself, though, showed little interest in worldly business—quite the opposite. He preferred the metaphysical to the material.

The spiritual spark set by Judge Darling was fanned in Philadelphia's Vine Street Presbyterian Church by the Reverend John L. Grant, a skilled preacher and an able Sunday school teacher.[9] By the time Mears was a teenager, his younger brother George later recalled, he "had begun to work for Christ, talking quietly to his companions and endeavoring to persuade them to start on the Christian life."[10] An early agitator, John espoused firm convictions while his father competed in business and his family coped with the loss of Mears's sister Lydia at the age of two, in 1838. In this environment, young Mears took himself seriously. "When his companions were enjoying themselves with hoop and kite and ball," George would write later, "he was busy poring over books."[11] While more slapdash lads would stumble, earnest John Mears memorized all 107 answers to the Westminster Shorter Catechism.

"The seventh commandment requireth the preservation of our own and our neighbor's chastity, in heart, speech and behavior," Mears would recite, adding at the next prompt that "the seventh commandment forbiddeth all unchaste words, thoughts and actions."

Like Noyes, Mears entered college at fifteen. Newark College was located in Newark, Delaware, about forty-five miles from Philadelphia. The school had opened in 1834, with three professors, several dozen students, and a demanding set of rules. Students paid an annual tuition of $20 and an additional $10 for a room in which they were instructed not to have "intoxicants (unless under doctor's orders), dogs, guns, swords, dirks or any deadly weapon."[12] Morning and evening prayers bound students in the practice of Christian faith. On Sundays, they needed a professor's permission to leave the campus, such as it was, and they were directed not to "engage in any diversion or unsuitable reading or study, or receive visitors, or otherwise profane the day."[13] Still, some struggled against the restraints. Students were disciplined for impudence, vandalism, and drunkenness. Intoxicating beverages posed a particular problem, prompting faculty members to petition Newark store owners to limit liquor sales and trustees to ask the Delaware state assembly to prohibit the sale of "spirituous liquors" to students.[14]

Newark College lacked amenities and stature. The library's collection was a pittance. The campus, a near-contemporary of Mears observed, looked "blown together in a storm."[15] For the committed, though, the place provided a foundation, and Mears persevered. He was one of twelve seniors to graduate in July 1844, in a ceremony where his recitation of a self-penned poem entitled "Progress of Truth" was greeted, one correspondent recorded, "as a masterly production indicating, we hope, a future progress in the acquisition of truth and in usefulness that will gladden the hearts of his friends."[16]

The next year, Newark College would change its name to Delaware College. By then, though, Mears had climbed the academic ladder.

• • •

Following his graduation, Mears spent two years at Yale College, taking a variety of courses, after which he enrolled in Yale Divinity School. The prevailing atmosphere was said to be one of "Lyceum lectures and debating societies," when everybody seemed to be writing essays and poems.[17] Mears fit right in. For the rest of his life, he would embrace debate and he would write, incessantly.

While in New Haven, Mears roomed for a time with his classmate James Thomas Hyde, a Yale College graduate who would go on to become a professor at the Theological Seminary of Chicago. Hyde had a lively mind and a talent for long, searching conversations that made him a suitably stimulating companion for earnest John Mears.[18] They could discuss, among many other topics, the provocative teachings of

Professor Nathaniel William Taylor, an influential Congregationalist whose previous students had included John Humphrey Noyes. Mears might well have heard of the by-then notorious Noyes for the first time while following his footsteps through the Yale curriculum.

Mears graduated from divinity school in 1851. The year before, he had traveled to Camden, New Jersey, and called upon a family disaffected with the city's Presbyterian church. Mears, inspired by possibility, suggested establishing a new church in the center of the city. The ambitious notion resonated, and on October 9, 1850, Mears made a formal presentation to the area's Presbyterian governing body.[19] Its members included the president of Mears's alma mater, the renamed Delaware College. Equally fortuitous for Mears was the position on the governing body of Albert Barnes, the influential minister who would prove as important in Mears's life as he was in the life of the Presbyterian Church.

Barnes was born in 1798, in the Oneida County city of Rome. He graduated from Hamilton College in 1820 and then attended Princeton Theological Seminary, after which he served churches in New Jersey and, for many years, Philadelphia. Barnes was an active abolitionist and a fervent crusader, fighting, Mears wrote admiringly, "his earliest battles for Temperance with the apple-distillers of northern New Jersey."[20] As Mears would, Barnes advocated absolute principle in the face of common practice. Adult American alcohol consumption at the time averaged up to seven gallons a year, double modern levels.

"I have exhorted the church to set an example of total abstinence," Barnes declaimed. "I have endeavored to show the manufacture and sale of ardent spirits for drinking purposes can be reconciled neither with the principles of sound morality or religion."[21]

Within the Presbyterian Church, Barnes was a leader of the so-called New School faction. New School ministers stressed evangelical effectiveness, while Old School conservatives hewed to a strict sense of decorum. The Old School clung to Calvinism, predestination, and isolation from other denominations. For Barnes and the New School, preaching was supposed to reach out and touch the congregant. Old

School believers considered the church to be exclusively a spiritual organization, and questioned the wisdom of joining forces with temperance, abolitionist, or other social reform campaigns. The New Schoolers valued revivalism, encouraged cooperation with other denominations, and envisioned universal salvation.[22] Barnes himself knew the power of revivals, having been turned around by one while a student at Hamilton College, and he questioned whether Adam's original sin could be imputed to all who followed.

Barnes's convictions led to his being put on trial for doctrinal deviations before the Second Presbytery of Philadelphia in 1835. Barnes's acquittal was later reversed by the Synod of Philadelphia, whose elders and ministers concluded Barnes's teachings were contrary to the standards of the Presbyterian Church.[23] Barnes stood firm even as he was suspended from his ministerial duties, successfully appealing his case to the Presbyterian General Assembly.

With his national reputation, tested by fire, Barnes was a powerful ally for Mears and a model of firm conviction. With Barnes's help, Mears secured a go-ahead from the Camden church committee and, following his divinity school graduation, was installed as pastor on April 15, 1852. Barnes offered the ordaining prayer, and Mears delivered his inaugural sermon based on a reading of Luke 5:4.[24]

"Launch out into the deep," Luke admonished.

• • •

Five months after his pastoral installation, Mears entered a different church for a different launch. He was getting married.

Phebe Ann H. Tatem was the daughter of a onetime farmer who later studied medicine. The good doctor was a strict Presbyterian, for whom religion could be a rock in hard times.[25] His first wife had died after barely a year of marriage, when they were both teenagers. He and his second wife, Martha, lost three children in infancy. Phebe was their oldest of four living children, born on April 14, 1824, in Delaware. She did not stray far. In her mid-twenties she was still living at home with her family in Caroline County, Maryland. Somehow, she met John, and they were married at a Denton, Maryland, church on September 2, 1852. Mears was twenty-seven; his new bride was twenty-eight. Their marriage lasted a good many years. Mears's Camden ministry did not.

During Mears's roughly twenty-one months as minister, the Central Presbyterian Church of Camden failed to thrive. Its membership stagnated at sixteen adults, even as the city grew to about eleven thousand residents.[26] Construction of a new building drove the church into debt. Neither Mears's sermons nor his shepherding could grow the flock, or even keep it whole, and in the face of intractable problems he surrendered the pulpit on January 19, 1854.

"All these facts had doubtless their bearing upon the decision of Mr. Mears to seek another field," a Camden church historian noted, adding that "upon the retirement of Mr. Mears from the pastorate, the process of dissolution was very rapid."[27]

The church was sold for use as a Camden public school before the year ended, punctuating Mears's failure. A driven young man, well-educated, and supported by powerful mentors, Mears had nonetheless flunked his first churchly test. The memory would sting and linger. From that bleak beginning, on October 31, 1854, Mears accepted a call to serve the Presbyterian church in Elkton, Maryland. He did not last there long, either. In November 1857 he moved on to another backwater post in Milford, Delaware, located seventy miles south of Wilmington. In that unlikely setting, Mears gave it his all. At the very least, he counted some successes, adding thirteen members to the congregation before he resigned on February 15, 1860.[28]

With his departure from Milford, Mears left the active ministry for good. All in all, he had not materially prospered since divinity school. His first church collapsed. He struggled in his two subsequent, short-lived callings. His challenges at all three, admittedly, had been severe. He had been tested in everything from fundraising and strategic planning to sermon writing and small talk. Mears excelled in some tasks more than in others. He was energetic and ambitious; he wanted to make his mark. He read carefully, thought deeply, and did not shy from conflict. Far from it—he sought out the fight.

Mears left the Milford church to take a position with the *American Presbyterian* newspaper. Henceforth, Mears would seek audiences larger than a single congregation. He had found the stage for which he was suited.

"The religious newspapers circulating in our families and congregations should be sufficient auxiliaries to the pastors in training the people to correct views of doctrine and duty," the Milford Presbytery stated in a farewell resolution, "and we believe Brother Mears, in his position as editor, is admirably qualified for such a work."[29]

Correcting the errant and defending the faith powered John Mears's lifelong personal ministry. In the *American Presbyterian*, he found his first sturdy platform. Its prior editor, Daniel Clay Houghton, held decided views that he, too, expressed forcefully. If anything, a eulogist recalled, Houghton was "perhaps too candid in his exposure of charlatanism in religion." With Houghton's death in July 1860—or, as the same Presbyterian eulogist elaborated, when Houghton "passed that mysterious barrier which separates time and eternity"—Mears stepped in as editor.[30]

For Mears, the editor's job opening was fortuitous. Writing would tap his talent for argument, and Philadelphia would educate him in ways that Milford could not. Philadelphia had been, for decades, the center of Presbyterianism in the United States, and the center's center was at 1334 Chestnut Street, about a mile from Mears's new home. The *American Presbyterian* shared space with church officials, the staffs of other church periodicals, and the Presbyterian Board of Publication, which, over the years, uncompromisingly produced brochures, pamphlets, and books. One characteristic volume published shortly after Mears left, entitled *Gaffney's Tavern, and the Entertainment It Afforded*, was described as a book that would "inspire its readers with a fresh zeal to suppress those fountains of sin and woe, the dram-shops."[31] Another, a seventy-two-page tract sold for ten cents, summed up a prevalent bias with its title, *Romanism, the Enemy of Civil Liberty*. Mears fit right in, sharing the anti-liquor and anti-Catholic sentiments of his time and place.

"We hold that this country, in its essential character as a land of religious liberty in law, is a Protestant country," Mears would write, adding that "its toleration in matters of religion cannot extend to what would prove openly subversive of its Protestant nationality."[32]

Albert Barnes was close at hand, serving as an editor of the *American Presbyterian and Theological Review*. One repeat contributor to this journal was a Union College professor named Tayler Lewis, who loathed the Oneida Community as much as Mears would come to. Henry Darling, Mears's childhood friend from Reading, could also be found around 1334 Chestnut Street as permanent clerk of the Presbyterian Church in the United States of America. Henry Darling had been instrumental in establishing the *American Presbyterian*, putting him in a position to help Mears. He also served directly with the ever-present Barnes, as both were members of the Presbyterian Publications Committee.

The newspaper Mears took over was typically eight pages long, and published on Thursdays with a claimed circulation of four thousand. For the two-dollar annual subscription, the *American Presbyterian*'s readers received a self-described "religious and family newspaper" that was published "in the interest of the constitutional Presbyterian church." By this, Mears meant the New School. The presumptive claim irritated some Old School proponents, a fact that would not have bothered the combative Mears in the slightest. His paper included a mix of stories and editorials that were, as the paper put it, "devoted to the promotion of sound Christian doctrine and pure religion." It was one of many religious publications—the country was replete with them. From Philadelphia alone, the 1863 city directory showed, came the *Catholic Herald and Visitor*, the *Episcopal Recorder*, the *Friends' Intelligencer*, the *Occident and American Jewish Advocate*, the *Lutheran and Missionary* and, for the German audience, the *Sunday Blatt*.

Mears undertook newspaper work with his characteristic certitude. He was, an ally said, a "bold, uncompromising advocate of the right." He addressed the pressing religious and social questions of the day, writing with what the same ally called "vigor, acuteness, breadth of thought and . . . a thoroughly candid, manly and wholesome tone."[33] Mears also showed a hard edge, denouncing the "Romish church," ridiculing death penalty opponents, questioning women's suffrage, and deriding those foreigners he identified as "John Chinaman."

"He lacks discernment to discover his own inferiority to the people among whom he has come," one unsigned *American Presbyterian* essay declared of the Chinese immigrants on January 6, 1870. "Perhaps he has never gone far enough in the slow workings of his mental machinery even to make a comparison."

Mears packed his paper with editorial comments, reports from scattered correspondents, snippets about other religious denominations, and fusillades in the Presbyterians' doctrinal war. At times, he also promoted himself. Positive reviews of his own book about the Reformation, *The Beggars of Holland and the Grandees of Spain*, landed on his paper's front page. For weeks on end in 1867, he published lengthy travel letters from abroad attributed to "Our Special European Correspondent." This otherwise unidentified individual's initials, G. W. M., were the same as Mears's brother George, the prosperous Philadelphia grain merchant. Mears also identified himself as editor with a certain typographical grandeur, his name larger and more ornamented than others on the page, even as he still grubbed for ads to pay the bills.

A typical issue might carry advertisements for Moffet's Life Pills, Mrs. Sherman's Corsets, an assortment of tempting French confections, and Batchelor's Hair Dye. Through the decade Mears spent in Philadelphia, he and his paper ventured into myriad social campaigns. He believed in order. He abhorred disturbances, and Philadelphia, a city of half a million residents, was filled with them.

Streetcars, for instance. Their clamor intruded on Sunday sermons, distracting congregants and compelling ministers to raise their voices. That was not all. Sunday streetcars drove people to sin. Mears and his allies thought the nickel-fare service facilitated the search for liquor and tempted the poor to squander their money. On Tuesday, October 2, 1866, Mears and Albert Barnes joined others in court to seek an injunction against Sunday streetcar operations. A commonwealth that professed itself as Christian, Mears argued, should not let city noises impede worship.

"The running of the streetcars on Sunday is . . . a violation of fundamental law, human and divine," the *American Presbyterian* stated.[34]

A devout judge welcomed the complaints. Pennsylvania Supreme Court Justice William Strong, an active Presbyterian, issued an injunction blocking Sunday operations of the Union Passenger Railway Co. Echoing Mears and Barnes, Strong wrote that "the noise of running the cars, the grating of wheels on curves, the clatter of horses' hooves on starting, the sound of the signal bell and the hallooing of those who wish to stop the cars for passage seriously annoy the occupants of the pews."[35]

Strong and Mears were cut from the same cloth. The year after Strong heard arguments in the streetcar case, he was elected president of the new National Reform Association, formed to pass a constitutional amendment declaring "Almighty God as the source of all authority and power in civil government."[36] To Mears's profound disgust, though, the Pennsylvania Supreme Court later dissolved Strong's injunction. While Mears complained that the streetcar company managers lacked either a soul or a conscience, in a November 1867 decision the state's high court ruled that the streetcar company could be fined for running cars on Sunday in violation of the state's Sabbath law, but it could not be preemptively enjoined from operating. Streetcar noises may be a general nuisance, and therefore subject to sanction, but churches enjoyed no special claim to command quiet. Unwittingly, by promoting and then losing the legal challenge against Philadelphia's Sunday streetcars, Mears had helped bring about that which he feared: a further unraveling of the connection between Protestant morality and the law.[37]

"The assault of ungodly men, of grasping corporations, of infidels, Romanists and foreigners upon one of the most venerable and effective safeguards of public order and morals" was encouraged by the insufficiently Christian court, the *American Presbyterian* declared on November 21, 1867.

Mears sought to cleanse other corners of the world, as well. In 1866, he wrote a series of articles warning of the pollution that threatened the purity of the Schuylkill River. Presciently, he noted that population growth, manufacturing, and tillage all corrupted the stream upon which city residents depended. More broadly, Mears associated clean water with clean living. It wasn't just a metaphor. There was a clear association, he observed, between access to potable water and the avoidance of disease.

A temperance man, like his mentor Barnes, Mears reported on a survey of 764 groggeries in Washington, DC; 440 of them, the *American Presbyterian* pointedly noted, were owned by Roman Catholics. From his newspaper's pulpit, as well, Mears denounced what he called the "amusement mania." While conceding that laughter had its place, he wanted limits. Man must restrain himself from excess. No less than Noyes, Mears advocated self-control. Modest enjoyment, Mears said, differed from the soul-eroding "gay parties lasting 'til midnight, in which everybody is overdressed or underdressed, in which dances handed down from those of the children of Israel around the Golden Calf are the main attraction."[38]

Thirty-five years old when the Civil War started in 1861, and thirty-seven when the draft was instituted two years later, Mears was not exempt from conscription, but with four young children under the age of ten, he had good reason to stay home. As an editor, though, he could cheerlead. Tens of thousands of copies of the *American Presbyterian* were sent to soldiers and hospitals. Mears also joined Barnes and several other ministers in helping circulate an 1863 selection of uplifting readings entitled *The Courtland Saunders Tract*, named for an ill-fated Union officer with the 118th Pennsylvania Volunteer Infantry, better known as the Corn Exchange Regiment of Philadelphia. The city's grain merchants had financed the regiment and given it its popular name, but nobody had properly trained the young men for war. Saunders, the twenty-one-year-old son of a Presbyterian minister, received a scant several weeks of basic training before being sent to Antietam in 1862. He died on September 20, in a botched attack undone by greenhorn martial confusion.[39]

Seeking to find order in young Captain Saunders's early death, Mears and his fellow civilians wrote at the beginning of the sixty-four-page booklet that the reading selections would "nerve their courage and endurance by reminding them of the righteousness and nobleness of their cause."[40] Mears and the others behind the inspirational booklet were on the same page with the members of the US Christian Commission, who sought through their own wartime book offerings to steer soldiers away from "all yellow-covered literature, lives of pirates and highwaymen [and] works against Christ and country" as well as the "great numbers" of "obscene books and pictures."[41]

• • •

Dr. James Francis Bourns, too, wanted to join his country's fight.

The forty-nine-year-old University of Pennsylvania Medical School graduate was living in Philadelphia at the time of the Battle of Gettysburg. Once the three-day battle ended on July 3, 1863, Bourns joined other volunteer civilian physicians on a mission to aid the survivors. More than fourteen thousand Union soldiers were wounded in the battle, along with some eighteen thousand Confederates, and most of the Army of the Potomac's medical staff had departed with the rest of General George Meade's battered army. Civilian doctors, nurses, and volunteers descended on the crossroads town to help.

Bourns was traveling the twenty-five miles between Chambersburg and Gettysburg when he and three companions, their wagon broken down, entered a tavern. There, they saw an ambrotype and heard a poignant tale that lay behind it. The ambrotype, a glass-plate photograph, had been found in the hands of a fallen, unknown Union soldier. The image showed three young children, their representation apparently the last thing the soldier ever saw. With his final breaths, apparently, the expiring soldier had gazed upon his children with an aching love, bidding them an unheard farewell.

But whose father was he?

Some 7,000 Union and Confederate soldiers had died at Gettysburg, and another 10,790 were missing. They were shades, with no fixed address. The father who died regarding the image of his young children represented them all. He had to be found and put to rest.

Bourns convinced the tavern keeper to let him take the ambrotype back to Philadelphia, where publicity might assist an effort to identify the fallen soldier. Once home, Bourns had several hundred copies made and circulated. The *Philadelphia Press* and the *Philadelphia Inquirer* both picked up the story on October 19, laying the sentiment on with a trowel.

"As he silently gazed upon them his soul passed away," the *Inquirer*'s reporter wrote. "How touching! How solemn!"

Historian Mark H. Dunkelman, in *Gettysburg's Unknown Soldier: The Life, Death and Celebrity of Amos Humiston*, speculates that Bourns next visited Mears at the *American Presbyterian's* Chestnut Street offices about a week after the first newspaper accounts appeared. However it happened, a revised version of the *Philadelphia Inquirer*'s story was reprinted in the October 29 issue of the *American Presbyterian*. A copy of the church paper eventually reached a subscriber in the small town of Portville in western New York, where a thirty-two-year-old mother of three named Philinda Humiston thought she recognized the description of the children in the ambrotype. Her husband, Sergeant Amos Humiston of the 154th New York Volunteer Infantry Regiment, had not been heard from since the battle.[42]

Mrs. Humiston wrote Dr. Bourns, who sent a copy of the ambrotype. The *American Presbyterian* reported the mystery solved in the November 19 issue. The dead soldier was, in fact, Sergeant Humiston. While the picture provided his widow and her three children with the "dread certainty of widowhood and orphanage," Mears's periodical declared, "the severity of the blow was tempered by the dying affection of the father [and] by the tender romance of mystery which enveloped the facts."[43]

Mears, showing the same persistence later demonstrated with his extended Oneida Community battles, didn't let the story rest. He published numerous follow-ups, promoted heavily a planned visit by Bourns to the Humiston family and, in December, announced that new subscribers to the *American Presbyterian* would receive a photograph of Humiston's children.[44] Mears's paper also sponsored a contest for the best poem about the Humiston incident. The winner was

James Gowdy Clark, a popular balladeer who set his "The Children of the Battlefield" to music.[45] Mears published it in the February 4, 1864, issue, with profits from sales of the sheet music dedicated to the Humiston family. The sheet music was also offered as a premium to new subscribers.

More ambitiously, Bourns and others founded the National Orphans Homestead Association to raise funds for a facility serving the children of those slain in war. Mears published an account of the association's founding in November 1865 and continued to follow up. In time, more than three hundred Sunday schools would pitch in contributions of $25 each.

"The fidelity and affection of the dying sergeant for his own little household has set in motion a stream of benevolent intentions designed to embrace many bereaved families," Mears's newspaper declared.[46]

The campaign succeeded. On the afternoon of November 20, 1866, the National Soldiers Orphans Homestead was dedicated in Gettysburg. Located in a large, handsome residence about a half mile from the center of town, the orphanage opened with twenty-seven children who were to receive a free education and the help they needed to make their way in the world. They also had friends in high places. Bourns served as the organization's general secretary. The other overseers included multiple ministers, two former governors, and Erastus O. Haven, then with the University of Michigan and several years away from taking up the post as Syracuse University chancellor. Mears served on the orphanage's six-member executive committee and spoke twice at the dedication, starting the day with a fervent prayer and ending, hours later, at the local Grace Church.[47]

The Gettysburg orphanage survived for a decade. The year after the orphanage opened, the *Evening Telegraph* in Mears's hometown of Philadelphia advised readers that "soon 500 orphans, an army of youthful soldiers, will find shelter under the imposing edifice in process of erection."[48] Funds, the newspaper noted, were sorely needed; they always would be, throughout the institution's increasingly troubled life. The *Evening Telegraph* repeated the plea on May 25, 1869, calling the care of the orphaned children "a sacred duty imposed upon our citizens." The fundraising efforts escalated, with the *Evening Telegraph* on November 29, 1870, alerting the "patriotic and humane public" that "the decline in its receipts threatens embarrassment to the institution." In May 1872, former general George Meade joined Philadelphia-based financier Jay Cooke and others in urging Congress to appropriate $50,000 for the orphanage's educational program.[49]

But for all its good intentions, the orphanage failed in a uniquely horrible way. The teacher hired to run it, Rosa J. Carmichael, was a harsh disciplinarian—sadistic, even. Reports emerged that the orphaned children were starved, beaten, and shackled. Girls were forced to dress as boys as punishment. Children guilty of infractions were kept in a dark, unventilated basement called "the dungeon."[50] Carmichael was eventually convicted in 1876 of aggravated assault on one of the orphans, and Bourns himself was charged with embezzling funds in 1877, the year the troubled facility closed for good.

From its energetic start and apparent success to its ultimately ignoble reputation, the Gettysburg orphanage campaign foreshadowed some aspects of Mears's later Oneida fight. It demonstrated his strengths and limitations. He was endowed with energy and earnest intentions. He could write up a storm, deploying the press to promote a cause, and he could rally the social and religious elite. He persisted. Mears could not, however, control what came after an initial triumph, nor could he determine how history would judge his works.

The site of the former orphanage is now described as "haunted," and is visited nightly by commercial Gettysburg ghost-hunting tours.

6 METAPHYSICS AND STRIFE

MEARS NEEDED A NEW JOB. His newspaper career was over.

In early 1870, the *American Presbyterian* announced that its debts and subscription list were being transferred to the *New-York Evangelist*, a weekly paper long affiliated with the church's New School faction. The move coincided with a broader healing of the decades-old schism dividing Presbyterians, a reunification that cast longtime combatants a little adrift. After a decade of standing fast and flinging words, the forty-four-year-old Mears required something different.

"The work of *The American Presbyterian* is done," the paper announced on February 17, saying that "without flinching or reserve, we have stuck to the great, scriptural, Christian principles of social order, of the sacredness of law, of human rights."

The newspaper's closing left Mears an editor without a journal, a preacher without a pulpit. Though he identified himself as a "Presbyterian minister" to the US census enumerator in June, specifying that he was "NSP," Mears lacked a portfolio. How he made ends meet, with a wife and four children, is not clear. He shouldered other weights, as well. His father, Henry Haller Mears, was also living nearby in Philadelphia and was in declining health.

At about the same time, Hamilton College officials had begun raising money to endow a faculty chair in honor of Albert Barnes, the esteemed Philadelphia-based Presbyterian minister who was one of the school's favorite sons. The Hamilton College endowment drive was led by the Reverend Nicholas Westermann Goertner who, as college pastor, tended the students' spiritual lives. Goertner also wore another hat: as college commissioner, he squeezed donations from those with money to spare.

Goertner was not a physically robust man. When younger, a eulogist subsequently recalled, "his physical system was wasting with lung decay,"[1] but as a fundraiser he excelled. The task rewarded patience, persistence, and a certain degree of shamelessness. Goertner had it all. The struggling college badly needed his services, as it was described by one as "hopelessly in debt [and] its buildings and credit were crumbling to decay."[2] Goertner set about connecting with men of means. He was the kind of man, a Hamilton College historian wrote, "who literally turned a deaf ear to rejections of his pleas for help."[3] Turn him down once, and he'd return. Give a little, and he'd be back for more.

"There is none so poor," Goertner reasoned, "that he is not able to do something. If he cannot bring a wreath with which to crown the head of the good old mother, let him at least pluck a single flower and place it on her brow or lay it on her bosom."[4]

For the sake of the proposed Albert Barnes's professorship, Goertner pressed his appeal on congregants of Philadelphia's First Presbyterian Church, among others. Hamilton College president Samuel Gilman Brown periodically raised the topic at monthly meetings of the college's board of trustees throughout the latter months of 1870. On December 21, the trustees once again discussed the endowment at length while meeting at Bagg's Hotel in downtown Utica. Brown mentioned one potential candidate in particular: John W. Mears, of Philadelphia.[5]

Something, or somebody, had brought Mears's name to Brown's attention prior to the December 21 board meeting. The board minutes do not explain how the connection was made between Mears and the fifty-seven-year-old college president, who had graduated from Dartmouth College in 1831, one year after Noyes, and then from Andover Theological Seminary several years after Noyes left. Brown himself did not share some of Mears's most combative characteristics. Notably, colleagues said, Brown was a genial soul who was neither by nature nor practice a controversialist.

"He had no fondness for the strife of words," Hamilton professor A. G. Hopkins said.[6]

No one would ever say that of Mears, who fed on conflict. Brown and Mears, though, did share an interest in metaphysics, the subject that Brown taught. Both men were avid readers and prolific writers, and both men had some connection through Albert Barnes. Barnes himself may well have been the one to suggest Mears as a candidate. Barnes had certainly helped the younger man in the past, beginning with Mears's first, ill-starred church posting back in Camden, New Jersey. In Philadelphia, the two at times worked in close quarters at 1334 Chestnut Street, the home of Presbyterian Publications. However it happened, Mears's name entered play. Following further discussion, the Hamilton board delegated the job search to the board's executive committee.

Barnes himself remained active in church affairs, though he was seventy-two years old and nearly blind. He had surrendered the First Presbyterian Church pulpit three years earlier, but the spirit still moved him. On Christmas Eve 1870, accompanied by his daughter, he walked a mile from his North Walnut Street home to make a condolence call to an afflicted family. Shortly after he arrived, Barnes slumped in his chair and passed away. It was a suitably peaceful death, but it would have shaken Mears, already grieving the loss of his father just two weeks earlier.

Barnes received a grand send-off on the afternoon of December 28, honored by the high and mighty. The pallbearers included US Supreme Court Justice William Strong, who several years before had ruled in support of Barnes and Mears in their fight against streetcars running on the Sabbath. Mears, though a close ally of Barnes, was not selected to join Strong and others as a pallbearer.[7]

Six weeks later, Hamilton's seven-member executive committee convened on February 16 to discuss filling the Albert Barnes professorship. The money was coming in, thanks to Barnes's repute and Goertner's relentlessness, but the new hire needed careful consideration. With the college so small, employing barely a dozen faculty members, a good fit was crucial. The discussion went on at some length but without resolution. On March 6, joined by Goertner, the executive committee returned to the Utica study of Presbyterian minister and college trustee Philemon H. Fowler. Goertner had succeeded in raising $17,200 for the endowment, nearing the $25,000 goal, and it was time to move. Brown, the college president, again had his say, while the other committee members weighed in after their own fashion.

College secretary and treasurer Othniel S. Williams was a former Oneida County judge whose weak voice masked a strong will. He was formal, dignified, and accustomed to having his way; he worked as a railroad lawyer, when he wasn't handling college affairs. Equally self-confident was William D. Walcott, whose Utica-area manufacturing business had brought a reported $100,000 salary during the Civil War.[8] The Reverend Amos Delos Gridley was a onetime Presbyterian minister who had graduated from Andover Theological Seminary about a decade after Noyes had departed. Ill health had compelled Gridley to retire from the pulpit, but he maintained an active interest in art and landscaping. An amateur painter, he had an eye for the beautiful, the right.[9]

Together, the men unanimously adopted a resolution supporting hiring Mears for the Barnes professorship, contingent upon reaching the endowment's $25,000 goal.[10] The offer was conveyed, and on March 24 Mears accepted.

"Relying upon divine aid and upon the sympathy of your committee and board, I shall endeavor to fulfill the duties laid upon me by the committee," Mears wrote.[11]

Mears had favorably impressed the board. His personal association with Albert Barnes himself surely helped, and his own religious credentials were sound even if his ministerial record was mixed. Though he had no prior college teaching experience, Mears was both learned and prolific. His scholarly record extended back to his time at Yale, when he had published a translation from the Greek of the orations of Thucydides. In 1867, his doggedness at the *American Presbyterian* had earned him an honorary doctor of divinity degree from Indiana University. He had published an astonishingly diverse set of works, from his twenty-four-page pamphlet, "Water Supply of Our Great

Cities," to his 477-page tome entitled *The Beggars of Holland and the Grandees of Spain*. He had energy to burn.

"In his editorials, he always met science with the welcome of a thoughtful, fearless faith, and always sought to illustrate the naturalness and necessity of a close alliance between the highest culture and the deepest piety," the *Utica Weekly Herald* recited on March 28, 1871.

Mears seemed altogether well-suited for the Albert Barnes professorship. In some ways, a sympathizer later wrote, "his preparations for it had been unconsciously going on during [his] studies and activities of the previous 25 years."[12] The full board of trustees subsequently ratified his selection, at the soon-to-be-disputed salary of $1,500 a year. The two dozen trustees who hired him saw in Mears a man, it was communicated on March 28 in the *Utica Weekly Herald*, whose "native gifts, culture and habits of intellectual work" would ensure his "usefulness and popularity" at Hamilton.

Mears loved, at first sight, the college located about nine miles from central Utica. He subsequently recounted the one-mile hike from the village of Clinton up College Hill to the fifteen-acre campus shaded by trees commemorating individual classes. Mears took in the college's chapel and gymnasium, the dormitories and the little observatory in which the school took great pride. He saw the Lombardy poplars, the carefully selected elm, maple, and ash trees. He felt himself in Arcadia.

"I was startled," Mears wrote later, "by the unexpected beauty and amplitude of the scene. The Hill Difficulty had become the Delectable Mountains."[13]

With his oblique reference to John Bunyan's *The Pilgrim's Progress*, Mears hinted at his own narrative of personal journey. He saw himself as a man for whom travails served a greater purpose. More than that, the panorama truly roused Mears. Sounding, uncharacteristically, like a besotted sensualist, he marveled at the wide valley "swept in soft curves." Thoroughly enamored, he confessed that the landscape "even in its undress, struck me as one of uncommon loveliness."

Following his selection, Mears was formally welcomed to campus on Tuesday, July 18, 1871. Hamilton College president Samuel Gilman

3. John W. Mears. By the Notman Photographic Co. Courtesy of Hamilton College Archives.

Brown spoke glowingly about the newcomer. Mears's position as philosophy professor, Brown assured members of the college community, required "enlarged reading, the most subtle and patient thought, the most persistent labor."[14] Mears, in turn, introduced himself with a midmorning recitation entitled "The Antagonisms, Perils and Glory of the Spiritual Philosophy." He had left the physical landscape behind. Instead, his address was pure Mears, an elevation of mind above body.

"The fact is," Mears told his audience, "man has fallen in love with this lower world, this earthly home of his."[15]

Sincere, humorless, and altogether too long, Mears's inaugural address warned against appetite and seduction. Man, Mears said, was being "bewitched into a new idolatry . . . an exaltation of material forces." He cautioned against the "madness of unrestrained indulgence," and insisted on turning the mind inward and upward. Materialists and natural scientists were, Mears said, "devoting their lives to tracing the physical relations of man downward to the lowest type of animal life"—a place, he said with disgust, of "dark and slimy depths."

Mears went on and on, showing no mercy either for his philo-sophical antagonists or for his wearying audience. Later published in the October 1871 issue of the *American Presbyterian and Theological Review*, Mears's written-out recitation extended twenty-eight pages. When Mears finally sat down, the *New-York Evangelist* later reported, with perhaps more insight than it knew, "the professor's reputation as a philosopher was made."[16]

Behind the scenes, his new colleagues were seeing another side of Mears's zest for combat.

The college's original job tender in March had been contingent on completing the fundraising. Until the college met its $25,000 tar-get, the endowed chair could not be occupied. At the moment of Mears's selection by the executive committee, the fundraising was nearly $8,000 short.

Mears's family stepped in.

His seventy-year-old mother, Anna, and his younger brother George Washington Mears could help out. The Philadelphia-based grain merchant firm begun by John and George's father, H. H. Mears & Son, had grown to become one of the city's largest. The *Success-ful American* magazine puffed H. H. Mears & Son as "one of the best known grain and commission houses in the United States,"[17] and George Mears moved in select circles. At various times, he would serve as president of the Philadelphia Commercial Exchange, founding vice president of Philadelphia's Maritime Exchange, and director of the Philadelphia National Bank.

In brief, George W. Mears had financial resources that his brother did not. He and his mother offered to complete the Albert Barnes endowment. And so they were, John Mears added pointedly in an August 21 letter, "somewhat surprised and puzzled" by the college's offer of a paltry $1,500 salary for the new Albert Barnes professorship. Mears's mother and brother thought $2,000 would be more like it; anything less would be inadequate. His relatives' distress was such, Mears said, that he felt his only escape from the awkward situation might be to resign his new position immediately. At the very least,

Mears warned shortly before the school year started, he could not promise a long stay at Hamilton College.

"The time of $1,500 professorships in respectable institutions is passed," Mears wrote. "Neither myself nor my relatives are willing to be connected with them, especially after having done all they feel able to do to raise them to a higher standard."[18]

Mears had not even begun teaching, and he was already disruptive. Somehow, though, he and college officials came to an agreement, and after this awkward beginning Hamilton seemed, in theory, like a good fit for Mears. The college took religion seriously, as did he. When Mears arrived, roughly half of the trustees and professors were ordained ministers. Students attended mandatory Sunday chapel, morning prayer services, and weekly student-run noon prayers. More Hamilton alumni had entered the ministry than any other profession.

The college enrolled 172 students during the 1871–72 school year. They paid an annual tuition of $60 for a rigid course of study. Freshmen began with a review of Latin grammar and courses in algebra, rhetoric, and the Bible. Seniors concluded with general chemistry, natural theology, and philosophy of the mind. Discipline was enforced by a system of warning marks, with expulsion the ultimate penalty. Rigidity also characterized social relations. Students would not talk to faculty members outside of class for fear of being labeled a "supe." Freshmen would not carry a cane or wear a hat until after the end of the second term. The penalty for violation was to have the cane seized and the hat smashed.

"The rule of the hats was never violated," an 1877 graduate named Louis Boisot recalled, "for a silk hat was expensive to buy, easy to smash and as impossible to restore as Humpty Dumpty himself."[19]

Still, for all its sincerity, the college was struggling financially. Its facilities were spare. The college's future at times seemed perilous. The faculty was underpaid, and students were graduating without paying their bills.[20] The college was operating at an annual deficit, and Mears soon recognized that improvements were urgently demanded.

"The college buildings include some substantial structures," Mears noted, "but with the exception of the handsome new library building, as yet unfinished, they are either much in need of repairs, or are too perishable for the treasures of minerals and apparatus they are beginning to contain."[21]

Students had their own complaints, which soon extended to their new philosophy professor. Hamilton College seniors, members of the class of 1872, were disappointed that the college president, Dr. Brown, would not be teaching metaphysics. For all his administrative shortcomings, Brown was a popular lecturer. Mears tried hard, but the novice teacher took some getting used to.

"It seemed an intrusion, almost," the *Hamilton Literary Monthly* candidly reported in February 1872, "that another, and especially one unaccustomed to teaching should take the place of our president in his favorite branch."[22]

Mears pushed students hard in what he termed mental gymnastics. He embraced intellectual conflict, the push and pull that strengthened the mind. Unsurprisingly, this made him, a eulogist acknowledged, "not always popular with students, especially those who proved derelict."[23] Mears would divide a typical class into sections and then allow students about seven minutes to elucidate a topic such as "Have we knowledge of the infinite?" and "Is sight or touch more important in gaining knowledge of the outside world?" Quoting Sir William Hamilton, a Scottish philosopher who was one of his favorites, Mears maintained that the professor's primary responsibility was "rousing students to a vigorous and varied exertion of their faculties."[24]

He lectured on the Book of Romans to juniors and taught intellectual philosophy to seniors. He taught German and French and, for seniors, he offered an optional course entitled Kant's Kritik der Reinen Vernuft. Mears revered Kant, the eighteenth-century Prussian philosopher who imagined as a thought experiment a world apart from "mere sensuous experience; color, hardness or softness, weight, even impenetrability."[25] Once free of the merely physical, metaphysicians, like Kant and Mears, could float among pure concepts such as the nature of God, freedom of will, and the meaning of time and space. The mere, filthy body was abandoned.

With intricately knotted sentences like "Conjunction is the representation of the synthetical unity of the manifold,"[26] Kant's *Kritik* (*Critique*) sorely tried the average undergraduate's patience. To Mears, though, it revealed the inherent power of the mind. Kant, Mears believed, should undergird every college curriculum. "All the thinking of centuries preceding seemed, in contrast to the 'Kritik,' to be shallow and purblind," he declared.[27]

Such metaphysics appealed to Mears far more than the newfangled theorists, like Charles Darwin. In the December 28, 1876, issue of the *New-York Evangelist*, Mears challenged the "materialism" and manifold errors of Darwin, enunciated seventeen years earlier in *On the Origin of Species*. Mears blasted the "preposterous claims," "numerous contradictions," and "self-conceit" of those who followed Darwin's "second-rate science," just as he denounced the "absurdity, presumption and contradictions" of Herbert Spencer, an evolutionary thinker who coined the phrase "survival of the fittest."[28]

However, Charles Darwin was not the biggest danger threatening John Mears's world.

7 BRIDLING THE PASSIONS

CLINTON could not contain John Mears.

The remote college town of about one thousand residents was far removed from bustling Philadelphia, the nation's second-most populous city, where Mears grew accustomed to the clash of competing ideas. As editor of the *American Presbyterian,* he had battled every single week. From Hamilton College's isolated hilltop, Mears saw all those distant battlefields and longed to enlist.

"Doctor Mears," a contemporary wrote, "was not content with the still air of delightful studies, and the quiet routine duties of the classroom."[1]

Mears sought the arena, where men compete before crowds. When he told his Hamilton students that "what the college wants is visibility,"[2] he was highlighting his own appetite as well as the college's lack. At Hamilton College, Mears missed the visibility he had found in Philadelphia while fighting for clean rivers, quiet Sundays, and sober citizens. Some of these campaigns were unique to the big city and could not be replicated in Clinton: the village had no streetcars, and the waters were fine. Intemperance, though, soiled even the smallest town, and it still summoned from Mears the utmost zeal.

"There can be no temperate use of alcohol as a beverage," Mears maintained, "any more than there can be temperate theft, adultery or murder."[3]

• • •

The founders of the American Temperance Society in 1826 had articulated a similar absolutist vision. While earlier efforts had focused on excessive drinking, the American Temperance Society and its progeny targeted the moderate drinker as well. Only strict prohibition could bridle the power of ardent spirits.

"All the drunkenness . . . that shall pollute our land must be traced to moderate drinkers," early temperance leader John Marsh had declared in a widely circulated 1829 tract. "They feed the monster. They keep in countenance the distillery and the dram-shop, and every drunkard that reels in the street."[4]

The message resonated. By 1833, more than six thousand state and local temperance societies had formed in the United States, with a million or so individuals having pledged themselves to total abstinence.[5] More than morality was at stake. Business leaders wanted sober workers. In New York State, the temperance movement from the 1830s on had seemed strongest in manufacturing towns like Utica, Syracuse, and others along the Erie Canal. In Philadelphia, a leading manufacturer of locomotive equipment patronized the city's First Presbyterian Church and heeded the temperance sermons of the church's minister, the influential Albert Barnes.[6]

Barnes, at one point, even shamed his fellow Presbyterian clergymen into forgoing the discreet sips that had warmed them prior to their synod meetings. He was willing to risk losing his congregation with his uncompromising rectitude. "I find I am the pastor of nineteen distilleries and some twenty grogshops," Barnes once preached, "and I find in the Bible where the future habitation of such men shall be." Feeling the heat, the guilty congregants gave up their "evil" ways.[7]

Mears, Barnes's acolyte, likewise distrusted alcohol. Drink, he cautioned, creates "a morbid thirst and craving, furious and insatiable as a wild beast."[8] Even moderate partaking would bring about a person's downfall. Alcohol, Mears said, was "destructive of reason, so crippling to the right exercise of the faculties in the daily walk of life" while it "ravages the bodily system, shattering the nerves, draining the vital force, arresting the natural processes, and exposing the system to every form of disease and to premature and disgraceful death."[9]

And still, people craved alcohol. In 1866, a survey sponsored by the Young Men's Christian Association (YMCA) in New York City identified more than 7,700 porter houses and beer halls as well as

223 concert saloons that employed "1,191 semi-clad waitresses, many of them prostitutes."[10] Smaller cities shared the thirst. By 1875, 249 licensed saloons operated in Syracuse, and temperance activists were denouncing "the enormous flooding of the city with low drinking houses."[11]

Even tiny Clinton was vulnerable. Edward North, a Hamilton professor of Greek, had warned the local Sons of Temperance in a July 4, 1848, address about the "besotted vassals" who toasted each other with "cups brimming of death."[12] Early in Mears's own Hamilton career, a fire destroyed the town's Clinton House Hotel. On the burnt-out site, an entrepreneur erected a slapdash shack for dispensing liquor until student vigilantes one night tried to pull it down. The lethally armed proprietor chased them off.

Other Hamilton students partook freely. "There was a great deal of drinking in college," Charles R. Kingsley, a member of Hamilton's class of 1878, recalled half a century later, "and trips to Utica were not always as they should be."[13] Nor were saloons the only purveyors of intoxicants. Local newspaper advertisements during Mears's Hamilton tenure promoted tonics like Lydia Pinkham's Vegetable Compound, Paine's Celery Compound, and Ayer's Sarsaparilla, each of whose alcohol content was a jarring 20 percent or more.

Women, though still disenfranchised, were at the forefront of the fight against the threat of alcohol. On February 21, 1874, a number of women convened in Plattsburgh, located in northernmost New York, and adopted a resolution opposing the granting of liquor licenses save for medicinal purposes. Identifying themselves as "wives, daughters, mothers and sisters," the Plattsburgh abolitionists declared that "our sex, even more than yours, are the sufferers from the sale of intoxicating beverages."[14] The next month, in Peterboro, located about seven miles from the Oneida Community, some thirty women swarmed the saloons on Friday and Saturday nights. Denied admittance, the women gathered on the steps for song and speeches. "Some hostile person threw flour upon the women from the second story," the *Lewis County Democrat* reported on March 25, 1874. "It was stopped by a constable, who received more than his share." Other tactics arose. A Mrs. Martin from Brooklyn proposed that same year to train attractive young women in temperance matters, then send them into saloons to spread the good word.

"The man does not live who can resist the persuasions of six pretty girls of the nineteenth century," Mrs. Martin reasoned.[15]

Mears wielded his pen in the fight. Always a prolific writer, he had authored a sermon entitled "The Church and Temperance," which was sold for fifteen cents by the National Temperance Society alongside other titles, including "Self-denial: A Duty and Pleasure" by Reverend J. P. Newman. Mears firmly believed the church should lead the temperance fight, and he took temperance to its most zealous extreme. Casting a sideways glance at other temptations, such as "dancing and the worldly amusements of modern society," Mears prescribed "a lifelong course of self-denial."

The alternative was hellish.

"It so robs man of the respect of himself and neighbors," Mears wrote of alcohol. "It so hurls him into poverty and disgrace [and] it opens the pores of his moral system to every kind of criminal solicitation."[16]

Mears preached to the choir, so to speak, at events such as the New York State Christian Convention held in Syracuse December 2–5, 1873. The speakers at the three-day convention included Erastus O. Haven, a future anti-Oneida crusader already known to Mears through their work on the Gettysburg orphanage and soon-to-be chancellor at Syracuse University. For one program at the convention, Mears joined a Methodist Episcopal minister from Elmira and a Lutheran minister from Albany in urging suppression of the liquor traffic. Despite their doctrinal differences, the three men of God agreed on the necessity of absolute temperance.

Following the convention, on a snowy April day in 1874, Mears and other members of the Utica Presbytery met to pass resolutions endorsing the "awakened zeal of Christian women on behalf of temperance,"[17] and calling for the total suppression of liquor trafficking.

Society required cleansing. No less than the individual, the civic body was a temple, not to be defiled by alcohol, tobacco, or gambling.

Or smut, of which there was plenty.

. . .

Pernicious literature spread faster than wildfire. New York City dominated the production, summed up in an 1862 mail-order catalog advertising "Books on Love." To the antebellum standards like *Memoirs of a Woman of Pleasure,* there existed other titles, such as *The Life and Adventures of Silas Shovewell* and *The Mysteries of Venus; Or, the Amatory Life and Adventures of Miss Kitty Pry.*[18] The Civil War accelerated the demand for such erotica, and this, in turn, prompted New York crusaders to secure legislation banning the publication and sale of obscene materials. By the end of the Civil War, twenty states had legislated prohibitions against obscene materials.

An old nemesis of the Oneida Community, prosecutor Samuel Garvin, brought the first indictment under New York's Obscene Literature Act. After pressuring the Community as Oneida County district attorney, Garvin had moved on to become district attorney for New York County. Urged on by the YMCA's Committee on Obscene Literature, in 1869 Garvin moved against the purveyor of such titles as *The Life and Amours of the Beautiful, Gay and Dashing Kate Percival.*[19]

"I am," confided Miss Percival, "what is called a woman of pleasure, and have drained its cup to the very dregs."[20]

With that, Miss Percival then spent the next several hundred pages recollecting one romp after another with "the Frenchman's instrument," and the "domain of Venus," enlivened by an assortment of "magnificent buttocks," "plump thighs," and the occasional "luscious grotto." These were inflammatory words, written deliberately to arouse men. Garvin ultimately secured a guilty plea from the seller, who nonetheless escaped with a suspended sentence.

"This setback," historian Donna Dennis noted, "would be the first of many that moral reformers would experience in prosecuting obscenity cases in New York County courts."[21]

State-by-state prosecutions failed in the face of a national danger. Congress started in 1842 with a tariff bill provision banning the importation of "all indecent and obscene" materials.[22] President Abraham Lincoln, in early 1865, had signed the first federal law making it a misdemeanor to mail an "obscene book, pamphlet, picture, print or other publication of a vulgar or indecent character." The bill lacked muscle. Though the law specified penalties of up to a year in prison and a $500 fine, Congress had neither specified an enforcement mechanism nor adequately detailed a definition of obscenity. The erotica continued spreading.

Anthony Comstock saw what was needed.

Comstock was a stout man who gave muttonchops a bad name, standing 5'10" and weighing two hundred-plus pounds. In time, when he had attained the public stature he hungered for, his physical appearance would be deployed against him as a caricature of well-fed self-righteousness. It took him time, though, to grow into himself. Raised as a Congregationalist, Comstock carried his faith into the army. While serving in the Seventeenth Connecticut Volunteer Infantry Regiment, he led Bible classes for his fellow enlisted men, who did not always appreciate his cleanliness. A typical army of the Potomac camp, one United States Christian Commission official reported, was "reeking with profanity and fetid with vulgarity and obscenity . . . card playing, profanity and ribald songs were the order."[23]

Comstock kept at it as a civilian. While working as a store clerk in 1868, he initiated a complaint against the seller of lewd books who had lured a friend into injurious temptation.[24] Comstock's resolute will ignited, leading him to work first with the Young Men's Christian Association and then, in 1873, the YMCA's spin-off organization, the New York Society for the Suppression of Vice. He soon needed sharper tools, for the 1865 federal law banning the mailing of obscene materials omitted reference to materials containing information about contraception or abortions, and it did not authorize search and seizure. Comstock, his way paid by businessman and philanthropist Morris Jesup, testified before the House Judiciary Committee on February 24, 1873, pulling from his brown leather briefcase an assortment of pornographic engravings, postcards, and contraceptive devices.

"It may well be doubted," declared Representative Clinton Merriam, a Republican who lived about thirty miles north of Utica, "if war, pestilence or famine could leave deeper or more deadly scars upon a nation than the general diffusion of this pestilential literature."[25]

By March 3, Congress had sent to the White House for President Grant's signature a bill that broadened postal restrictions. Formally called the Act for the Suppression of Trade in, and Circulation of, Obscene Literature and Articles of Immoral Use, the law was popularly dubbed the Comstock Act in honor of its most fervent champion. Drafted with the help of Supreme Court Justice William Strong of Pennsylvania who, as a state judge, had once sided with Mears's crusade against Philadelphia's Sunday streetcars,[26] the law made it a federal crime to advertise or communicate through the mails material that was "lewd or lascivious," or obscene, or "of an indecent character." In language that alarmed the Oneida Community, the new law also prohibited the mailing of information concerning "the prevention of conception or procuring of abortions."

Since the beginning of his career, Noyes had written frankly about sex. While neither pornographic nor gynecological in the details, and intended to instruct rather than arouse, Noyes's writings were vulnerable to denunciation. His essay *Male Continence, or Self-Control in Sexual Intercourse*, first published in 1866 and subsequently expanded to a green-covered, twenty-four-page pamphlet in 1872, could quickly excite Comstock's scrutiny. Noyes's "appeal to the memory of every man who has had good sexual experience," and his declaration that a properly disciplined man should "be able to enjoy the presence and the motion *ad libitum*"[27] cut too close to the bone.

Noyes shared, in his own way, Comstock's and Mears's loathing for obscene material. He viewed it, like prostitution and masturbation, as an interference with the proper relationship between man and woman. The men radically differed, though, on what constituted obscenity, and Comstock took a hard line against the "free lusters," for whom "marriage is bondage, love is lust, celibacy is suicide [and] fidelity to marriage vows is a relic of barbarism."[28] It would not be hard for Comstock or his allies, like Mears, to cast Oneida's literature as obscene. One Oneida pamphlet, a writer fumed in *Frank Leslie's Illustrated Newspaper* on April 23, 1870, was "so filthy that no average gambler or courtesan would, for one moment, linger over its pages."

The way Noyes saw it, he did not write to excite, but to educate. He was, in fact, an amateur scientist, and his experiments extended beyond sexual performance to include human breeding. Ever the tinkerer, Noyes had been reading Charles Darwin and reached certain conclusions about offspring. The betterment of the human species should not be left to chance, even if that required breaking yet more conventions. He coined the term *stirpiculture*, from the Latin for root or stock. Fifty-three young women and thirty-eight young men signed up for Noyes's experiment in 1869. The participants would apply for permission to propagate. Noyes and his lieutenants evaluated the applicants for their spiritual fitness as well as physical and intellectual capacities. Noyes, Oneida's baron, would father at least nine of the fifty-eight live children born as part of the stirpiculture venture.

Noyes wrote candidly of the human breeding experiment as well as the practices of male continence and ascending fellowship. He knew his heart was pure, but he could not be sure of how *Male Continence* would be taken by Anthony Comstock, so zealously patrolling the postal frontiers. Noyes was therefore prudent to pull back some publications, though the retreat didn't come soon enough for John W. Mears and his growing collection of Oneida Community evidence.

8 VISITING ONEIDA

IN EARLY AUGUST 1873, Methodist ministers met in Perryville, about four miles from the Oneida Community. There, Reverend Reuben C. Fox denounced his neighbors down the road.

The Oneida Community, Fox said, harbored "the hideous thing that hides away from the light of day and in dens and midnight balls revels in debauchery and shame."[1] Even the Mormons, as abominable as they might be, could not compare to the shameful outrages practiced by the Oneida Community's free lovers, Fox declared.

"Flaunting its vices in the face of the public, and sending out its indecent publications to propagate its free lovism, it is a disgrace to civilization that it has been so unmolested," Fox said.[2]

Fox, an 1854 graduate of the Boston University School of Theology, was still new to his post as minister for the First Methodist Episcopal Church in Waterloo. From this pulpit, located about seventy miles west of Oneida, Fox saw the Community more as an abstraction than a flesh-and-blood neighbor. Indeed, his distance enabled him to perceive how Oneida's commercial success and entanglements had blinded those in closer contact and made it, Fox admitted, "almost hopeless to arouse public sentiment" against the Community. Underscoring the truth of Fox's lament, dozens of "gay and happy" visitors from more than half a dozen villages descended upon the Community several days after Fox's speech for a meal and a tour that participants described as "delightful."[3]

"A visit to their place disarms much of the prejudice that exists against them," one of the August visitors observed.[4]

Nonetheless, Fox's rousing words against Oneida stirred some twenty other Methodist ministers and congregants to join the cry. From their Perryville meeting, they issued a statement urging the public to "drive out the social vermin from their midst."[5] The Methodist session subsequently seemed to spur the Synod of Presbyterians of Central New York.

The Presbyterians were gathering in Utica in October 1873 for their annual conference, shortly before the appearance at the Utica Opera House of P. T. Barnum's traveling aggregation of gymnasts, ventriloquists, and exotic species. Starting on October 22, more than 140 Presbyterian clergymen and laymen convened. They sorted through some administrative matters, but most important to Mears was the necessity of confronting Oneida. During the daytime session of October 23, one of the Presbyterians sought to put the synod on the record as denouncing the Community and calling for combined action along with other denominations. In a rush, the resolution was adopted. Then, some reconsidered. The vote on the resolution, it was noted, occurred amid confusion and noise as synod members were coming and going. The resolution was withdrawn, in time for a field trip.

In the afternoon, ministers and church elders boarded a special train for the twenty-five-minute ride to Clinton. They toured the Hamilton College campus, heard presentations by Mears and others, and feasted on a meal served by the young women of the nearby Houghton Seminary.[6] Upon returning to Utica in the evening, refreshed by their outing, the synod reopened the Oneida Community question. In quiet conversations, some might have more or less tolerated the Community, but a room full of fellow ministers demanded righteousness. With no public objection, the Presbyterian Synod declared it was time to "record its testimony against a notorious evil and flagrant violation of divine law, which for many years has disgraced the name of the county."[7] The synod further declared that it "cannot regard the outward prosperity of the Community as, in the eyes of Christian people, any extenuation of the palpable fact that it is founded in a systematic prostitution and adultery." The Community's practices were worse than Utah's polygamy or Africa's heathenism.

"Its existence," the Presbyterian Synod said, "is a blow to the most sacred of our social ties and institutions."

Mere words would not suffice. The time for action had come. Seven top men would be selected to investigate and, as they saw fit, challenge the Oneida Community. The committee members were to confer with other religious bodies and consider the feasibility of joining forces. The Baptist state convention meeting in Hornellsville, about 130 miles southwest of Syracuse, that October would, in fact, appoint their own committee to cooperate with the Presbyterian Synod.

The Presbyterian committee may not have been Mears's idea alone, but he would become the undisputed leader. The other members joining him were Theodore W. Dwight, the Honorable John C. Churchill of Oswego, Judge Scott Lord of Utica, attorney Daniel Ball, Reverend Samuel Jessup, and Peter Stryker. These were men well positioned to dig deep and strike hard if the moment required.

Theodore W. Dwight, born in 1822, had graduated from Hamilton College after reportedly working his way through all four thousand books in the college's library.[8] Dwight then studied law at Yale, where his grandfather was former president. He had preceded Mears as a professor at Hamilton before joining the Columbia University faculty. Dwight could legally dissect the Oneida Community, and his many civic affiliations could reinforce any follow-up campaign. John C. Churchill, too, was powerfully connected. Born in 1821, he was a Middlebury College graduate who had studied law at Harvard. He served as Oswego County district attorney and then was a county judge during the Civil War before serving two terms in the US House of Representatives.[9] Ball likewise brought a prosecutor's perspective, as the Hamilton College graduate had served as Oneida County district attorney from 1868 to 1872. Together, Dwight, Ball, and Churchill could calculate the Oneida Community's legal vulnerabilities.

Samuel Jessup was younger, a graduate of Princeton and Union Theological Seminary. In 1871, he had become pastor of the Presbyterian church in Oneida. He brought some neighborly insight into the Community. Peter Stryker was a published Christian poet in his late forties. A former member of the *American Presbyterian*'s editorial committee in Philadelphia, since 1870 Jessup had served the First Presbyterian Church in Rome, New York. Stryker was, like Mears, an anti-alcohol agitator and a lover of intellectual combat.[10] Scott Lord was a courtly, dignified man in his early fifties who had served as judge in Livingston County for eight years before moving to Utica in 1871, where he was a law partner of the irrepressible Roscoe Conkling.[11]

The committee covered all the bases: legal, political, and spiritual. The members also started their business properly, not as witch-hunters but as seekers after the truth. They were conducting their study, they let it be known, "within the bounds of the Oneida Community." The phrase nonetheless amused Community members who resided, after all, a full twenty-five miles away from Utica. "We knew that we lived at the exact center of New York," the *Oneida Circular* drily observed on November 10, "but were not aware that we *were* central New York."

The *Circular*'s editor, Harriet M. Worden, counseled soft words to turn away the synod's wrath. Reasoning that it was prudent to let others speak on their behalf, the thirty-three-year-old Worden at first simply reprinted a favorable editorial from the *Fulton Times*. Tactically, it made sense. The *Fulton Times*, founded in 1868 as a politically unaffiliated newspaper, was fair-minded and unexcitable in its assessment of the Oneida Community. Though published from a town some fifty-five miles away, the *Fulton Times* spoke familiarly of the Oneida Community as a good neighbor.

"They preach charity, kindness, forbearance in their daily demeanor," the Fulton paper stated. "They illustrate in their dealings with men their faith in the power of the Golden Rule. They abstain from hypocrisy, dishonesty, lying, profanity and all manner of what they conceive to be immorality."[12]

The *Oneida Circular* followed up with an explicit defense of its own on November 17, authored by Noyes's lieutenant William Hinds. Hinds dismissed the synod's denunciations as falsehoods propounded by "ignorant and prejudiced men." The Oneida Community, Hinds declared, practiced precisely the opposite of licentiousness. "The intercourse of the sexes in the Oneida Community," Hinds wrote, is "the great subject of scientific and conscientious study, instead of being left, as it usually is, to the sensual drift of fashion and ignorance." By and large, though, the Community's members handled the latest rhetorical assault with equanimity. They had, after all, endured previous crusades.

In 1864, an *Oneida Circular* writer recounted, there was what became known among Community members as the "Mills' war." This involved a Community member named William Mills, who had allegedly set about seducing as many young women as he could. Alienating others, he was summarily ejected from the Mansion House.[13] Mills brought his complaints to Syracuse attorneys Charles B. Sedgwick, a prominent Hamilton College graduate, abolitionist, and former member of Congress, and Charles Andrews, a former Onondaga County district attorney. Sedgwick and Andrews were not to be trifled with.[14] A settlement followed, and Mills was paid off and departed for parts unknown. This "Mills war," the *Circular* recounted, was followed by the "horse-barn war" of 1867 and the "Royce war" of 1870. In each, critics of the Oneida Community had arisen, fanned the flames, and then fizzled out. Now the cycle had revolved again. "If it comes," a Community member reasoned, presciently, "we shall have to call it the Ministers' War."[15]

As in the previous fights, Oneida's neighbors came to its defense. The neighbors knew the character of the place. They had done business with the Community and had been employed by it. They had enjoyed its strawberry shortcake. One local Presbyterian elder confided that he didn't understand what the Mears-led agitation was all about, telling a Community member that while he disagreed with Oneida's social theory, neither did he advocate its suppression by anything other than moral suasion or the setting of a superior example.

But the Community leaders also recognized some vulnerabilities. Their pamphlets on male continence and scientific propagation, some feared, could be construed as obscene by anyone who had that inclination. Oneida leaders knew the threat was real. The dogged Comstock would arrest *Toledo Sun* editor John Lant for writing about sexual physiology in late 1875, and reformer E. B. Foote would face charges for publishing an instructive volume called, benignly enough, *Plain*

Home Talk.[16] Prosecutors maintained that the educational intention was irrelevant; what mattered was whether the words or illustrations had a tendency to deprave or corrupt the viewer.[17] In an act of preemptive self-defense, the Oneida Community eventually stopped circulating the potentially offending pamphlets.

The Community's literature had already attracted the attention of Comstock's men. In the bound ledgers of the New York Society for the Suppression of Vice, now stored at the Library of Congress, there are several unexplained listings for "Oneida Community," suggesting complaints had been filed or materials had been collected. The ledgers include, as well, evidence of the stiff price paid by those who ran afoul of Comstock's enforcers, with enumerated punishments ranging from two years hard labor to stiff fines. Oneida Community members challenged convention, but they also knew which fights were best avoided.

Community members prepared, as well, to welcome into their midst the man who most wanted them gone. In the summer of 1874, Professor Mears was coming to visit.

• • •

Eden drew a crowd.

Thousands of people visited the Oneida Community each year, curious to see the communists in their natural habitat. Of complex marriage, the underlying mystery that drew outsiders like filings to a magnet, they saw barely a hint. The private rooms stayed off-limits, and Community members avoided public displays of physical affection. Mostly, the visitors were confined to an impeccably polished surface that could impress even the John Mearses of the world.

"The people saw the handsome buildings, the well-kept grounds, the graveled walks and the beautiful flowers," one former Community resident recalled. "Visitors observed the neatness and the appearance of order everywhere, and were shown about by smooth talkers, who put everything before them in the best light."[18]

The New York Central Railroad dropped visitors off at the Oneida station, about four miles from the Community. Some walked the remainder of the way. Others hired a carriage, or for fifteen cents took a seven-minute ride on the Midland Railway to the station named

"Community." Syracuse visitors leaving at 10:00 a.m. could connect with the Midland at Oneida, arrive for afternoon supper, return at 5:18 p.m. at Midland, and be back in Syracuse by 6:30 p.m. However they arrived, the visitors found themselves in "a sort of Arcadia," a correspondent enthused in 1869.[19] The landscape undulated. Lush meadows alternated with cultivated fields and plots of trees. The grounds ripened in spring, when the tulip and locust trees blossomed and white daisies bloomed. Groomed lawns alternated with square plots of flowers. More distant, to the north and west, were the orchards and vineyards, producing apples, pears, and grapes.

"Your scribe has seldom, that is hardly ever, seen anything to equal the cool, deep shadows of that grand orchard with its solitary, big-headed, white-collared trees, standing there independent of drought and insects," a visitor from Saratoga declared.[20]

The heart of it all, by the 1870s, was the brick Mansion House. It commanded attention with a tower, an observatory, large windows, and a piazza in front. Like the community it served, the main building was both handsome and designed, one critic said, by a man who held convention in contempt. The structure, another visitor said, suggested "strength, roominess and comfort."[21] To others, however, the building seemed a brooding, somewhat sinister, presence. Some thought it resembled a well-endowed orphanage, or perhaps an insane asylum.

Visitors entered the Mansion House and made their way to a reception room where, the *Oneida Circular* explained on March 21, 1870, they would "usually find a gentleman or lady attendant who will answer his inquiries and give him directions for making a tour of the place." Across from the reception room was the visitors' dining hall, for which one might buy a ticket. Visitors toured the large kitchen, serviced by the newest contrivances, such as a potato washer and a dishwasher. They visited the ground-floor library, equipped with a long reading table and lit by overhead lamps. It was a place even Mears could appreciate. The library had about six thousand volumes, about half the size of Hamilton College's collection. Nearby, a small museum room displayed curiosities collected by Community members in their travels and arrayed in glass cases, including the tooth of a mastodon, some stalactites, and, courtesy of Noyes's brother George, a pair of Chinese chopsticks.

"The collection of birds' nests and eggs is very interesting," a visitor enthused in 1874.[22]

The visitors saw the second-floor main hall, which could seat about seven hundred persons. It was frescoed and handsomely furnished, with small tables and chairs arrayed before a stage. Paintings of allegorical figures festooned the high ceiling. The hall hosted lectures and entertainments, which might range from readings from the works of Charles Dickens to performances of Shakespeare's plays. Music was particularly key to the Community, which by one later account featured "two orchestras (one with twenty-two pieces), a brass band, a choir of twenty-five singers, two male quartets and a club of eight male voices."[23] Visitors might pay sixty cents for the full community dinner or thirty-five cents for a plain dinner, which was generally meatless but rich with fruits, vegetables, bread, cheese, and cake. After dinner, an extra twenty-five cents paid for performances that included dramatic readings, songs, and pantomimes.

"The girls and women were arrayed, the older women in their strange Turkish trousers, and they sang a song in French," visitor Alonzo J. Grover recounted in a January 19, 1879, *Chicago Tribune* story. "I was told it was called 'Song of the Socialist.'"

Visitors reported coming from England, Denmark, Scotland, Ireland, Germany, Russia, and throughout the United States. They included the famous, from suffragist Susan B. Anthony to pint-sized circus celebrity Tom Thumb, as well as just plain folk. Most came away impressed. By the 1870s, the Community was fielding upwards of fifty or more requests for membership every month.

"They have often been represented as coarse sensualists," one visitor from the *Providence Journal* noted in 1874. "Those whom I saw were intelligent, well-mannered ladies and gentlemen."[24]

Prominent abolitionist and editor Thomas Wentworth Higginson arrived in early 1872. Higginson was a graduate of Harvard Divinity School, a Unitarian minister who once had been a radical abolitionist and supporter of John Brown. After the Civil War, he helped found the American Woman's Suffrage Association and served fourteen years as co-editor of the *Woman's Journal*. He was a progressive soul, open to new ideas. In the March 18, 1872, issue of the *Woman's Journal*, Higginson recounted his visit. He savored the Oneida Community's food and its presentation, praising the "delicious bread and butter and snowy tablecloth" that reminded him of the Shakers' purity. After dinner, Higginson enjoyed the "really excellent orchestra of six or seven instruments, led by a thoroughly trained leader, while a boy of eleven plays the second violin."

"They play good German music," Higginson wrote, approvingly.

Like other visitors, Higginson scrutinized the faces of the Community members, seeking evidence of moral rot or carnal exhaustion. Reading critically into the appearances of the Oneida Community's women was a standard part of the public intellectual's tour. Oneida visitors analyzed faces the way phrenologists palpated skulls, seeking evidence of inner character. Alonzo J. Grover bluntly addressed the question as to whether the Oneida women were "inferior, care-worn and dispirited," before concluding that "to all appearances they are happy and cultivated."[25] Higginson, too, acknowledged that he "looked in vain for the visible signs of either the suffering or the sin." He thought the faces certainly compared favorably to the "pallid joylessness" of the abstinent Shakers or the "stupid sensualism" of the bigamous Mormons.

"I saw some uninteresting faces, and some with that look of burnt-out fire of which every radical assembly shows specimens," Higginson reported, "but I did not see a face that I should call coarse, and very few that I should call joyless. I saw men and women there who I felt ready to respect and love."

A female visitor assured *New York Sun* readers in 1870 that from their unornamented simplicity of their dress and "from the expressions on their faces" the Oneida women were both "free from fashion's trammels" and apparently "happy and contented with their position."[26] Higginson and the unnamed *New York Sun* correspondent were both sympathetic and reliable narrators. The unsympathetic and unreliable narrator who took the name John B. Ellis voiced a contrary but common presumption about Oneida's sexual brigands. The Oneida women appeared to Ellis as coarse and unrefined, heavy lidded from sexual excess. Their countenance was one of "lustfulness," he wrote.

"All bear marks of the frightfully licentious life they lead," Ellis wrote. "Nature has branded them as habitual violators of her law, and they cannot remove the mark."[27]

A more reliable visitor from the *New York Times*, too, saw shadows in the Oneida women, describing in an 1878 article their pallid and dejected faces, while a visitor from Saratoga observed that the "women's faces are not pretty, but show . . . expression, anxiety and sometimes weariness."

"They look," the Saratoga visitor said, with a combination of compassion and fascination, "like roses which have lost their dew."[28]

Mears came to see all this for himself on Friday, July 3, 1874.

Beyond Oneida, agitators were fighting corruption of all kinds. In Bloomington, Illinois, participants in the Illinois Prohibition Convention had just endorsed total suppression of the noxious liquor traffic. Temperance advocates had likewise convened in Syracuse in late June to consider whether to stay within the Republican Party or spin off a political challenge. Underscoring the dangers of drink, a July 1 *New York Sun* headline informed readers about the "latest rum murder," a crime about which the drink-addled perpetrator could remember not a thing. Even a comet tracing its way across the night sky was illuminating some hidden fire.

"Spooney young men and women occupy the piers and lake banks, studying astronomy," the *Oswego Daily Palladium* reported on July 3.

More troubling, to some, was the viral spread of sinful coupling schemes. On Lake Champlain's Valcour Island, newspapers were reporting on plans for something "similar to the notorious Oneida Community," a place that would be devoted to "absolute social freedom, and whose only governing law would be 'complete, universal free love.'"[29] Nonetheless, despite the threats all around, in the nine months since the Presbyterian Synod's Oneida Community investigating committee formed, interest had flagged among all but Mears.

Singularly focused, he was the only member to take part in the July 3 visit, in the company of Philip Schaff, a professor at Union Theological Seminary in New York City. The Switzerland native was, like Mears, a practicing Presbyterian and a prolific writer.[30] Like Noyes, he knew the pain of procreation. Five of his eight children had died young.

Together, Mears and Schaff took the Oneida tour. They admired the impeccable grounds and spic-and-span Mansion House. They could appreciate the capacious library, remark upon the foreign curios displayed under glass. In the social hall, they gazed up at the frescoes. Some corners were off limits, but for every question, they received a response.

"It was with undisguised satisfaction that we showed these gentlemen the practical working of Christian Communism in our family, answered their queries and listened to their criticism," the *Circular* reported on July 13.[31]

Mears, it seemed to the *Circular*'s reporter, respected the benefits of social and business cooperation even as he "made it evident that he does not yet sufficiently appreciate the improvements that we have made to the monogamic system." While remaining civil, Mears brought his love of debate to the Community. Schaff seemed less judgmental, more open-minded. He struck the Community members as a genial, sophisticated man who, the *Circular* reported, "seemed to study us as an interesting phenomenon, wondering meanwhile that we could keep in check the passions of envy and jealousy under our peculiar order of life."

Mears returned to Clinton with his fervor unchecked; he had seen nothing to moderate his views. The July 3 visit was apparently Mears's only on-site work during his investigation, and it fell short of thorough. Had he returned the very next day, Mears would have seen firsthand the neighbors' high regard for the Oneida Community. Many attended a Fourth of July celebration featuring croquet, musical performances, and tours of the Community's silk and trap manufacturing plants. Mears might have broadened his perspective had he joined the good, clean fun. Instead, he confined much of his inquiry to his own study. What purported to be an investigation, a searching after material facts, had, in fact, become a sermon. In Mears's hands, the work turned into a moral exercise with a predetermined outcome—right versus wrong.

In the fall of 1874, several months after his July visit, Mears presented a draft of the report to the synod, where it apparently provoked considerable discussion. Some of the language may have seemed excessive, and some modifications were considered. Mears, though, would not be denied or delayed. Under his own name, in several periodicals, Mears unleashed his fury in late October.

"For twenty seven years, the people of the center of New York have been suffering themselves to become accustomed to this moral monstrosity," Mears wrote.[32] Oneida's sinners, Mears went on, "invent impure devices by which lustful desires may be gratified without any inconvenient results." He meant male continence, though he didn't use the phrase. Similarly, Mears refused to use the term *stirpiculture*, instead denouncing how the Community "put the sexual instincts of men upon a level of those of brutes, by their plan of raising a breed of men."

Shortly after Mears fired his solo shot, the Presbyterian Synod committee's report was published. It was both harsh and unsigned. The absence of signatures incited speculation that some of the committee's distinguished members were embarrassed at the result. The real responsibility, in any event, seemed obvious to those familiar with Mears' exhortations, especially his most recent published essay. Certain phrasings were identical.

"It was the product of Prof. Mears' busy zeal," the *Oneida Circular* assessed on December 7, "and was allowed by courtesy to have its course in the hands of the committee and through the Synod."

The synod's report certainly laid it on thick, in Mears's fashion. Though the Presbyterian Synod had included three lawyers, the report's tenor was pervaded, the Oneida Community's newspaper correctly assessed, more by a "spirit of ignorant and reckless vituperation" than by neutral fact-finding. The Community's practices were, to Mears, a "monstrous aggregate of lust and shame" that were "totally unfit for public mention or discussion." The residents were "filthy dreamers" who had sunk into "scandalous impurity." Their views of religion were "perverse, fantastical and devilish." Tolerating their existence caused "the stimulating of impure and licentious passions." Whatever off-setting virtues like economy, industry, and the timely paying of debts might be suggested, the Community remained "a pestilent and organized iniquity." The Community was founded on "systematized prostitution and adultery," and it manifested "a notorious evil and flagrant violation of humane and divine law."

The pestilential details, though, were left to the imagination. Complex marriage was neither named nor explained. The biblical argument for the Community's belief in common ownership of both property and bodies was ignored. The specifics of male continence and stirpiculture were ignored. There was no explanation of ascending fellowship.

"There are certain species of impurity whose grossness is their very protection," the report explained. "There are certain filthy devices that are the product of a mind which must have groveled long on sensual associations, and which no one can study without peril of contamination."

The report then identified multiple lines of attack. The Community's poisonous literature must be kept out of the US mail system, to prevent spread of the infection. Social relations with the Community should be discouraged, to keep the gross impurity quarantined. Additional legislation should be procured as necessary, and assistance sought from other religious bodies.

"Noxious weeds do not disappear of their own accord from our pastures, our fields and our waysides," the Mears committee counseled. "Unless the people rise against them with sickle and with plow, they take a deeper hold year by year."[33]

Therein, for the crusaders, was the problem. The people who knew the Community best were the ones least likely to rise against it. The Community had ingratiated itself over the years, contributing to local charities and the area's volunteer fire department, loaning books and, during the Civil War, paying bounties to help local men sidestep the draft.[34] By the mid-1870s, as many as two hundred outsiders at a time were employed by the Community. The Community members did not noisily proselytize or seek converts. The Mears committee acknowledged that the Community members' thrift, industry, and activity had improved not only their own lot but that of their neighbors.

"People easily grow indulgent to an evil which increases their worldly prosperity," the committee complained.

In truth, individual journalists and periodicals regularly denounced the Community. Isaac G. Reed Jr. of *Frank Leslie's Illustrated Newspaper* set the standard with his April 23, 1870, fulminations against Oneida's "abominable filth" and "foul and unnatural horrors." The *Independent*, in praising the Presbyterian committee's work, likewise repeated its declaration that Oneida was a "thousand times worse" than Mormonism, while on April 8, 1875, the *Saratogian* termed the Community "one of the most vicious institutions this side of Utah."

The *Saratogian*'s slur was, moreover, alerting readers to the publication of a full-throated ninety-nine-page volume by a certain A. L. Slawson entitled *Behind the Scenes; Or, an Exposé of Oneida Community*. Purportedly based in Oneida's hometown, the 1875 book praised Mears and denounced the "depths of animal degradation" and "shocking and impure" behavior found at a place where "a set of men banded together for the sake of practicing shameful immoralities."[35]

Still, the Mears committee was correct in observing that many newspapers treated the investigators skeptically and the Community sympathetically.

"We look in vain for any earnest, outspoken words of condemnation on the part of the daily press generally, which prides itself on being the specific guardian of the interests of the public," the committee stated.[36]

The press was a pet peeve of Mears, who raged against the "editors of certain journals, who can become almost pathetic" in their lavishing of praise upon Oneida.[37] The reporters, Mears wrote, were like "dumb dogs that cannot bark." Instead, it was Mears who got bit. However right-thinking the crusaders might be, the *Oswego Times* predicted on November 20 that most "expect to see the Oneida Community stand a fixed and permanent institution after their report has been forgotten." Others attacked the report and its authors more directly. The *Fulton Times* typified the journalists' scorn, stating that "we do not learn from this report that the peculiar theories and practices of the community have had deleterious influence upon anything but the imaginations" of the critics. The Fulton paper, with a bit of cheek, further noted that anyone might be criticized for their matrimonial arrangements.

"On what system the Oneida Community manage their domestic or family concerns, we don't know," the *Fulton Times* stated, "and we have no more right to inquire than we have to inquire into the family affairs of Prof. Mears or Judge Churchill."[38]

9 THE UTAH AT HOME

TRY AS HE MIGHT, Mears could not rattle the Oneida Community.

For most Presbyterian Synod members, this failure meant relatively little. They had already moved on. Theodore W. Dwight, the Columbia University law professor, was tapped in 1874 by New York governor John A. Dix for a commission handling an overflow of cases from the state's court of appeals. Scott Lord was running for Congress that same year, making it prudent for him to avoid antagonizing a successful local business. Lord, who learned something about politics from his Utica law partner, Roscoe Conkling, won the election and served one term in the House, without further attacking the locally entrenched Oneida Community. Another politically ambitious member of the synod, John C. Churchill, the former congressman and district attorney, spent part of 1874 under consideration for appointment by Governor Dix to a judicial vacancy. Though he was passed over, Churchill kept himself in competitive shape, finally securing a New York Supreme Court seat.

Mears, more or less alone, owned the report. He stuck to his guns; that was his way. Mears insisted upon maintaining, as he once summed up proper Presbyterianism, "a system of strong and clear convictions . . . [whose] grasp upon the will, therefore, is clear, strong and regulative."[1] Convictions were to be held, with a deathless grip.

At Hamilton College, Mears shouldered his usual course load of German, philosophy, and Bible studies. His college remained an intimate setting, with only twenty-eight seniors starting off the 1875–76 academic year. A new library held the college's expanding collection, not all of it enticing to callow undergraduates. The Hamilton collection included, the college's catalogue proudly announced, "all the Scotch decisions, in the Judiciary, Senior Courts and House of Lords, and the Irish reports in Law and Equity."[2] Mears, serving part time as college librarian, added to this dreary lot by raising nearly $400 for the purchase of various volumes on metaphysics. He also undertook the librarianship with a high-minded focus that made him, 1876 Hamilton graduate Archibald P. Love recounted, "hardly the man to see the needs of young boys in the reading line."[3]

With equal seriousness, Mears drilled students in the classroom. He asked probing questions: What does vision apprehend? What is the nature of imagination? What is sensation? Sensation, specifically, troubled Mears. He did not trust it. He considered sensation a seductress, luring man away from proper philosophical inquiry. The material, sensory world, to Mears, was gross and luxurious, the latter word an insult. He wanted to isolate the mind from the fleshy phenomena of nature.

All the while, Mears continued his off-campus crusading. He was not done with the Oneida Community, nor had Community leaders forgotten him. Sometime around January 1876, in what was described, perhaps disingenuously, as a courteous gesture, the Community sent Mears a "Bulletin of the Turkish Bath." The putative invitation smacked of goading, though Noyes did believe, sincerely, in the toxin-releasing benefits of steam heat. He habitually prescribed Turkish baths as a cure-all, and the brochure he sent Mears included illustrations depicting the cleansing experience. Mears, no stranger to excessive metaphor, countered that what was really needed was a "moral Turkish Bath" in which the "sentiment of the people of New York was roused to the necessary temperature" so that the filthy Oneida Community could expel its poisons amid the "pummeling and scraping of wholesome laws administered by uncompromising judges and juries."[4]

On January 27, 1876, three weeks after the college's winter term commenced, Mears wrote in the *Independent* a screed entitled "Our Utah at Home." Noyes, himself, took pains to distinguish Oneida Community and Mormon social practices, but to Mears they were identical. Utah was, like Oneida, morally foreign. The state's pioneering

Mormons threatened the nation's spiritual integrity, Mears and others believed, and the professor praised President Ulysses S. Grant for publicly denouncing Mormons' unconventional marriage practices. Polygamy, Grant had declared in his State of the Union, on December 7, 1875, "should be banished from the land" and the "scandalous condition of affairs existing in the Territory of Utah" should be set right. Mears believed that, and more. Then, having invoked the Mormon threat, Mears turned toward Oneida.

"If we owe it to our nationality, our law, our morality to seek the overthrow of the polygamy of Utah, what is our duty to this organization?" Mears asked in the *Independent.*

The Community's own publications, Mears said, were "exposing with a free hand the disgusting peculiarities" of Noyes's followers. Since Madison County authorities seemed indifferent, Mears suggested new legislation might be needed to force action, "unless we can bring the weight of public sentiment to bear upon the good people of Madison County sufficient to bring an indictment" by a grand jury.

The *Independent* was a proper outlet for Mears. Founded in 1848, the periodical engaged serious-minded readers interested in the betterment of society and themselves. Oneida, moreover, was not the editors' only concern. Elsewhere in New York, Governor Samuel Tilden had exposed the Canal Ring, the latest in a cycle of patronage and contracting scandals along the Erie Canal. A scathing 1876 report of the New York State Canal Investigating Commission prompted by Tilden determined that "the interest of the public has been systematically disregarded" while the state put itself at the "mercy of the predatory classes."[5] It was a year for rings. In Mears's former hometown of Philadelphia, a Gas Ring led by a Republican political boss was revealed to have siphoned off nearly $8 million.[6] Congressional committees exposed corruption and cronyism in the Grant administration. In its January 1876 annual report, the New York Society for the Suppression of Vice recounted that some one hundred thousand volumes of filthy books had been seized the prior years, along with an otherwise undescribed "63,000 implements for immoral use." Such material, the society warned, was "designed and cunningly calculated to inflame the passions and lead the victims from one step of vice to another, ending in utmost lust."[7]

Against these corruptions, the forces of virtue rallied where they could. In January 1876, Anthony Comstock arrested physician Edward Bliss Foote Sr., author of *Medical Common Sense* and *Plain Home Talk*. Though advertisements for contraception were the focus of the criminal charges, Foote included a frank and sympathetic discussion of the alternative marriage arrangements practiced both in the Mormon Church and the Oneida Community.[8] Foote was convicted and fined $3,500, prompting the doctor and his son to start publishing *Dr. Foote's Health Monthly* as a vehicle for promoting free speech and attacking Comstock, pointedly dubbed "the Agent" and leader of the "American Inquisition."[9]

• • •

The Oneida Community, meanwhile, was changing.

Noyes had been looking to retire from direct leadership, and in 1875 he had proposed that his thirty-six-year-old son, Theodore, take over. Theodore was a Yale graduate, a bright, corpulent man of considerable talents, but he lacked his father's charisma and unflagging Christian faith. His selection as leader was not greeted well, particularly by those who thought themselves better suited for leadership. Some turmoil followed before Theodore fully ascended in May 1877 to the position he neither sought nor was suited for.

Theodore administered a stricter accounting of sexual assignments. At the Community's Wallingford outpost, he had reviewed weekly written reports of who was sleeping with whom. Brought to the main Community, the sexual bookkeeping irritated those accustomed to a lighter touch. It also incited, Jessie Catherine Kinsley recalled, an enforcement regime of "policing and espionage" that set members of the Community against one another.[10] Theodore's interest in systems and science, moreover, led him to question some Oneida Community fundamentals. At the least, he kept his eyes open. In his own research, he had bluntly assessed the occurrence of nervous disorders among Community residents. He noted, without sentiment, the case of a twenty-nine-year-old female with a "nervous derangement which is evidently hysterical [and] much aggravated by sexual intercourse."[11] Theodore simply wanted the facts. He didn't always appreciate their danger.

In the autumn of 1877, Theodore confided in a fellow physician, Dr. Ely Van de Warker of Syracuse. The two men had known each other for about a year, and Theodore felt comfortable telling his peer about a growing sense among Community members that complex marriage and male continence might be unhealthy. Perhaps some further research might prove illuminating? Van de Warker said he was interested.

"He returned to the community," Van de Warker subsequently reported, "and in about a week I received a letter inviting me to Oneida, to make a study of the subject."[12]

Van de Warker was well suited for the sensitive study, for he was not easily shocked. After graduating from Troy Polytechnic Institute and Albany Medical College, Van de Warker had enlisted in the 162nd New York Volunteer Infantry. He served as an assistant surgeon as the regiment bled its way through the Shenandoah Valley and other campaigns, and left the service as a major. Even after war, death was not done with him. His first wife died within a year of their 1865 marriage.[13]

The thirty-five-year-old physician circulated in elite society. He was professor of "artistic anatomy" at the Syracuse University medical school and a leader of regional medical organizations. He cast a wide net and showed personal courage that could verge on the foolhardy. He tested abortifacients, known more delicately as "female pills," by sampling eleven different varieties so he could describe their physical effect. Van de Warker was also prolific, writing regularly for the likes of *Popular Science Monthly*, and he held firmly conventional views about women's proper place in society. He doubted the value of coeducation and the introduction of women into higher forms of labor. He believed that men and women were equipped with different kinds of brains, and so had different social roles. Men were born to strive; women, to nurture. Van de Warker spelled out in *Popular Science Monthly*'s February 1875 issue his belief that every healthy woman felt compelled to marry.

On the selected day, he traveled to the Community and, starting after breakfast, began a daylong round of interviews in Theodore's Mansion House room. Van de Warker and the women he interviewed spoke candidly. Neither the physician nor the subjects saw any reason for shame in what they discussed; it was simply sex.

Van de Warker identified a "peculiar sexualism" permeating the Community, to which he speculatively attributed an early onset of menstruation. An unnamed Oneida Community woman told Van de Warker that she knew of "girls no older than sixteen or seventeen years of age being called upon to have intercourse six or seven times a week and oftener, perhaps with a feeling of repugnance to all those whom she was with."[14] Conversely, the doctor recounted, "it was very rare for a young man under twenty years of age to associate with a woman who had not passed the change of life."

Van de Warker methodically interviewed about a quarter of those he termed "lady inmates." Of those he questioned, the median age of first sexual intercourse was thirteen. The youthful introduction to sex was not necessarily unlawful. The legal age of consent in New York would not be raised to sixteen until 1889. Oneida stood out, though, for its concentration of sexual experience, widely shared and ideologically justified.

"I am knowing particularly of at least four women of my own age who had sexual intercourse at the age of ten, and one case of nine years of age," one woman advised Van de Warker. "Boys of thirteen and fourteen years old were put with old women who had passed the change of life and instructed about such things before they had begun to think about it at all."[15]

The women seemed well-adjusted, and hysteria, Van de Warker found, was "remarkably absent." The women appeared to conform, in health and vigor, to the condition of conventional wives, though Van de Warker did note some abnormalities. Their vaginal temperatures, he found, were higher than average, prompting the doctor to speculate that the "frequent sexual acts" might explain the heat.

"There is a question," Van de Warker conceded, "that would require a long series of observations to determine."[16]

But Van de Warker would not have the chance to make those observations. When John Humphrey Noyes heard about the study, he immediately apprehended the threat it posed. Unlike Theodore, the intellectually acute but politically obtuse scientist, the elder Noyes knew how raw facts might be apprehended by the public, or a prosecutor. Noyes terminated the study, and Van de Warker's findings remained secret, so far as is known, until they were published in 1884, well after the Oneida Community had ended its unconventional sexual practices. It was dangerous information Van de Warker held in his hand during the years between his truncated study and his eventual publication. Even a whisper of his findings might have emboldened the Oneida Community's enemies, some of whom were among Van de Warker's own Syracuse University colleagues.

Theodore's approval of the Van de Warker study unsettled those who already questioned his judgment. Theodore eventually stepped down, and in early 1878 his father resumed leadership. The elder Noyes sought to set things right, ending Theodore's strict sexual accounting. Still, the Oneida Community that John Humphrey Noyes returned to lead had lost some of its spirit. The flawed installation of Theodore as leader redoubled doubts about the elder Noyes's judgment. There were other reasons for concern. Noyes turned sixty-seven in 1878, and he was facing competition from younger lions. James William Towner, in particular, seemed a dangerous man.

Towner had first contacted the Community in April 1866, introducing himself as a searcher after salvation. Towner was forty-three at the time, a Michigan lawyer and former Universalist minister who had lost an eye while fighting in the Civil War. He had since come to consider communism the natural fruit of a love for Jesus Christ, and he wished to explore firsthand the workings of the Oneida Community. Married to a rather sickly wife, with three children in tow, Towner had assured the Community in his introductory letter that he was prepared for change.

"I believe that my wife and self are measurably free from the bondage of marriage spirit," Towner had informed Community leaders in his April 4, 1866, introductory letter.[17]

Towner finally came to Oneida to stay in 1874, following residence in a free-love community in Berlin Heights, Ohio. The seasoned veteran carried himself well. As his own self-confidence within the Community grew, Towner challenged Noyes's tight-fisted control of sexual partners. He struck a chord among the younger members, who increasingly resented the strictures of ascending fellowship. Noyes himself had grown more rigid and dictatorial.

"He has grown so positive in all his beliefs that he does not care to hear the ideas of others," Community member Francis Wayland-Smith wrote.[18]

Some later suspected that one of Towner's followers might have been preparing to inform on Noyes in a prosecution for sexual crimes. It wouldn't have been out of the question. There were about thirty adults ultimately aligned with Towner's faction, out of several hundred.[19] Any aggrieved parent of a young girl discomfited by Noyes's self-appointed role as first husband, the sexual initiator, might have had evidence to share. Noyes himself insisted that he never took advantage of unwilling young women, though his defense might not have survived serious cross-examination. In some cases, Noyes said, he had been "accused of sexual intercourse with them, when there was only sportive familiarity in the way of external contact."[20] In other cases, while acknowledging sexual activity, Noyes declared his partners were willing.

"I swear," Noyes said, "that I have never had sexual intercourse with anyone who did not give what I considered evident tokens of a mature state of passional and physical development."[21]

Noyes's sexual dominance was resented. His judgment was failing. His health was waning, and his leadership was under attack. The common religious commitment that had once unified the community was dissipating.

• • •

Mears, too, was facing upstart youth.

In July 1877, during a three-day conference held in Plattsburgh, several hundred educators elected Mears president of the New York State Teachers Association.[22] Mears used his new bully pulpit to denounce college rowdyism, which seemed rampant. Students kept disrupting the scholarly calm of Hamilton College. One dark night, high-spirited lads had guided a horse from the nearby Chenango Canal up several flights of stairs into the South College dormitory. The next morning, responsible adults found the befuddled animal, head sticking out of a window as it tried to make sense of the situation. Other venturesome students would scramble up the Hamilton Chapel tower and ring the bell at unseemly hours.

"Certain acute and crafty spirits do occasionally resort to such exhilarating sports as seat painting and blackboard greasing," the *Hamilton Literary Monthly* reported.[23]

Hamilton sophomores would invade dormitories early in the new school year and toss freshmen's furniture from windows. Other indignities occurred during rowing season, as it was called. Older students would sometimes torment younger students with tobacco smoke as an emetic. Sophomores, their own memories of being hazed still fresh, would muscle a freshman out at night, raggedly cut his hair, and fraternally abuse him. During the day, catcalls and flung objects would interrupt student recitations. One Hamilton alumnus from Mears's time recalled that "the waters of the well by the old library building were certainly cold in the autumn . . . when applied direct from the bucket to the naked person, as the writer well remembers."[24]

Hamilton was not alone. Hijinks bedeviled college leaders through the 1870s. Yale's president warned sophomores they would be expelled if they kept abusing the freshmen. Ohio's Kenyon College suspended an entire sophomore class for hazing. Mears, ever the scholar, assessed the ancient roots of the widespread hazing rituals. He likened the sophomoric actions to the Egyptian and Pythagorean atrocities that had welcomed the ancients into the secret brotherhoods of their time. The Hamilton College boys were but the latest in a long line of initiatory prospects. Mears understood that. He, too, had been a young man, once.

This modern hazing, though, went too far. In the August 29, 1878, issue of the *Independent*, Mears expounded on "the evil so deeply seated" that required to be met by "stern and uncompromising laws." He praised, as salutary, the suspension of an entire Princeton

College class. Mears prescribed gymnastic exercises for working off the superfluity of "animal spirits." "The buoyancy and overflowing spirits of youth must have an outlet," Mears wrote approvingly elsewhere, citing the "large amount of spare vigor" and the "excess of animal spirits" found among young men. He insisted it wasn't the sap of youth, per se, that he was opposed to. He pronounced it, after all, a "real joy to hear their shouts upon the campus, to see their vigorous blows with the bat." At the same time, warning not to "replace rowdyism with the regatta," Mears said excessive attention should not be placed on athletics.[25] Instead, Mears urged the use of his standard tonic: dutiful study, chased by rigorous testing.

Along with rowdyism, modern technology was infiltrating Hamilton College. In 1878, natural philosophy professor Chester Huntington installed, as an experiment, a telephone line connecting his house to the Mears's home. One evening, Huntington's class marveled to hear Mears's voice conveyed clearly from over one hundred yards away.

"Scientifically, it is most interesting," Huntington assured the students, 1879 graduate Charles Hitchcock reported years later, "but I doubt very much if any of us live long enough to see the telephone of much practical or commercial importance."[26]

Hamilton alumni remembered Huntington for decades. Other professors, too, left warm and lasting impressions. Mathematics professor Oren Root, inevitably dubbed Cube, was recalled with affectionate respect. Archibald B. Love, an 1876 graduate, described Root and Greek professor Edward North as "true friends of the boys" and "genuine men through and through with marked personalities but no swagger of pretense."[27] Mears rarely merited the same regard. Some students did appreciate his better qualities, which unexpectedly included, an 1881 graduate of Hamilton named Edison E. Dayton recalled, a good sense of humor. Behind his back, though, students put the ever-serious Mears down as "Johnny." None who graduated during Mears's decade-long tenure, however, summoned extensive memories about him fifty years later for the college's traditional alumni half-century memorial letters. Professor Mears seemed to be more endured than loved.

Outside the small Hamilton campus, though, Mears was an authoritative antagonist, the man to call upon.

In an in-depth examination starting on August 8, 1878, the *New York Times* purported to reveal serious dissension at Oneida. One of the Community's original founders, Abiel Kingsley, was reported to have left with a $10,000 payoff. Others were said to have abandoned the Community as well. The *New York Times* reported that Theodore Noyes frankly acknowledged that deeper causes than the discontent of a few restless members have been at work. Piecing together the evidence, the *Times*'s reporter revealed that John Humphrey Noyes's grip was growing weaker. It seemed unlikely, the *Times*'s reporter assessed, that the Community would survive Noyes's demise.

"The older members still adhere to the doctrines promulgated by Noyes," the *New York Times* recounted, "but younger members are skeptical of his apostolic claims."[28]

Oneida's women, the reporter added, appeared "pale, sickly, dejected and discontented." They were growing weary, it was said, of bobbing their hair and wearing the eccentric short skirts and Turkish trousers. The paper's observations were, in some cases, pretty much on the money. The Community was unsettled, its leadership shaky and its cohesion frayed. The *American Socialist*, the Community's renamed house periodical, retorted "there has not been so great a degree of harmony in the Community for years as at the present time,"[29] but the facts were otherwise. The Oneida Community was newly vulnerable, an exposed target for crusaders. Chasing the *New York Times*'s exposé, the *Utica Morning Herald* dispatched a reporter to speak with Mears.

Mears offered what was, for him, a nuanced perspective. He had visited the Community, he told the *Herald*'s reporter, and he had been kindly treated there. Mears forthrightly acknowledged Oneida's upright business practices, and he agreed the founders were sincere in their religious beliefs. He conceded Oneida's neighbors held it in a positive light. Practically speaking, Mears observed, this complicated the prospects of legal action.

"He admits also that there is no law upon the statute books which the members of the community can be said to violate," the *Utica*

Morning Herald reporter recounted. "He thought that if the community was ever disturbed, it would have to be by the passage of a special statute which fit their case."[30]

The *New York Times*'s accounting of internal dissent encouraged the Oneida Community's critics. They had not gone away in the four years since the Presbyterian Synod's Mears-led committee had completed its work, but their efforts had subsided. Now, perhaps, it was time for another charge.

• • •

On Tuesday, October 15, 1878, members of the General Association of the Congregational Church of New York and the Presbyterian Synod of Central New York opened their respective annual meetings in Oswego. Over the course of three days, the Congregationalists heard talks on temperance, aid for the indigent, and what one speaker called, ominously, "The Christian View of Popular Amusements." The Presbyterians, meeting in town on the other side of the Oswego River, discussed work among the freed slaves of the South, the woefully low salaries provided ministers, and the persistent money shortfalls that hindered Presbyterian performance.

"Rev. A. F. Lyle," the local *Mexico Independent* newspaper reported, "presented the cause of church erection."[31]

Mears, moderating the Presbyterian Synod's session, pressed for a renewed campaign against Oneida. On the second day of the conference, the Presbyterians followed a discussion of women's issues with a vote to communicate to the Congregationalists a proposal that the churches unite against the free lovers. The following day, the Presbyterians and Congregationalists discussed the campaign directly, as they gathered for a joint celebration.

The Congregationalists selected a team to prepare a paper on the Oneida Community: Reverend James Douglass, Reverend Martin L. Williston, and Reverend Edward Payson Thwing. Thwing was a graduate of Harvard College and Andover Seminary. A prolific writer and leader in the Long Island Temperance Alliance, he had authored sermons urging watchfulness against riotous appetites.[32] Williston, minister at the First Congregational Church in

Jamestown, New York, had visited the Oneida Community during a fourteen-day, three hundred-mile walkabout the year before and so had formed some immediate impressions of the place.[33] He had been sharpened as a Civil War sergeant in a disease-riddled Massachusetts infantry regiment and then as a minister in a succession of pulpits.[34] Douglass, a fifty-five-year-old graduate of Hamilton College and Auburn Theological Seminary, was known for his efforts with the Oswego County Sunday School Association.[35] Augustus Beard, the energetic minister at the Plymouth Congregational Church in Syracuse, would end up leading the Congregationalists, while Mears led the Presbyterians.

The new committees enlivened Mears, who unleashed himself in an October 31 piece that characterized the Oneida Community as an "outgrowth of lust." The essential trinity of Christianity, civilization, and monogamy must be maintained, Mears declared, against John Humphrey Noyes and his polygamous forces of heathenism, despotism, and semi-barbarism.

"One cannot divest oneself of the feeling that an impure mind has as much to do with the shaping of Noyes' scheme as an enthusiasm for social progress," Mears wrote.[36]

The Oneida Community literature, Mears wrote, "has such a taint" about it that it should draw the attention of Anthony Comstock and the New York Society for the Suppression of Vice. The Community's instructions on male continence, Mears wrote, "do not breathe of purity. They belong to the nastiness of the Epicurean sty. Their purpose is to show how Nature's law is to be evaded without sacrifice of indulgence. They are precisely calculated to raise a race of Sybarites, to imbrute and degrade to bestiality those following them."

Mears was just getting started. The very air breathed at the Oneida Community was, he wrote, "loaded with the vapors of sensuality," while "the outcome of their miasmatic lucubrations is the introduction of the principle of the stockbreeder in place of the sanctity of the marital relation."

"Every principle of Christian morality," Mears added, "calls out for their suppression."[37]

The same month that Mears turned his latest torrent toward Oneida's sty, the Oneida County Prohibition Committee nominated him
as the party's congressional candidate. The selection suited Mears.
Intoxicating drink and the Oneida Community were of the same sin,
doors to the brothel. As historian Helen Lefkowitz Horowitz noted,
in the nineteenth century, one of the recurring reasons for opposing
alcohol consumption was "how it relaxed men's control of their passions, unbridling their lust."[38]

The temperance movement had started with the acceptance, by
many, of moderation as a rule. Alcohol, per se, was not considered
evil. The relatively tolerant attitude was realistic, given the widespread
alcohol consumption in the early years of the American republic. As
early as 1816, though, the Presbyterian Synod of Pittsburgh declared
that "ardent spirits ought never to be used, except as a medicine."[39] By
1829, the Presbyterian General Assembly went on record in support
of total abstinence, followed by the Dutch Reform Church General
Synod in 1830, and the Methodist General Conference in 1832, which
urged its members to "banish the evil from our Church altogether."[40]

In time, the focus expanded beyond the salvation of individual
souls. If civil society stopped providing licenses for the sale of alcohol,
the problem would be yanked up by the roots. Local selectmen in a
number of Massachusetts towns had stopped issuing licenses, effectively imposing local prohibition, through the 1830s.[41] The sentiment
spread. By the Fourth of July celebration in 1835, Mears's mentor
Albert Barnes was orating in Philadelphia on the connection between
temperance and Republican freedom. Two hundred of Connecticut's
220 townships banned liquor licenses by 1845. When county com-
missioners challenged the local decisions, the no-license advocates
took their campaigning to the county level. Historian Ian R. Tyrrell,
in his thorough study, noted that by 1846 all but one of Maine's
counties had imposed prohibition.[42]

When checkerboard, county-by-county enforcement left too many
loopholes, advocates sought uniform state laws. Maine led the way in
1846 with the first statewide prohibition law, later given more muscle
in 1851. Though Governor Horatio Seymour vetoed New York State's

first prohibition-type bill in 1854, legislators and a new governor resurrected it the next year as "an act for the prevention of intemperance,
pauperism and crime."[43] The New York law empowered magistrates
to issue warrants to constables to seize some forms of liquor. Other
states followed suit. Subsequent court rulings had curtailed some of
the state laws, demoralizing crusaders but also spurring comprehen-
sive action like that sought by the National Prohibition Party, established at a convention in September 1869.

"Both of our existing political parties are in such homage to the
interests and policies which cluster around and uphold the dram shop
that neither of them will ever consent to demand its suppression,"
New Yorker Gerrit Smith told the Prohibition Party conventioneers
in Chicago.[44]

A wealthy graduate of Hamilton College, where he had been two
years ahead of Albert Barnes, Smith resided not far from the Oneida
Community and periodically corresponded with its members. He was
also, even more than his fellow Presbyterian Mears, an all-purpose
morality crusader. Smith had been an early abolitionist, a secret financial supporter of anti-slavery advocate John Brown, and a temperance
advocate for decades. On the side, Smith publicly denounced tobacco
and Freemasonry while he advocated vegetarianism and, along with
Noyes, women's dress reform.[45]

Smith and the New York prohibitionists, meeting in Syracuse
several days before Christmas 1869, agreed with the new national
party organizers that neither the Democrats nor Republicans were
willing to suppress the liquor traffic or dissolve their corrupt union
with the dram shops. Singularly dedicated crusaders rather than
political trimmers were needed. In 1871, a well-known temperance
lecturer running on the Prohibition ticket was elected to the Massachusetts legislature, showing political success was possible. By 1872,
the Prohibition Party was running candidates for president and vice
president, though they finished dead last with fewer than six thousand votes nationwide. They did little better in the 1876 presidential
election, with the head of the ticket garnering fewer than ten thousand votes.

Still, crusaders mobilized against the pervasive threat. An 1876 investigation in Philadelphia had detected liquor being sold at 8,034 places throughout the city, with the sellers reportedly including "497 Scotch, 568 English, 2,179 Germans, 304 Irish and 672 whose nationality is unknown."[46] The next year, President Rutherford B. Hayes's wife banned intoxicants from the White House. At the other end of Pennsylvania Avenue, the House of Representatives would vote in 1879 to establish the House Committee on Alcoholic Liquor Traffic. The temperance movement that had begun with securing individual sobriety pledges had advanced up through local and state statutes to its natural conclusion, the call for national prohibition.

In Oneida County, a dedicated constituency had supported since 1873 the publication of a weekly temperance periodical, the *Living Issue*. For $1 a year, temperance advocates could receive each Thursday the periodical described as "radical in sentiment but courteous in manner."[47] Like the temperance movement itself, the journal sometimes drew cynical laughs for its seriousness.

"The Living Issue asks, in great mental agony, 'can our girls marry drunkards?'" the *Ogdensburg Journal* observed in early 1878. "We don't see anything to prevent it if the girls don't object."[48]

In the face of public mockery or indifference, the activists could claim some success. In 1877, a prison reformer reported to the Oneida County Board of Supervisors that the temperance movement had reduced the local jail population. Statewide, Prohibition Party candidates came forward in about one-third of New York's thirty-three congressional races in 1878.

Mears made sense as a candidate for the cause. He had long paid attention to politics, writing sharp analyses of Oneida County's political environment for the *New-York Evangelist*. Temperance, in particular, had captivated him going back to his years alongside Albert Barnes in Philadelphia. Certainly, Mears welcomed the attention that came with a public campaign. Upon hearing the news of Mears's nomination, seniors in Hamilton's class of 1879 marched at night to the professor's home adjoining the campus. Mears may not have been beloved, but his political ascension was a good excuse for a student rally. After massing before Mears's home on College Hill, the students quieted so that senior Lawrence Winfield Baxter could speak.

"It is one of the most gratifying signs of the times that the people are awaking to realize the necessity of instituting some genuine movements of reform," the future lawyer enthused.

The students urged Baxter on, some, perhaps, ironically. Hamilton undergraduates knew the Utica groggeries all too well. The students' yearbook carried full-page ads for McQuade Brothers wine merchants, among others. While Mears dedicated himself to eradicating pleasure spots, students sought them out. Still, Baxter rolled on.

"Who, gentleman, is more worthy to take the initiative?" Baxter declaimed. "Who is more competent to carry it to a successful completion than our revered and learned professor, Dr. Mears!"

Mears drank it all in. He was accustomed to student obedience, heads bowed as they copied his words, but this gathering was animated by the freer spirits that accompany young men spontaneously gathered at night. Mears felt the political moment.

"I suppose, gentlemen," Mears said, when young Baxter was done, that "you have come here and want to know how your professor got into politics. Your professor of metaphysics in politics!"

Mears and the students shared the humor, though they may have been tuned to different jokes. Students, wearied by Mears's recitation hall demands, might laugh at the notion of him winning a popularity contest.

"A little sound metaphysics would not do politics any harm," Mears said. "Politics ought to be gotten out of the dram shops, our politicians of all parties would be safer and sounder men if they were separated from the fumes of the bottle."

Mears continued.

"You know that geese flying south form a wedge in flying, with the angle in front, and it is said they choose the toughest bird in the flock and put him in the angle to lead off. Somehow, though I am not very old, and do not regard myself as very tough, I have been selected as the toughest bird and have been put in the front. Perhaps we are on a wild goose chase and will never get very far on our journey."

"We hope you will get all the way there," one student shouted.[49]

Maybe that was yet another joke. If the dreadfully serious professor reached Congress, then he would be far away from Hamilton, for good. Or, maybe the student was sincere. However it was, the speeches finally done, Mears invited the seniors in for refreshments. His campaign would never swell higher.

10 ON BATTLE'S EVE

THE PROHIBITION PARTY candidate stumbled and fell.

The odds against Mears, of course, were long from the start. Liquor pervaded Oneida County, notwithstanding the local temperance constituency. A veteran Oneida County assemblyman, a Mr. Jones, summed up the prevailing sentiment when he observed in 1878 that he had been drinking ale and whiskey for decades and had never been drunk once.[1]

Realistically, everyone knew Mears didn't stand a shot. He lacked money, organization, and electoral experience. Uncharacteristically, moreover, Mears himself seemed rather low-key between his October nomination and the early November election. The Rome, Utica, and Clinton newspapers followed politics avidly, and Mears was all but absent from each of them. At the least, he might have tried rallying hometown forces at Clinton's Scollard Opera House; it would have been an apt venue. A fellow Prohibition Party candidate, running for a state assembly seat, spoke in late October at Scollard to a small audience. A certain Professor Reynolds appeared a few days later to demonstrate his mesmeric powers. Several days after that, suffragist Elizabeth Cady Stanton took the Scollard stage.

Mears, though, seemed to confine himself to the lecture hall, chapel, and recitation room, and the political cognoscenti dismissed him— at least, in part.

"Doctor Mears," the *Utica Morning Herald* bluntly stated on October 24, "cannot hope to receive one-twentieth of the popular vote in any contingency, and probably will receive less."

Even so, partisans recognized that even a watered-down campaign could taint the final outcome. Most Prohibition supporters, including Mears himself, were Republicans. The Democrats, as newspaper editor Horace Greeley had once put it, were the "whiskey and lager beer" party.[2] A vote for Mears thus likely drained a vote away from the Republican candidate and aided the Democrats. It had happened before. Some twenty years earlier, vigorously advocating prohibition, abolitionist Gerrit Smith had taken about six thousand votes away from the New York Republican gubernatorial candidate. The question, then, was not whether Mears would lose, but who he might take down with him.

"When will the Prohibitionists receive the returns?" the *Utica Sunday Tribune* asked on November 3. "People will want to know the size of the dent in the Republican column."

In the end, Mears barely left a scratch. He pulled a little more than four hundred votes, fewer than the third-party Greenback candidate and less than 5 percent of the total claimed by the winner, Republican railroad lawyer Cyrus Dan Prescott. Mears won a scant sixty-seven votes in all of Utica, and even in his hometown of Clinton, he lagged far behind the other three candidates. Mears's low vote tally, though, did not undercut his stature among New York State prohibitionists, nor did it permanently discourage Mears. He would fight on.

"The Prohibition Party, it seems, made rather a poor show as to numbers," the *Watertown Re-union* observed on November 21, several weeks after the election, "yet we must admire it for its pluck and commend its principle in the abstract."

Mears sought the admiration, yes, but he craved more than that. He needed to fight and he also needed, at long last, to win. A lifetime of lost battles takes a toll. The Pennsylvania Supreme Court had restored Philadelphia's Sunday streetcar service. The Gettysburg orphanage had collapsed. Mears was politically savvy enough to recognize a Prohibition Party candidacy as a quixotic gesture. The Oneida Community, though, was a target that could be hit.

• • •

Mears's election defeat was about two and a half months old in early 1879, a season of threats. In Wyoming, heathens still defied suppression. An army board of inquiry was reexamining the evisceration, nearly three years earlier, of George Armstrong Custer's command. From outside, immigrants pressed upon US shores. In Washington, DC, lawmakers were considering legislation to curtail Chinese immigration, with House members explaining that "homogeneity of ideas and of physical and social habits are essential to national harmony and progress."[3] From inside, Utah's Mormons were, a New York editorialist warned in early 1879, "silently and insidiously stretching out their line over neighboring territories and establishing Mormon colonies."[4] Senators were considering the further regulation of Mormon polygamy in the wake of the January 6 Supreme Court decision upholding the federal anti-bigamy statute. Other moral threats, too, required containment. In Massachusetts, Governor Thomas Talbot warned in his early 1879 message to the state legislature that, with liquor, "the unchecked appetite evades law and mocks its officers."[5]

There was more. Obscenity polluted the streams of commerce. Reverend Josephus Flavius Cook of Boston denounced in one early 1879 New York State sermon "the ghouls and ogres of the city slum" who were making "debauched use" of the mails, the *St. Lawrence Herald* reported on January 25. Cook had also warned about the "moral lepers and assassins, [who] secretly, at night, through the cover of mails, throw their poison into seminaries of all grades."[6] Case in point: in November 1878, agents for the New York Society for the Suppression of Vice in Rochester, New York, had required six horse-drawn wagons to haul off a stock of vile literature. Cook, famed for a series of noontime Monday lectures in Boston, saw a related threat in the Oneida Community, which he termed "an example of false religion more loathsome than Mormonism or Mohammadanism."[7] He respected Mears's prior crusading work for throwing a "red-crooked thunderbolt through that infamy of Oneida,"[8] and the two men would arrange to meet in Syracuse.

Amid this tumult, on Friday, January 17, Episcopal bishop Frederic Dan Huntington braved Syracuse's wintry streets to call upon Reverend Augustus Field Beard.

Beard was a highly principled, forty-five-year-old Congregationalist minister, tapped for the Scroll and Key secret society while at Yale. He had gone on to Union Theological Seminary and then served a flock in Bath, Maine, before becoming a minister in 1869 at the large Plymouth Congregational Church in downtown Syracuse. Plymouth was a prominent perch, with a congregation famous for its pre–Civil War abolitionism. Beard suited its sentiments. He put his faith into action through the American Missionary Association, which espoused equal brotherhood through the founding of black colleges and universities.

"People who believed in God looked out upon another people, children of a common Father, who were born under the skies of a common country," Beard would write, "and saw them, not only with no legal rights, but not even with the rights of their own persons, chattels under the laws, bought and sold as things, in sin and degradation, and without hope in the world."[9]

Beard overflowed with spirit. A friend described his "sparkling wit, his playful humor, his enthusiasm and his big-hearted friendliness."[10] This spirit would be tested, sorely. His first wife, Eliza, had died after only two years of marriage. A daughter from his second marriage, Ethel, would not live past the age of three. Beard himself would survive to the age of 101; at 100, he would take his first airplane ride.

Beard was younger than Mears, but in some ways more formidable. He was a fixture in the Central New York establishment, and could move smoothly among elites without radiating the raw missionary zealotry that could overheat Mears. "Dr. Beard," a Yale acquaintance would recall, "is a man of broad culture, large and varied experience and of a national reputation."[11]

He was meeting a man of similar stature.

Bishop Huntington was fifty-nine years old and had been the head of the Episcopal Diocese of Central New York since 1869. He oversaw religious activities in a fourteen-county region that included 106 parishes and missions. The youngest of eleven children, Huntington was class valedictorian at Amherst College and a graduate of

Harvard Divinity School. Like Beard, he was accustomed to moving in rarified circles, as the onetime Plummer Professor of Christian Morals at Harvard. Personally, he tended toward the austere, urging ministers to renounce self-indulgence, self-will, and self-promotion.

"No others can rouse the nation from its spiritual deadness in materialism, in indifference, in frivolity and carnal luxury," Huntington would declare.[12]

Full-bearded, with a high forehead and white hair curling over his ears, Huntington appeared a man of distinction. In meetings of his fellow bishops, he sometimes stayed silent, while at other times he could drone on. Mears said Huntington could be "brusque and self-assertive . . . and his voice like that of a captain rather than an orator,"[13] and his sermons, fellow priest A. L. Byron-Curtiss allowed, tended to be "overlong" and "a bit top heavy with ponderosity." Attending a service at Hamilton College one Sunday, Huntington was observed to bow lower, chant louder, and stand more erect than anyone else.

"We all loved, revered and esteemed him," Byron-Curtiss said, "despite his few crotchets."[14]

A Unitarian before he switched denominations, Huntington supported the rights of Indians, the protection of juvenile prisoners, and the cause of women's suffrage. He knew misfortune firsthand. Years before, he and his wife had lost a child when it was just two weeks old. He was also acutely aware of temptation and taint. A summertime encounter with an "evil-minded companion" and several, unspecified, experiences in college "caused him to look back with repugnance to what came near to becoming sources of hidden corruption," Huntington's daughter Arria would later ambiguously recount.[15] As an adult, having avoided these earlier lures, Huntington was much vexed, Arria would write, by "two plague spots of moral corruption" festering in his New York diocese. One, Arria recounted, was the "strong Pagan influence" among the Onondaga Indians living near Syracuse.[16]

The other plague spot, Arria reported, was the Oneida Community.

By 1878, Huntington was publicly denouncing Oneida. During Lent, filled with the spirit of self-denial, he castigated Oneida's carnal excesses. He struck a chord. That October, leaders with both the Presbyterian Synod of Central New York and the General Association of the Congregational Church of New York had established their committees to assail the Oneida Community. Beard chaired the Congregationalists' effort. The Presbyterians' renewed effort was led by Mears. With the religious forces rallying, Mears began corresponding with Huntington and reported finding him "ready at once to join in initiating active measures."[17]

So it was that on a cold January day in 1879, Huntington and Beard quietly convened at Beard's home at 236 East Genesee Street to contemplate what might be done.

Previous individual sallies had failed to dislodge Oneida. Sermons had been preached, essays written, prosecutions considered. Nothing had availed. Beard and Huntington concluded that a broader meeting should be convened. The key would be to gather men of common cause. Together, they might form a clenched fist. Beard and Huntington considered potential allies. Mears, of course, was already on board. Syracuse University's chancellor, Erastus O. Haven, would make sense. His university's spacious new Hall of Languages could suitably host a meeting. Huntington and Beard decided that "four or five" representatives each from Presbyterian, Methodist, and other denominations should gather. But the conference, Beard advised Mears, was not going to be very large; "not over 30 or 35 persons," Beard wrote.[18] Nor, it went without saying, would the meeting be open to all. Though Syracuse alone had seven Roman Catholic churches and three synagogues or other Jewish associations, no rabbis or Catholic priests were apparently invited. No women, either.

And no reporters. This was meant to be private.

At his comfortable home on College Hill Road, adjoining the Hamilton College campus about fifty miles east of Syracuse, Mears readied himself. A renewed crusade was just what he had been agitating for. If anything, he wanted the Syracuse conference larger. The conference grew, at any rate, from its original conception. The impeccably handwritten letters were sent from Syracuse on January 23.

"The great wrong done to society by the institution known as the Oneida Community, from its deadly opposition to the principles of Christian morality, appears to demand some unified counsel and action on the part of teachers of the gospel and defendants of public and domestic virtue in this part of the country," the invitation stated.[19]

The recipients were asked to attend a "preliminary meeting, at Syracuse, in the University building, on Friday the 14th day of February at 2:30 o'clock P.M." Though responses were directed to Beard, Mears was the first signatory among five.

Another signer was Edward G. Thurber, who had served as minister at the Park Central Presbyterian Church in Syracuse since May 1870. The graduate of the University of Michigan and Andover Theological Seminary knew Mears from past Presbyterian duties, and they could be equally stern. Thurber would warn, in his preaching, that "love of ambition, wealth and pleasure gives only ephemeral success."[20]

Haven, Syracuse University's chancellor, also signed the invitation. A fifty-eight-year-old graduate of Wesleyan University and the divinity program at Union College, Haven could seem tightly wrapped emotionally. He was kind enough with his children, but not outwardly affectionate as a rule. With his wife, he seemed invariably proper; he was content, a colleague said, so long as she was dutiful in bringing him his books and papers.

"In neither did I ever see an exuberance of love or any other emotion," a friend recalled. "Neither was demonstrative in the slightest degree."[21]

Haven had previously served as president of the University of Michigan and Northwestern University and as secretary of the Methodist Board of Education, until Syracuse hired him in June 1874 at a delicate juncture for the three-year-old university. The previous September, the influential Philadelphia banking house Jay Cooke and Company had closed, an early spark in what became the Panic of 1873. Railroads defaulted on their bonds, bank deposits plummeted, and financial pledges made in flush years evaporated. Syracuse University was stretched close to snapping.

4. Erastus O. Haven. Portrait Collection, University Archives, Special Collections Research Center, Syracuse University Libraries.

Haven himself was accounted to be "weak bodily and discouraged mentally" by the time he took over as Syracuse's chancellor.[22] His skills—which in his prime were many—did not always satisfy the peculiar demands of a financially struggling new university. The Oneida Community, put simply, was not Chancellor Haven's greatest worry at the moment. Still, his recruitment seemed both inevitable and crucial. As one Syracuse University colleague noted, Haven faithfully "lent his help to every public measure of the city where he resided, and thought it his duty and privilege to do what he could to make and guide public opinion on matters of public policy."[23]

And so the movement's leaders presented themselves. Mears: the ambitious philosophy professor. Haven: the tightly stretched university chancellor. Huntington: the ever-righteous Episcopalian bishop. Beard: the spirited Congregationalist comfortable in elite society. Thurber: the capable Presbyterian minister. Each of these reverential men came to the cause well-armed. Each could write, speak, and rally a congregation. Together, they resolved to cleanse the Oneida Community.

• • •

The secret leaked, as secrets will.

On February 10, a telegram sent from Syracuse arrived at the *New York Herald*'s newsroom in Manhattan. The boisterous newspaper was run by men who knew a good story when they saw one, even if they had to make it up themselves. Under *Herald* editor James Gordon Bennett Jr., truth could be subordinate to spectacle. Several years earlier, luring readers with subheadlines like "Savage Brutes at Large" and "A Shocking Sabbath Carnival of Death," the *New York Herald* had captivated New York with a thoroughly fictional report about wild animals running amok out of the Central Park Zoo.[24] But with the Syracuse telegram, the New York City paper was put on to something real. The tipster wrote that many prominent men, including the presidents of several colleges, were expected at a Syracuse conference targeting the Oneida Community's notorious immoralities.

Other newspapers received the same tip, and the *Syracuse Morning Standard*'s February 11 edition declared that at least one hundred delegates were expected at a conference attacking Oneida. The *Syracuse Daily Courier* followed the next day, announcing that "another war has been declared against the Oneida Community." The paper further stated, in the passive phrasing reporters sometimes favor, that "it is understood" that Mears instigated the conference.

At first, the reporters could not obtain a copy of the actual invitation. One night, though, several days before the scheduled February 14 meeting, reporters called upon Haven at his Syracuse home. "Though the worthy chancellor had disrobed and retired, they were graciously granted, not only an interview but a copy of the Call," the *American Socialist*, the Oneida Community's periodical, subsequently reported on February 20.

Slowly, information trickled out. On February 13, the *Syracuse Morning Standard* reported that Beard had received positive responses from about fifty prominent clergymen and others. Although "a large number of others have expressed regret at being unable to be present," the *Standard* stated, presumably echoing Beard's account, "they will use their influence to second any action which is taken."

The story grew, for the Oneida Community always made for sensational copy. The *Albany Evening Times* typified the sensational coverage, with its February 12 declaration that the Oneida Community's "social system is only to be named with horror and disgust." Newspapers outdid one another in their denunciations of Oneida's social—that is to say sexual—system. No one wanted to be mistaken for a defender of the libertine. At the same time, newspapers respected the Community's civic and commercial virtues. The *Evening Times* followed the ritual moral denunciation by taking note of the "plain, thoughtful people, well behaved . . . attending to their daily duties, which are light and pleasant, under apparently the most cheerful and agreeable circumstances."

It was complicated, the way newspapers portrayed the Oneida Community and the renewed fight against it. The Community's unconventional sexual practices excited dismay and fascination alike. Business-wise, the sexual exotica presented an opportunity. Sin sells. Editors summon spectators with the promise of sensation. Reporters, moreover, tend to be sardonic toward the self-righteous. The February 13 *New York Herald* hinted at this with its headline about the "religious crusade" brewing against the Oneida Community:

Episcopal and Presbyterian Bishops and Priests in War Paint!

What a semi-comical sight, underlined by the exclamation point: bishops and priests in war paint! The phrase *religious crusade*, too, sounded a little snide, like something spit out by a cynic with one foot on the bar rail.

Preparing for the conference, the *Herald*'s unnamed correspondent journeyed through a dense February snowstorm to call upon the Community, whose members he reported had the reputation among neighbors as being "industrious, temperate, frugal, courteous, honorable in all their dealings." If it were up to the neighbors, the reporter determined, the crusade would never have started. The reporter met the patriarch Noyes, who could not speak at length because of his chronic throat affliction. Instead, the reporter interviewed William Hinds, editor of the Community's periodical, the *American Socialist.*

Hinds was a longtime confidante of Noyes, having first joined the Perfectionists as a sixteen-year-old apprentice in the original Putney, Vermont, outpost. Educated in his mid-thirties at Yale's Sheffield Scientific School, Hinds was famed for his powers of concentration.[25] Stories were told of his having memorized, for the reward of $1, a forty-page essay by Noyes entitled "Salvation from Sin in This World." Hinds was himself a bit of a scholar. In 1878, he published through the Oneida Community a 175-plus-page book entitled *American Communities,* examining the likes of Shakers, Harmonists, and the since-forgotten Separatists of Zoar. Defending the Oneida Community put Hinds in a poignant position. Unbeknownst to outsiders, he was part of a restive faction that had grown unhappy with Noyes's leadership. Loyally, though, he insisted in public that the Community was unconcerned about the upcoming Syracuse meeting.

"This is not the first time that Dr. Mears has agitated on this subject?" the *New York Herald* reporter asked.

"No, sir," Hinds said. "He brought the community to the attention of the Presbyterian Synod of Central New York and other like bodies several years ago."

Hinds further cited a letter to the *Utica Morning Herald* on August 10, 1878, in which Mears allowed it might take passage of a special statute to uproot Oneida. Perhaps, the reporter suggested, the Supreme Court's recent ruling against Mormon bigamy was a sign that the political winds now favored Mears.

"It has doubtless given momentum to this movement," Hinds said.[26]

Hinds, though, was fearless and smart. Before the conference, Hinds had previously called upon the editor and publisher of the *Syracuse Morning Standard,* Moses Summers. The two men could use each other. Born in Ireland, the bearded, sixty-year-old Summers had toughened his hide while serving as an army quartermaster during the Civil War.[27] Swearing, after the fashion of both soldiers and newspapermen, Summers told Hinds he didn't know why the clergy couldn't mind their own business. With what might have been a touch of mischief-making, Summers referred Hinds to a young man who could hand out copies of the *American Socialist* to the meddlesome ministers.

February 14 arrived. By early afternoon, dozens of ministers, educators, editors, and uninvited others had ventured up the hill toward the university's Hall of Languages. The young man recommended by Summers was among them, and, whether from courtesy or curiosity, many of the clergymen accepted copies of the *American Socialist*. By the time Hinds arrived with two reporters at about 2:00 p.m., he saw twenty or thirty men reading the paper and milling about on the second floor.

Mears, Haven, and Beard greeted everyone, but it was Mears who seemed, Hinds subsequently reported, "to be the ruling spirit of the occasion . . . dodging about with a black patch over one eye, presenting a very comical appearance."[28]

And then the conference came to order.

11 THE MINISTERS' WAR

THE CAMPAIGN looked promising from the start.

As he surveyed the Hall of Languages's parlor, Mears saw men capable of carrying on the good fight. Universalist minister Richmond Fisk, for one, had studied at Union College under Tayler Lewis, the learned battler against the Oneida Community.[1] From the ministry, Fisk had ascended to the presidency of St. Lawrence University in 1868 as a precocious thirty-two-year-old. He stuck with it through early 1872, when he embarked on a series of Universalist church assignments.

John J. Brown, a bespectacled fifty-eight-year-old professor of physics and chemistry, was a former pastor who had left Cornell and joined the embryonic Syracuse University faculty because of the new school's Methodist Episcopal affiliations.[2] He had arrived at the Hall of Languages about the same time as Professor George Fisk Comfort, a Syracuse colleague who specialized in modern languages and aesthetics and who had helped found the Metropolitan Museum of Art in New York City before coming to Syracuse to serve as dean of the College of Fine Arts. He was a cultured forty-five-year-old man, keen on building the university's scholarly reputation.

Reverend Philemon H. Fowler, the sixty-five-year-old former Presbyterian minister who, as a Hamilton College trustee, had helped hire Mears, sat not far from Reverend Evert Van Slyke of the First Reformed Church in Syracuse. An 1862 Rutgers graduate, Van Slyke had much on his mind beyond the cleansing of sin. The previous February, shortly after Sunday school had been dismissed, a fire destroyed Van Slyke's beloved James Street church. He was busy raising the funds for a new stone building, one built to last.[3] The forty-six-year-old Orris H. Warren was a regent of the University of the State of New York and editor of the *Northern Christian Advocate*, a Syracuse-based weekly serving the Methodist Episcopal Church. Warren had studied at Oberlin College under the presidency of Charles Grandison Finney, the evangelist whose fervent preaching had once helped inspire Noyes as well as Mears's own father. Warren was well-armored for crusading against Oneida's wrongs.

"Courage and inflexibility, not compromise and conciliation, were the dominant notes of his character," an ally recounted.[4]

. . .

Chancellor Haven, as the Syracuse University host, started the proceedings politely.

"We are here," Haven intoned, "because certain gentlemen, ministers of the gospel among them, have thought it proper to consult on the subject of whether Christian people possess a certain obligation, a certain duty, shall we say, to perform with regard to what is known as the Oneida Community."[5]

Mears declared it a closed session, off-limits to the uninvited press. Secrecy, some thought, seemed inappropriate for a university devoted to disseminating knowledge. The reporters grumbled, as did some ministers. Some were simply confused. They had not received a personal invitation, either, but had tagged along through word of mouth. Did Professor Mears mean to expel them, as well? Some ministers stood to leave, while at the front the leaders tried to calm the waters. Reporters made their own case, with John J. Flanagan, city editor of the *Utica Morning Herald*, arguing that publicity was in the ministers' best interest.

The thirty-eight-year-old Flanagan could speak with some authority. A military telegrapher during the Civil War, where he had reportedly worked alongside inventor Thomas Edison, Flanagan had served as a police and fire commissioner in Utica.[6] He moved in informed circles throughout Oneida County and was not easily intimidated. Some ministers agreed with Flanagan's assessment, but Mears was adamant that the session be closed, and at his insistence the reporters departed.

5. Jesse Truesdell Peck. Portrait Collection, University Archives, Special Collections Research Center, Syracuse University Libraries.

Privacy having been obtained, Bishop Peck was called upon for the benediction, an appropriate choice. When Jesse Peck boomed out his plea, heaven above was sure to hear. Beneath his bulk, though, Jesse Truesdell Peck was vulnerable. As president of Dickinson College in Pennsylvania from 1848 to 1852, it was said, "the undergraduates did not take to him kindly."[7] Once, so a story went, Peck was visiting Staunton, Virginia. Student pranksters sent a telegram to the warden of the local insane asylum, advising that an unmistakably large man would soon be arriving by train. The deluded giant, the telegram warned, called himself president of Dickinson. He required careful tending. The warden knew his duty. He went to the station and found Peck, just as massive as had been described. The warden soothingly took his visitor by the elbow and prepared to escort him off to the asylum, until a mutual acquaintance chanced by and greeted them both. The jig was up.[8]

Though Peck acted as if he appreciated the joke, he spent weeks trying to nab the perpetrators.

Married but childless, Peck lectured other families in a book entitled *The True Woman: Or, Life and Happiness at Home and Abroad.*
Chapters covered topics such as "how to get a good husband" and
"a true woman in her proper sphere." Under no circumstance, Peck
directed, should a woman marry before the age of eighteen, but by the
age of twenty-five she should definitely be attached. The true woman
should ensure that her betrothed avoid vicious company and intoxicating drink. She, in turn, must not flirt or play the coquette.

"Do not scold," Peck added.[9]

Peck's business done, the Syracuse conference participants selected
Augustus Beard as secretary and settled in for a protracted roll call.
One man after another announced himself and his affiliation, regi-
mental representatives reporting for duty. Presbyterian, Episcopalian,
Methodist, Congregationalist, Baptist, the Reformed Church, and
more were all accounted for. The Oneida Community had succeeded
in uniting, in opposition, much of the Protestant diaspora.

Mears then summed up the history of the Oneida Community,
with a reasonably fair accounting. He described John Humphrey
Noyes as an intelligent Dartmouth College graduate who showed real
potential before veering into sexual communism. Mears allowed some
light to shine through the vituperation.

"I may say," Mears acknowledged, "that these people are good
citizens, orderly and cleanly in the manner in which they conduct
their home."

But as he went on, Mears unleashed himself. He complained that
newspapers invariably sympathized with the Oneida Community even
though it was, he declared, "the product of vile passion." Raw lust
and licentiousness were rampant, Mears said. The Community's social
practices violated every norm of decent society. Reverend Philemon
Fowler interrupted, asking whether Mears believed the Oneida leaders
were sincere in their beliefs.

"I presume they are sincere," Mears allowed.

"Is it dying out?" Fowler asked.

"It shows no sign of it," Mears said, ominously.

Bishop Huntington added his two cents. The Oneida Community, he said, should be exposed to the light of righteousness.

"There is an impure emanation from it," Huntington said. "Young people go there and return with these impure thoughts and associations in their minds."[10]

A letter was read from Congressman William Henry Baker, a Republican born in a town close to the Oneida Community. Several weeks prior to the Syracuse convention, Baker had received petitions from women living in several villages including Hamilton, Vermillion, and Bridgeport; they had urged some action with regard to the 1862 federal anti-polygamy statute. The petitions may not have specifically identified Oneida, but they reminded the congressman that some of his constituents cared about marriage morality. Baker, a former Oswego County district attorney, wanted to throw the book at the free lovers. He called it a disgrace that Congress should admit a Mormon delegate from Utah, or that New York should tolerate a community such as Oneida. This system, the congressman opined, is a foul blot on civilization.

No one disagreed. The conference participants had worked themselves up, and they were ready to talk tactics.

Huntington called on Levi Wells Hall, a sixty-year-old Syracuse attorney, for a legal assessment. Hall had served three years as Onondaga County's district attorney and had retired from private practice in 1878, turning his attention to the Syracuse Chilled Plow Company.[11] A man who loved a good joke, Hall still moved easily through the city's Republican clubhouses.

Hall reported that Massachusetts and Connecticut, among other states, had legislated against adultery and lascivious cohabitation. These statutes could be extraordinarily severe. At one point, the prescribed penalty for adultery in the colony of Massachusetts was death. Public whippings, of up to forty lashes, and the enforced wearing of a two-inch-high capital *A* were lesser punishments imposed on colonial adulterers. Though criminal prosecutions had become rare, legal prohibitions remained. Several years before the Syracuse convention, a married South Carolina man named Daniel Carroll, who had been having an affair with a single woman, had been convicted on charges of breaking a state law against "habitual" sexual intercourse outside of marriage. The South Carolina Supreme Court upheld his conviction, for which he received a sentence of six months imprisonment and a $200 fine.[12]

"But in our own state," Hall told the ministers gathered in Syracuse, "adultery has not been made a penal offense. Not in its specifics. It is not a crime."[13]

That news unsettled those who assumed civil law would follow the Ten Commandments. Hall went on. The Oneida Community, he said, might require specific legislation. It would not necessarily have to be broad and sweeping. If public sentiment were set against the Community, and if the popular mood was turned just so, Oneida might be struck down with a well-placed statutory word or two. Here, Hall offered specifics. If the existing New York law concerning disorderly persons included the words "all persons living in concupiscence and adultery," Hall hypothesized, it would implicate the entire adult Oneida Community.

"Rouse a general feeling," Hall advised, "and the legislature will act."

Hall's summation set the ministers on a path. Now, they needed to organize their campaign. For a bit, like disputing faculty members, they bogged down in process. Mears suggested forming separate committees to investigate the law and the Community's practices. Haven favored a unified committee, inquiring into every facet of the Oneida problem as well as potential solutions. The ministers discussed how explicit they should be in spelling out their goals. Haven thought the resolution should be open-ended, letting the future work come to its natural conclusion.

All the bureaucratic blather about procedures, committees, and resolutions frustrated Reverend William Smith, of the Congregational Church in Oswego. A Rutgers College graduate and Glasgow, Scotland, native, Smith had been leading the Oswego church for the past several years, where he was known for his strict orthodoxy.[14] He had been among the first ministers Beard and Huntington thought of when they were planning the Syracuse conference.

Sarcastic at first, the forty-eight-year-old Smith soon heated up.

Every man, woman, and child must be made to understand the Oneida Community's immorality, Smith said. The crusaders should neither fear nor equivocate. It was time to take decisive steps. Smith was Robert the Bruce, rebuking the battle shy, and Chancellor Haven, a man accustomed to professorial circumlocution, took exception. He assured Smith that he was not afraid. Former St. Lawrence University president Richmond Fisk echoed Haven. Mister Smith was laboring under a misapprehension, he said. Everyone in the room, let it be understood, had the courage of their convictions. But Smith was not alone in demanding firm action to suppress Oneida's evil, however difficult the task might prove. Reverend J. T. Brownell, a Methodist, tried to speak for all when he summoned the rousing phrase attributed to Hannibal: "we must either find a way, or make one," Brownell said.[15]

The conversation sallied back and forth. If the community stood alone, without sympathy from the outside public, it might be overcome with a popular uprising. But given current circumstances, with Oneida's roots sunk into the soil, Peck moved that a committee be established to investigate questions of fact and law. The follow-up work would ensure the Syracuse conference would have the permanence necessary to succeed. This war would be long.

"The evil is too deep-seated to be easily eradicated," Peck warned.

Huntington called upon Reverend G. M. Pierce, editor of the Salt Lake City–based *Rocky Mountain Christian Advocate*, a monthly Methodist periodical, to share his insights. Since arriving in Utah in 1870 to launch the state's first Methodist church, Pierce had studied the Mormons firsthand. Guided by questioning from Mears and others, he described the Mormons' fraught relations with the US government and assessed the dissatisfactions of Mormon women. Pierce was echoing a common refrain about the ostensible association between Oneida communism, Mormonism, and general heathenism. Not only was Mormonism, as one Congregational minister declared in 1879, a "national shame and peril," but the Mormon-populated state of Utah amounted to "our American Turkey."[16] That same year, Presbyterian evangelists likened Utah's residents to the "idolators and the cannibals of the Sandwich Islands."[17] By summoning such a dread topic, the Syracuse crusaders could reinforce, at least in their own minds, the linkage between Oneida and Utah.

It was time to wrap up.

Huntington, Mears, and Beard were named to the committee that would conduct the follow-up work. The conferees also intended to put themselves on record. Some questions later surrounded exactly what transpired, but according to the *Utica Morning Herald*'s version, a resolution was offered demanding the suppression of the Oneida Community. Haven, the *Morning Herald* reported, proposed softening the resolution, to specify that it was the immoral features of the Oneida Community, and not the Community in its entirety, that was to be suppressed. Mears later insisted that no one had proposed suppressing the entire Community. The mistaken reports, he said several weeks later, were due to someone who was not paying attention when the resolution was first read. This knuckle rapping greatly amused the reporters who had to piece together what happened after Mears kicked them out of the room.

Professor Comfort noted that since the announcement had gotten into the newspapers, the reporters should be provided with the resolution and other information. Comfort's position may have been subtle. Perhaps, it was later suggested, he intended to funnel all reporting through a single officially sanctioned channel, limiting disclosure to the barest of formal resolutions. However it was meant, the clergymen agreed to issue a statement.

"We have nothing to be ashamed of," Haven agreed. "Let the people of the state know what is done."[18]

Bishop Huntington wasn't so sure.

Huntington, it was said, subsequently beseeched reporters not to make public his name or that of the other participants. Any hope of keeping the secret, though, faded by that night, when Syracuse reporters made clear they would publish everything they knew, including the full list of participants. Reporters had set upon the departing ministers the minute the meeting broke up, and participants who thought it imprudent to lock the reporters out freely communicated all that had transpired. Mears's effort at confidentiality had failed utterly. In truth, it backfired, as the subsequent newspaper accounts cited the attempted secrecy as proof that even the ministers thought they had something to hide.

That night, several reporters met with the Oneida Community's William Hinds at the Vanderbilt House, a handsomely appointed hotel in downtown Syracuse. The launch of this latest campaign did not faze Hinds. From his studies and his own experience, Hinds knew that the unconventional would always draw public rebuke.

"That's nothing new," Hinds said. "It has been tried over and over again."

"Then your people are not greatly disturbed?" a reporter asked.

"Oh, no," Hinds said. "Why should we be?"

The Oneida Community, Hinds elaborated, had never been accused of theft, murder, fraud, or arson. Its members, currently numbered at 145 men and 161 women, were not being dragged before the courts. Unlike Mormons, Oneida Community members were law-abiding. They lived harmoniously with one another and with the neighbors, and persecution would inevitably backfire.

"That is the old story," Hinds said. "The blood of the martyrs is always the seed of the church."

Hinds then recalled, with relish, the self-defeating ruckus raised by previous anti-Oneida agitators.

"The result," Hinds said, "was the increased sale of our products to a public made more aware of our existence. I can only hope that this latest crusade will have a similar effect."[19]

12 AROUSING A SENTIMENT

REVEREND WILLIAM SMITH of Oswego, the Scottish firebrand, ascended his own pulpit the day following the Syracuse conference for a sermon he entitled, pointedly, "Muscular Christianity."

What a perfect example of Christian muscle-flexing it would be, Smith declared, to arouse public sentiment and crush the Oneida Community. Elsewhere, too, the religious press urged on the anti-Oneida troops. The agitators who convened in Syracuse were, after all, representatives of the leading Protestant denominations. They spoke for the faithful, particularly those physically distant from the Oneida Community, who could loathe the Community's principles from afar without ever meeting its members as flesh-and-blood neighbors.

"We trust that the committee created to carry on this reform will prepare a suitable bill, and we can promise it the support of all the best citizens of the State," the New York City-based *Independent* proclaimed, calling "Oneida communism the most flagrantly vile system of social life ever organized."[1]

Outside the religious realm, though, the clergy's campaign incited skepticism if not downright derision. The *Utica Morning Herald* dismissed the February conference as a "ridiculous failure," not least for the attempt at secrecy. "Any body of men which is afraid of the reporters, and the publicity that follows their presence is not capable of inaugurating any great movement," the paper opined.[2] Beyond the discontent over secrecy, skeptics noted the Oneida Community had been condemned for years, without any visible effect. The place seemed a Leviathan, impervious to assault.

"Darts were counted by it as stubble," one wrote. "It laughed at the sticking of a spear."[3]

Critics assailed the Syracuse agitators instead of the communists. In the days following the conference, the *New York Star* called the anti-Oneida effort "conspicuously foolish," the *Catholic Telegraph* of Little Falls, New York, dismissed the Syracuse conference as an "almost ridiculous failure," and New Jersey's *Vineland Independent* assessed that "zealous clergy showed a hand singularly devoid of trumps." On February 26, the satirical magazine *Puck* lampooned Mears et al. with a cover cartoon showing smug, Comstock-like clergymen pointing at the Community and exclaiming, "Oh, dreadful! They dwell in peace and harmony and have no church scandals. They must be wiped out!"

"I suggest," another skeptic offered, "that these crusaders employ themselves in repressing the scandals of their own holy orders, of which the whole world is cognizant."[4]

Practically speaking, the *Albany Evening Post* noted, a criminal indictment brought against the Community would be futile, for local Madison County juries would "ensure their acquittal every time."[5] The *New Haven Sunday Register* praised the communists as "thrifty, industrious and honest," and the *Memphis Appeal* remarked on the orderly, clean, good citizens of the Oneida Community.

The reactions encouraged Oneida Community members, who at several evening meetings following the Syracuse conference read aloud excerpts from the newspaper accounts. They wanted, moreover, the ridicule properly aimed. When on February 17 the *New York Tribune* credited Bishop Huntington and Chancellor Haven for the conference, but omitted any mention of Mears, Oneida Community members set the record straight. Mears's name was first among the invitation to the conference. He was, by all accounts, the most active participant in the conference itself.

"His previous career made him the natural fugleman of the Crusade," the *American Socialist* declared. "The *Tribune*'s representation is a manifest injustice to the gentlemen which it thrusts into the leadership, as well as to Prof. Mears, the actual leader."[6]

The Community's public posture, though, masked internal problems. Behind the scenes, Noyes was losing his grip. He was sixty-seven years old, tired, and unwell. His voice was shot, his legendary vigor drained. Within the Community, Tirzah Miller confided shortly after the Syracuse conference, "evil thinking of the administration and general independence have become more widespread and outspoken."[7] Younger members, in particular, were questioning Noyes's leadership abilities. Noyes sensed the turmoil. Privately, he had begun voicing discouragement about the state of the Community. Evening meetings were growing ugly. Doubt and anger tainted the atmosphere. About ten days after the Syracuse conference, Noyes confided to Francis Wayland-Smith that he had been seriously thinking of proposing that the Community disband.

"I cannot stand it any longer with things going as they are," Noyes told Wayland-Smith, adding that "I shall have to ask the Community to dismiss me. They evidently want and need a new leader."[8]

Noyes's demoralized state remained a secret known to but a few. To outsiders, the Community's members maintained their composure. They would not allow themselves to be beaten down by the likes of John Mears. In a show of confidence, Oneida Community leaders invited the clergymen who had attended the Syracuse conference to visit and see the Community for themselves. All of the workings and habits would be explained, the clergymen were assured. The Community's neighbors, rallying as they had during past crises, also stepped up and wrote letters of endorsement to local newspapers.

"Professor Mears spoke of the women as being low in the scale of intellect," one resident of nearby Lenox wrote in the *Syracuse Daily Journal* on February 26. "I think the professor must have had his mind on their short dresses, short hair and calico pants, which, I admit, make them appear to a great disadvantage." But intellectually, the neighbor opined, the Oneida Community women would be "entirely competent to hold a discussion with Professor Mears himself."

Mears could handle such retorts well enough. If anything, he relished the recognition as an invitation to debate. He wanted precision, though. Erroneous reporting vexed him like a student's stumbling recitation. Aggrieved, Mears wrote the *Utica Morning Herald* a letter, published on March 20, challenging the report that advocates had ever sought to "crush the Oneida Community." By some published accounts, this initial proposal to dismantle the entire Oneida Community was softened on reconsideration. The impression conveyed was that hotheads like Mears were reined in, and more diplomatic language was chosen for the Syracuse conference's concluding resolution. Mears insisted that the Syracuse resolution was, all along, targeted strictly at the "immoral features" of the Community rather than its overall existence.

"Someone, who was not paying due attention when the resolution was first read, misunderstood or failed to hear the exact form of the clause," complained Mears, the very man who banned reporters from the meeting.

In March, Mears sought to undercut Oneida's neighborly support by helping circulate a statement to be signed by local church leaders. A village of about five thousand residents, Oneida housed diverse manufacturing concerns whose products ranged from carriages to caskets. It was also served by a number of churches. Tellingly, none of the local ministers had attended the Syracuse conference. Either they hadn't received an invitation, or they hadn't been willing or able to take up arms. Mears and his allies calculated that a direct request would be hard to deny, bringing the siege lines closer to the Mansion House. Some local church leaders declined to sign the new missive, but four ministers joined the movement.

Reverend Samuel Jessup, a graduate of Princeton and Union Theological Seminary, was called to head Oneida's First Presbyterian Church in 1872.[9] He endorsed Mears's latest screed. So did Reverend George P. Hibbard, who had been rector at St. John's Episcopal Church, the oldest in the village, only since 1877.[10] A third minister, Reverend William A. Ely, was in his early thirties and likewise a relative newcomer to the village's Methodist Episcopal Church.[11] Neither Hibbard nor Ely had been in town long enough to get to know the Oneida Community intimately. A Baptist minister also signed on to the circular dated March 5. The town's Roman Catholic priest did not participate.

While they conceded the Community's members were hard workers and good businessmen, the four signing ministers denounced the
Community's "unconcealed vulgarities." Let there be no mistake, the
ministers attested: they heartily sympathized with the call to suppress
the Oneida Community's immoral practices. "We cannot withhold
our condemnation when we see views and practices that we regard as
outrages upon decency and good morals upheld in the name of religion and the Bible," the ministers declared.[12]

Rallying the Oneida village church leaders reinforced the crusaders' effort to undermine the Community's traditional local support. It
was only the start. Bishop Huntington appeared in the village's Presbyterian church on April 15, and again in a Rome, New York, church
on April 27.

"And thus," Mears said, "the impression so industriously sought
to be made that the people of the vicinity were in sympathy with the
community was dispelled."[13]

Step by step, the campaigners were advancing on multiple fronts.
They sought to arouse public sentiment, pursue new legislation,
and deploy existing law. There was considerable evidence to be collected, including incriminating documents from the institution itself.
Though the Community had prudently curtailed certain mailings following passage of the Comstock Act, Mears and his allies could still
imagine an obscenity case.

Comstock himself had shown how it might be done. In 1877,
using a false name, the morality enforcer had ordered a copy of a
twenty-three-page pamphlet entitled *Cupid's Yokes*. An earnest free-
love plea authored by anarchist Ezra Heywood, *Cupid's Yokes* was
frank in its praise for love unfettered by convention. A true believer in
free love, Heywood criticized the Oneida Community for not being
liberal enough in the distribution of affections. The Oneida communists, Heywood wrote, "are mistaken in supposing that Free Love and
Free Labor are possible only within their ironclad scheme of Socialism."[14] Noyes himself would not entirely disagree with Heywood's
characterization, rejecting as he did the applicability of the term *free
love* to the Oneida Community's well-ordered social practices. In

other ways, though, Heywood prescribed sexual measures similar to those promoted by Noyes, including "reason and self-control over the whole human system" as a means of preventing conception—sexual continence, in other words.

"Though my experience is quite limited," Heywood admitted, "facts within my direct knowledge enable me to affirm without fear of refutation that Lovers' exchange, in its inception, continuance and conclusion, can be made subject to Choice; entered upon, or refrained from as the mutual interests of both, or the separate good of either, requires."[15]

This was as racy as it got in *Cupid's Yokes*, but for Comstock it was still much too much. On November 2, 1877, he had made a grand show of arresting Heywood at a meeting of the New England Free Love League in Boston's Nassau Hall. Heywood's subsequent criminal conviction in January 1878 and his sentencing that June to two years in prison sent a signal readable by Oneida as well as its opponents. Though President Rutherford B. Hayes later pardoned Heywood, Comstock throughout 1878 kept up the pressure by arresting other individuals on charges of mailing *Cupid's Yokes*. Some of these arrests and subsequent trials shadowed the Oneida Community, too.

DeRobigne Mortimer Bennett, born in upstate New York in 1818, had once lived in a celibate Shaker community before leaving to marry and undertake a varied career that eventually brought him to the freethought newspaper, *Truth Seeker*, in the 1870s.[16] A vocal critic of Comstock, Bennett was duly arrested after Comstock used a pseudonym to order a copy of *Cupid's Yokes* by mail. During Bennett's March 1879 trial, his attorney repeatedly quoted from Noyes's *Male Continence* while noting that it had been freely sent through the US mail.

The federal prosecutor, William P. Fiero, countered in a closing flourish that the United States was "one great society for the suppression of vice."[17] The jury agreed, after being instructed by the judge that the test for obscenity was "whether the tendency of the matter is to deprave and corrupt the morals of those whose minds are open to such influence and into whose hands a publication of this sort might fall."[18] Bennett was found guilty on March 21, 1879, and subsequently sentenced to thirteen months of hard labor. The successful obscenity prosecutions heartened Mears and his allies. In the right hands, they were assured, the law could be a sword.

. . .

On June 9, about fifty circulars signed by Mears, Huntington, and Beard invited clergymen to a follow-up conference, intended to reinforce the February 14 meeting. Though they did not know it, the clergymen were moving at an opportune time. Within the Oneida Community itself, dissent was still increasing. On the same June day that Mears, Huntington, and Beard sent out their invitations, Francis Wayland-Smith recounted that the "disaffection continues" at the Community, with leading members "practically alienated" from Noyes.[19]

About twenty-five clergymen, most of them Presbyterian, responded to Mears's latest summons. At 7 p.m. on Wednesday, June 18, they discreetly convened in the parlor of the First Reformed Church on James Street in downtown Syracuse. The hosts kept tight watch on those arriving; secrecy was key. Beard and others had concluded the initial Syracuse conference was undone by publicity and the ensuing ridicule. They would not make the same mistake twice. Recipients of the invitation to the follow-up meeting were directed to bring the circular with them to Syracuse. To gain entrance, ministers had to show the invitation.

Huntington presided, and the ever-reliable Beard served as secretary. The ministers could talk about the Community and the state of the fight without worrying how meddlesome reporters would make them look foolish. Word finally did leak out, though, prompting a *Syracuse Morning Standard* reporter to question Huntington about the private meeting.

"There was little done beyond continuing the old committee," Huntington said.[20]

The reporter kept pressing. Sounding increasingly agitated, Huntington insisted that he could not offer any details. It would be, he insisted, premature.

"What localities were represented by those present?" the *Standard*'s reporter asked.

"I do not recall them just now," Huntington insisted, repeating that "the meeting was a private one."

"Could you give me the names of the delegates in attendance?" the reporter pleaded.

"That would be a difficult matter," the bishop said.

The Reform Church's minister who hosted the meeting, Reverend Evert Van Slyke, likewise clammed up. Perhaps, Van Slyke said, the reporter should try asking some of the other ministers.

"Which proposition would have gladly been accepted," the *Standard*'s reporter noted, "had not the reverend gentleman again declined to give the names of such parties."[21]

In fact, Mears and the other agitators had set upon a course of action. They were going to continue to spread the word. The sermon delivered by Bishop Huntington in April, with some modifications, was going to be reprinted and circulated. As Mears later reported, with some ambiguity, "in seeking these signatures, certain developments appeared, which decided the committee, in addition to the address, to a definite course of legal action."[22] Mears did not elaborate on the "certain developments" that "appeared." The implication, though, was that documents or an informant came to the attention of the committee. The possibility of a leak like this had certainly alarmed Noyes and his lieutenants, who feared turncoats. The precise nature of the relevant information, while unspecified by Mears, must have pointed to some crime. It was evidently sufficient to convince Mears that Noyes or his lieutenants could be prosecuted not through "new legislation, but upon the basis of existing laws."

Charges of incest or statutory rape posed the greatest danger to Noyes. The required evidence, or at least suggestions of it, could have arisen from several sources. The Community's own publications had been diligently collected by Mears and sifted through for incriminating details. Even more specific information about the Community's sexual practices had been collected by Dr. Ely Van de Warker as part of his truncated study of the Community's sexual practices. Noyes had stopped the study, but the prominent Syracuse physician still retained his records, incendiary findings that fairly screamed for publication.

Then there were the Oneida Community's own dissidents, members unhappy with Noyes's faltering leadership and resentful over the skewed administration of sexual favors.

Whoever it was, someone seems to have spoken out of school.

On Thursday, June 19, Mears, A. F. Beard, and about fifteen other allies met again at Huntington's Syracuse home. The house on Waverly Avenue was well known to visitors, with floor-to-ceiling bookshelves and Huntington's favorite rocking chair situated in front of the fireplace.[23] This, too, was meant to be a secret session. By the next day, though, word was circulating, and the *Syracuse Morning Standard* broke the story on its front page on Saturday, June 21. The *Standard*'s account made clear that the anti-Oneida crusaders meant business. They were not simply fulminating, they were plotting legal action. Some of the state's top attorneys had been consulted. Oneida literature had been collected, and testimony taken.

"The arrest of Noyes, the leader of these socialists, is to be made," the *Syracuse Morning Standard* reported, "and his trial is to be pushed by gentlemen who are prepared to go to the very foundation of this thing."[24]

The *Brooklyn Daily Eagle* elaborated the same day, reporting without attribution that "a number of witnesses have been obtained and the committee will take legal steps to arrest the leader of the community and others on the charge of incest." Mears, coyly, would only say that "other testimony, too, has been obtained, which stamps the Oneida Community as far worse in their practices than the polygamists of Utah."[25]

"And what use will be made of this?" a reporter asked.

"Upon this latter testimony," Mears said, "the arrest of Noyes, the leader of the socialists, shall be made."

The reporter pressed to know the basis for a potential arrest. Mears demurred, cautioning that to be forewarned was to be forearmed. Nothing must interfere with the working up, carefully, of the case.

"Rest assured," Mears said. "Warrants will be sworn out, and the movement of February, which everybody thought amounted to little or nothing, and at which you and the rest of the press were content to laugh, will in fact mark the most important crusade that has ever been made against the sin of this so-called American socialism."

• • •

Augustus Beard subsequently wrote Huntington on July 26 to report on further progress.[26] Beard had traveled to Oswego. There, he called on state Assemblyman George B. Sloan, a forty-seven-year-old Republican who had served a term as speaker of the state assembly. Beard also visited the former Oswego County judge, district attorney, and two-term congressman John C. Churchill, who had previously served with Mears on the Presbyterian Synod's 1873–74 committee attacking the Oneida Community. Churchill was still a man with many political ties, and he would in another two years win appointment to the New York Supreme Court.

Churchill and Sloan were both in "hearty sympathy" with the anti-Oneida sentiments, Beard reported, and Churchill urged Beard to develop a definitive plan.[27] During other consultations, Beard heard the suggestion to contact Samuel Colgate, the Baptist soap manufacturer and sin-cleansing president of the New York State Society for the Suppression of Vice. In Buffalo, Beard met with Reverend Wolcott Calkins, who had one year ahead of him at Yale. The minister at Buffalo's North Presbyterian Church, Calkins was a man who knew, as he once wrote, that "every Christian, in the process of proving himself for the Lord's Supper, will find many hateful lusts to destroy."[28] He passed along the names of several other influential men in western New York for Beard to contact.

James O. Putnam proved particularly helpful. Another Yale graduate, Putnam tolerated neither sin nor false religion. Like Mears, Putnam turned a splenetic eye toward the Roman Catholic Church. He once decried the "priesthood, panoplied with all its power over the pockets and consciences of its people, armed with the terrible enginery of the Vatican."[29] A New York state senator for a term during the 1850s, Putnam knew his way around the political world. He counseled Beard that simply amassing the names of ministers carried little weight. Even gathering support from legislators only went so far. Politicians routinely endorsed causes and then dropped them when it was expedient. Instead of merely gathering signatures, Putnam urged Beard to collect hard evidence and hide his hand until he was ready to strike.

But for all their diligent plotting and gathering of intelligence, there was one crucial fact the crusaders didn't yet know. The mortal blow had already landed: Noyes was gone for good.

13 ONEIDA TURNS A PAGE

AN ANXIOUS JOHN HUMPHREY NOYES visited Francis Wayland-Smith's Mansion House room on June 22, 1879, the day after the newspaper reports about imminent legal action against the Oneida Community.[1]

Wayland-Smith, called Frank by some, was a lawyer who could offer learned counsel. Noyes, he subsequently recounted, sought his opinion about a will "drawn up to dispose of the presidency of the Community in case he should be taken away by any cause."[2] The ominous "taken away" reference might have meant anything, from voluntary departure to sudden death or prosecution, but it hinted at the shadow following Noyes. That same day, Oneida member Myron Kinsley discussed with Noyes the fear that hostile community members or Mears's group, acting alone or in collaboration, might bring criminal action. Kinsley, though several decades younger than Noyes, was an energetic and trusted lieutenant to whom the Community's founder would listen carefully.

Once mocked, the latest crusade was proving more nettlesome than its predecessors. In Mears, the Community faced an unusually dogged opponent. Year after year, since he first targeted Oneida in 1873, Mears had sustained his drumbeat. At first, he seemed just another gust of hot air. But over time, Mears's dogged will revealed itself. John Humphrey Noyes's son Pierrepont, who was young at the time of Mears's final fight, recalled half a century later how Mears appeared to be a "sinister" figure, whose very mention caused the men of the Community to look worried and his mother to look "prayerful."

"I remember my very definite mental picture of Professor Mears," Pierrepont Noyes recalled. "The shoulders were broad and truculent, the head large, the face made coarse by a mottled redness, predatory by a huge nose and pharisaical by a long smooth gray beard."[3]

With the June 1879 report of pending indictments, Mears changed from a caricature of intolerance into an honest-to-God threat. While the nature and source of the new ammunition remained ambiguous, it sounded explosive. Kinsley told Tirzah Miller on June 22 that there were Community dissidents who would be willing to turn the law against Noyes.

Three decades earlier, Noyes had fled Vermont to escape justice. Withdrawal suited him. It was, after a fashion, the foundation of his sexual practice, and it sometimes seemed to be his instinctive response under pressure. One must learn, he had preached, the art of vanishing. On June 22, Noyes and Kinsley decided that Noyes should vanish once more.

Late that Sunday night, Noyes stepped quietly out of his third-floor room in the Mansion House's south tower. He made his way downstairs and outside to where Kinsley and another man waited by a carriage. Noyes was conveyed to a rail station in Holland Patent, north of Utica. There, Noyes and a companion went by train some 111 miles to Morristown, and then took a ferry across the St. Lawrence River into the safety of Canada. The way Noyes saw it, he had barely escaped with his life.

"I only know," Noyes wrote, "that indictments, mobs, imprisonment and even death were in the air at Oneida when I took my flight to the north."[4]

On Monday morning, Community members awoke to learn that their founder, their patron and, for a good number, their lover, had skipped town. Where he had gone, no one knew. His presence in Canada was not revealed for several days. But what became slowly apparent was that, after months of publicly shrugging off the Mears-led movement, Noyes had withdrawn from the field.

"We who loved him wept, and our grief was terrible," Jessie Catherine Kinsley recalled, while "they to whom Mr. Noyes appeared evil, rejoiced."[5]

Several days after Noyes departed, the *New York World* happened to send reporter Frederick William Eddy to check up on the Oneida Community. The *World* was a struggling Democratic Party organ, not yet led by editor Joseph Pulitzer, but in F. W. Eddy it employed an up-and-comer. The Rome, New York, native and 1874 Tufts College graduate would, in time, ascend to the *New York Times* and win acclaim for his reporting on the Boxer Rebellion in China.[6] His aggressive approach to the Oneida Community story showed the stuff of which he was made.

Eddy worked all the angles. He approached Madison County district attorney John E. Smith, first elected to the office on the Republican ticket in 1877. Smith had learned independence from a young age, having lost both his mother and his father by the time he was four, and he was not one to be rushed. He bluntly told Eddy that he saw no cause for investigating Oneida.

"I am at a loss to know," Smith said, "in what respect the community has offended against the law."[7]

The Community's literature had stopped circulating years before and could no longer be the basis for prosecution, Smith explained. Noyes himself had already sought to put the obscenity issue to bed, with an April 3 letter to the *Utica Morning Herald* in which he noted that "long ago we withdrew from sale all works which we had reason to suppose, after taking legal counsel, might be considered by others as coming under the prohibition of [obscenity] laws." The withdrawal of potentially taboo literature, the *American Socialist* added on May 29, was done "in deference to the fastidiousness to the Comstockian era."

The Community's members, Smith added, were industrious, frugal, and honest. They treated their workers well, and were orderly in every respect. They abided by the law, so far as he could tell, and he found no reason to move against them. Maybe the Oneida County district attorney over in Utica had something cooking, Smith said.

So Eddy called upon Milton Delos Barnett, the young Oneida County prosecutor. An 1867 Hamilton College graduate, the Republican Barnett was in his second and final two-year term as district attorney. Married but childless, he struck some as excessively nervous—prone to fretting and bouts of insomnia.[8] His career as a public official would end ignominiously, with a subsequent indictment on bribery charges. The charges would not hold, but his subsequent run at a business career would fail as well. Barnett, though, was not entirely infirm during his service as district attorney. Flawed as he was, he approached the Oneida Community rationally. Like Smith, Barnett had concluded no legal basis existed to dislodge the communists. They were seated as firmly as a rock.

"It's easy enough to say their social habits are wrong, because they don't conform with ours; that is, with what we say ours are," Barnett said. "But if indictments could be procured on the grounds of general immorality, then who would not be liable?"[9]

"They are good citizens," Barnett added. "They mind their own business. They have the respect of their neighbors and of their customers. They furnish employment to hundreds of people at good wages, and they are altogether too serviceable to warrant doing anything to cause them displeasure without very good cause."

The two district attorneys' tolerance aligned with the general view among Upstate New York business and political men. They respected the Community's commercial successes, and saw no reason to interfere with potential trading partners who did not actively proselytize. Instead, it was Mears and the other agitators who came across as zealots. Community leaders, it was said, treated Mears with a glacial courtesy and local legislators declined, when explicitly asked, to enlist in the crusade.

Assemblyman George Berry, a Democrat who represented Madison County, had advised the Community on June 5 that "two men from near Utica" had made efforts during the prior legislative session to foment support for anti-Oneida legislation.[10] The two unnamed men had spoken to legislators from Albany and Brooklyn as well as to Berry himself, but they struck out across the board. The legislators from other regions called the Oneida Community a local affair, leaving it up to Berry to intervene or not, and Berry stood by the Community, his constituents. Berry was an eminently practical man then in his late fifties, a former director of the Oneida National Bank. He had either had commercial dealings with the Oneida Community, or he knew people who had. Everyone agreed the Community conducted its business honorably and well.

From those close to the US Attorney for the Northern District of New York, a former Republican congressman and devout Presbyterian named Martin I. Townsend, Eddy learned that no federal consultations concerning the Oneida Community had taken place. Eddy had touched all the outside law enforcement bases. On June 25, he traveled to the Community itself. Though Noyes had departed just a few days before, the permanence of his absence was not yet apparent, and the Community's leaders fended off some of Eddy's questions. Eddy advised Wayland-Smith that he had a "considerable list" of individuals who had departed the Community. These so-called seceders, the reporter indicated, were being targeted by the clergy as potential sources for inside dirt on the Community's practices. Wayland-Smith did not seem fazed. The Community was accustomed to hearing unfounded claims of its imminent demise and it remained, Wayland-Smith assured Eddy, on sound footing.

Eddy traveled to Clinton for a chat with Mears. The chief crusader offered his own assurances that the clergymen had plans to deal with Oneida. The reporter pressed for details, and Mears, ever the teacher, offered up a morality tale.

"You know," Mears intoned, "if a farmer finds boys in his apple trees, he takes a gradual approach toward removing them. First, he asks them to come down, courteously. If they refuse, he escalates, until finally he may be throwing pebbles at them.

"That's about our plan," Mears continued. "We are starting with a moral effort, and only if necessary will we advance to the law."

"If it comes to that," Eddy asked, "do you think you have the law on your side?"

"Without doubt," Mears said.

"For what?" Eddy pressed. "I thought adultery was not a crime."

"It is not," Mears conceded.

"For keeping a disorderly place?"

"No," Mears said, "though their place is just as bad. But perhaps incest; that is a crime, and I rather think they could be prosecuted for that."

It's unclear what evidence Mears possessed. Among Noyes's lovers was his niece Tirzah Miller. Tirzah's mother, Charlotte, was Noyes's younger sister. Noyes was almost exactly thirty-two years older than Tirzah. She called him "Father Noyes" and "Mr. Noyes" in her diary. He spoke to her of having sexual intercourse on stage, of having a child together. "I have felt rather bad lately, fearing that if I remain so unmagnetic Mr. Noyes will not love me anymore," Tirzah confided in her diary one day. "Tonight, he asked if I would like to sleep with him."[11]

There was more. Noyes spoke, in theory, of having sexual relations with a sister, with a daughter. The heavenly sexual revolution would burn down all barriers. Noyes had declared that in overthrowing the worldly notion about incest, he was conquering the devil's last stronghold. The prohibition against siblings having sexual relations was, Noyes said, "the last citadel of social falsehood." In his 1872 "Essay on Scientific Propagation," Noyes opined that the animal breeder's rule of breeding "in and in" could be applied to humans though it implies incest. By identifying and segregating superior families, human thoroughbreds might be produced regardless of the conventional outrage it might incite.

"It is well known," Noyes wrote, "that animal breeders pay very little attention to the principles of the law of incest in any stage of their proceedings."[12]

He could look at his own family for support. All four of his uncles on his father's side had married close cousins.[13] From the Bible, Noyes cited the example of Abraham and his clan. Abraham the patriarch married his sister, Nahor married his niece, and Jacob married two of his first cousins. Strictly speaking, Noyes reasoned, the social laws against incest reflected sentiment rather than physiology. Noyes practiced, after a fashion, what he preached. Besides Tirzah Miller, historian Robert Fogarty concluded, there is evidence that Noyes was the biological father, and possibly the lover, of a woman named Constance

Bradley.[14] Rumors, and more, had been circulating for years. As early as 1871, a visitor had cited Noyes's "reported experience with his own sisters and nieces; nay, more, with his own illegitimate daughter."

"Nightly," the visitor lamented, "these poor women are sacrificed to his damnable passion."[15]

Technically, Noyes might have been safe, albeit dangerously close to the border of right and wrong. Though by the middle of the nineteenth century every state had enacted statutes prohibiting incest, definitions varied. As historian Brian Connolly noted, "the list of prohibited kin was in nearly constant flux."[16] The rationale for the prohibition was shifting, too, as it moved away from the biblical admonitions found in Leviticus that underpinned colonial-era and early nineteenth-century laws. The sacred, which led colonies and early states to prohibit marriage with the sister of a deceased wife, shifted to the secular, and states sorted through the rules in different ways. In Connolly's words, they were "adding and subtracting prohibited kin with little logic or uniformity."[17]

"On no point have writers of all ages and countries been more united than in the conviction that nature abhors, as vile and unclean, all sexual intercourse between persons of near relationship," lawyer and prolific historian James Schouler wrote in 1872. "But on few subjects have they differed so widely as in the application of this conviction."[18]

In some states during the 1870s, it was still legal for an uncle to marry a niece or an aunt to marry a nephew. Ohio's 1872 law required seminal emission as an essential ingredient in the crime of incest—a requirement that, were it in place in New York, would uniquely shield the Oneida Community's practitioners of male continence. In New York, incest was still legally confined to relations between parents and children, between grandparents and grandchildren, and between siblings. It might well be, a New York–based federal judge and former Syracuse mayor would note in 1880, that marriages between uncles and nieces or aunts and nephews "are felt to be so unnatural and revolting that they have been very rare, and but few persons have been found willing to contemplate such a union."[19] Even so, the judge added, such relations could be recognized unless the state explicitly outlawed them. New York law would not expand coverage to include aunts, uncles, nephews, and nieces until 1893.

The law was complex but, taken together, Noyes's physical practices and his philosophical speculations rendered him vulnerable, at least in the court of public opinion. Community insiders, including those chafing under Noyes's leadership, would have known of any damning facts. Noyes himself had lost strength, and a tip-off to the agitators could be just enough to topple the aging patriarch. It was not out of the question. About this same time, some within the Community were warning that James Towner, the one-eyed Civil War veteran and former judge, was quietly amassing evidence about Noyes's sexual behavior for possible use in a lawsuit.[20] In conversing with Eddy, Mears offered that legal action did not have to be criminal. Civil actions, too, might be brought.

"And then," Mears told Eddy, "there is the obscene literature they distribute through the mails. I have a stack so high of the filth."[21]

Mears spread his hands about five inches apart as he denounced the publications as "disgraceful, horrible." Somewhere in the philosophy professor's house, the filth was shelved, ever ready for examination. Mears had been assiduous in its collection, like an anthropologist in Madagascar, or a special agent with Comstock's crew.

"And so who, then, would you have arrested?" Eddy asked.

"Time will reveal all things," Mears promised, "but you may say that we, the committee, believe it likely that in a few weeks, if not days, the matters will be laid before the public."

• • •

On July 20, clergymen meeting in Saratoga further cogitated about the Oneida Community. Mears was absent from the Sunday meeting, but Reverend Samuel W. Duffield from Altoona, Pennsylvania, took it upon himself to first explain and then tear into the Community. Though the thirty-five-year-old, Yale-educated Presbyterian minister had not yet visited Oneida himself, he had heard the stories. Like others before him, he cast Oneida as a germ spot threatening to infect nearby cities. Right-thinking men of all occupations, Duffield said, would have to unite against it. Ministers, he added, must be reinforced by members of the press, who might have more leeway than men of the cloth in describing the Community's detestable practices.[22]

A Hamilton College faculty colleague of Mears's, Edward North, offered for the Saratoga meeting a somewhat more measured account. Affectionately known on campus as "Old Greek," for the subject matter he taught, the fifty-nine-year-old North had been teaching at Hamilton since before the Oneida Community came into being. While he matched Mears in his denunciations of alcohol, long familiarity with the Oneida neighbors subtly softened his assessment of the communists. North praised the Community's business acumen and the overall integrity of its members while including an obligatory denunciation of its immorality.[23]

Shortly thereafter, Duffield visited Oneida. He conversed with thirty-nine-year-old George Cragin, one of the Community's two doctors, in addition to getting a full tour and a chance to talk to Noyes's son, Theodore. Duffield assured Theodore that he wanted to discuss the general health of the community, a safe enough topic, but he persisted with questions about the sexual practices until he was finally told that everything was secondary to the religious sentiment. Duffield finally departed, taking with him $2 worth of Community publications.[24]

Like others before him, Duffield subsequently reported that he had read deeply into what he saw as an "Oneida face." He detected a "flatness and sinking of the eye, with dark lines frequently below it," as well as a "close-set, repressed expression to the lips."

"Of the women," Duffield wrote, "I can say that only one or two are good-looking, with any roundness of face or figure."

Duffield gained one other impression.

"Of Dr. Mears," he recounted, "they speak contemptuously."[25]

A week after Duffield visited Oneida, he reported on his findings to other ministers gathered again in Saratoga. The seeds of the Oneida Community's destruction were fixed so long as the communists clung to complex marriage, he said.

"The 'Saratoga Movement,' as they called it at Oneida," Duffield explained, "was no more than this, that the public attention of earnest men had been directed to the Community in a definite way."

What neither Duffield nor other outsiders could yet discern was how unsettled the Community had become. Though Mears later reported he had picked up hints of internal distress, he had little tangible evidence. But behind the Community's closed doors, fissures were opening. Harriet Skinner decried, in a letter to Noyes, the "awful state of disrespect and rowdyism"[26] that had come upon the Community's younger members, and in a July 19 letter Wayland-Smith advised Noyes that there had arisen "among the young women a popular sentiment in favor of marriage, pure and simple."[27] Instead of short hair and Turkish pants, Wayland-Smith noted the women were demonstrating "a noticeable leaning toward long dresses and long hair." It was becoming clear, Wayland-Smith said, that the Oneida Community system that had been in place for some three decades was "pretty well broken up already." It might be prudent, Wayland-Smith suggested, to adopt a new system and announce it through the local newspapers.

"That would put an immediate and final end to all thoughts of persecution and you would be perfectly free to come and go as you please," Wayland-Smith advised Noyes. "Otherwise, I do not see but this threat of arrest, prosecution, etc., will hang over you indefinitely."[28]

Myron Kinsley, the loyalist who had accompanied Noyes to Canada, wrote him on August 3 to speculate that the clergymen were getting their information from a Community informer. It seemed, Kinsley warned, that "someone inside has been talking."[29] Kinsley had confided a similar fear in private conversations with Tirzah Miller. Kinsley, she wrote the day Noyes had decamped for Canada, "says there are certainly folks inside the Community who would use the law against Mr. Noyes."[30]

Whatever information the campaign possessed, they were closer than they knew to victory. In an August 20 letter, Noyes offered a "Proposal for a Modification of our Social Platform." He reminded everyone that, several years before, as the Comstock anti-smut movement escalated, the Community began to withdraw potentially objectionable items from sale. He reasoned that a similar retreat could be sounded once more.

"I propose that we give up the practice of complex marriage, not as renouncing the belief in the principles and prospective finality of that institution, but in deference to the public sentiment which is evidently rising against it," Noyes wrote.[31]

Noyes went on. There would be two classes of Community residents: the married and the celibate. The latter would be preferred, following the inspired guidance of Paul, but both would be legitimate. Outside the sexual realm, communism would be retained. Property would be held in common. Members would live together as a common household, eat together at a common table, and meet together in the evening.

"With the breeze of general good will in our favor, which even Professor Mears has promised us on the condition of our giving up the 'immoral features' of our system, what new wonders of success may we not hope for in years to come!" Noyes declared.[32]

Noyes's proposal sparked heated Community debate. It made sense, Theodore Noyes argued, to take public sentiment into account. The wave of antipathy against the bigamous Mormons, having attained both legislation and legal victories, was bound to turn toward the Oneida Community, with leaders more capable than Professor Mears. Wayland-Smith echoed the point. The national campaign against Mormons would divert toward the Oneida Community unless it was headed off. The Community's leadership council adopted Noyes's proposal, with Hinds the sole dissenter.

The Oneida Community's complex marriage system ended at 10 a.m. on Thursday, August 28, 1879. In the final forty-eight hours, Community residents embraced their final opportunities. The energetic Tirzah Miller enjoyed relations with two men and then encountered a third old friend.

"I can hardly tell how it happened," Tirzah recounted, "but there seemed to be a subtle fire between us, and before we barely knew it he hurried me into the inside bath-room where we . . ."

And there, the diary breaks off.[33]

The surrender to convention became public with the *American Socialist*'s August 28 edition, which printed in full Noyes's letter urging the end of complex marriage. "The community," the editors wrote, "will now look for the sympathy and encouragement which has been so liberally promised in case this change should ever be made."

The *Syracuse Standard*'s editors sent their own reporter on the morning of August 29. In the village of Oneida, the reporter found no one knew anything about the change, though one "distinguished citizen" was said to deliver a "thumping whack on the table with his fist" to underscore his faith in the word of the Community's leaders. If Noyes had signed a statement forsaking complex marriage, by God, then it was credible. The reporter also talked with one of the men who organized the February conference in Syracuse. The unnamed clergyman peered at the words on the page presented to him and questioned whether it was really John Humphrey Noyes.

"I see his signature there," the minister said, "and yet I can barely credit my senses."[34]

William Hinds, the Oneida editor who had hovered around the Syracuse conference in February, repeated Noyes's explanation that complex marriage was being given up "in deference to the public sentiment which is evidently rising against it." The Community, he went on, "has always held itself ready to recede from the practical expression of its peculiar social principles as a matter of expediency." Contrary to some other reports, Hinds further noted that, to his knowledge, neither Mears nor any other member of the crusading clergy had been to visit Oneida or meet with its leader since the February conference.

"If they have," Hinds said, "they have not made themselves known as such."

The *Utica Morning Herald* dispatched a reporter to Clinton for a conversation with the triumphant lead agitator. Mears read the Oneida Community's statement in the presence of the reporter, rustling the paper as if testing its strength.

"It says here," Mears said, "that henceforth the community will divide itself into two classes, the celibate and the married. I do not intend to express or harbor distrust, but it would, perhaps, be useful for them to announce themselves in their *American Socialist* or some other publication who will be living together in the sacred relation of man and wife."[35]

Mears then wanted to clear up some misunderstandings.

"There is a mistaken idea that has gone abroad," Mears said, "that our goal is to crush the Oneida Community. That is wrong. Our efforts have been against its immoral features alone, the game the community now abandons."[36]

The reporter asked about the future of the crusade.

"Bishop Huntington is the head of that committee," Mears said, disingenuously, "and its disposition will be up to him. But as for me, I can say unreservedly that if it has indeed forsaken its immoral features, then our occupation is gone. There is nothing more for us to do."

At the Community, the *Morning Herald* reporter was given a bit of misdirection. Asking to meet with John Humphrey Noyes, he was told the Oneida Community's founder was out west on a tour for recreation. Noyes was, in fact, permanently sequestered in Canada, although this would not become public until the next year. Instead, the reporter heard from Noyes's son Theodore, who explained that the abandonment of complex marriage was designed to "avoid conflict with outside opinion, and put ourselves on a platform to which the world says it cannot object."[37]

Some Oneida Community wags proposed inviting Mears up to perform a conventional marriage ceremony. In a September 3 letter, George Miller, a resident of the Community's Wallingford, Connecticut, outpost, suggested that the Community could pay Mears suitably for his trouble. The resulting publicity, Miller figured, would boost the Community's businesses.[38] Mears, no doubt, would have accepted the invitation, but none was ever offered.

But on Wednesday, October 1, accompanied by a Mr. McKinney of Utica, Mears paid a personal call upon the Community. It was, apparently, only his second visit to the place against which he had been railing for so long. His first had come five years before, as part of his initial foray with the Presbyterian Synod. During his October 1 visit, for about two hours, over dinner and before, Mears grilled members. He wanted to know how the public, whose interests he said he represented, could be assured that the Community had truly reformed its social practices. The Community, he was told, had given its word, and its word had always been considered good. Mears pressed on, ever the professor probing for illogic.

"Mr. Noyes," Mears said, snaring the devil on his own words, "has taught that marriage is a sin. How then can he recommend the Community to adopt a condition of sin?"[39]

An Oneida member asked where it was that Noyes called marriage a sin.

"In the *History of American Socialisms*," Mears said, revealing the breadth of his study.

The Oneida member challenged Mears's understanding and Mears, who loved mental combat, insisted on the point. Didn't Noyes believe communism to be incompatible with marriage? It was true, Mears was told, that Noyes had found that successful communities had tended to modify the customary marriage arrangements, but Noyes would certainly be content to see marriage succeed.

"Mr. Mears went away with good feeling, apparently," the Oneida diarist wrote, adding that Mears invited one and all to visit him at the college.

Oneida Community members, though, were too busy adapting to their newly reordered lives. They had also been attacked by Mears for so long that hard feelings would be hard to put away. Mears himself hardly sheathed his own sword.

In early October, not long after his visit to Oneida, Mears joined Huntington and Beard in making it known that their "report in full is nearly ready for publication, and is partly in print."[40] But in view of the Community's declarations, the committee members offered, "we deem ourselves bound in both courtesy and good faith to hold materials of our report in abeyance and to suspend proceedings."[41] There was, the trio said, no need to convene further meetings. Finally, on the afternoon of October 22, when the Presbyterian Synod of Central New York met in Binghamton, Mears presented the Oneida

Community missive. He explained the background, how the Syracuse convention was initiated to suppress an evil long tolerated in the state.

"It seemed," Mears acknowledged, "as if we had entered upon a long and doubtful strategy, as if the synod had embarked on a long and quixotic enterprise or had undertaken to lead a forlorn hope with absolutely nothing to encourage it but an absolute sense of duty."[42]

Mears's acute sensitivity to the press pervaded the final summing up. With rare exceptions, he complained, the press had supported the communists and dampened the fire of its opponents. The reports of the Syracuse meeting were "garbled, incorrect, injurious and absurd," while the accompanying editorials were invariably "contemptuous or disparaging." The Utica papers, in particular, were said to have "pursued a policy of indifference and skepticism on the one hand or of open hostility to the movement on the other." Moving to the Community itself, the crusaders welcomed Oneida's disavowal of complex marriage, but simple concession was insufficient. Mears wanted complete capitulation. The committee, Mears said, thought the Community should offer "some token of penitence for the grievous errors and shameful immoralities which they now promise to abandon."

"We do not ask them to follow precisely the model of the converted Ephesians who brought their magic books together and burned them," the Mears committee offered, "but we have a right to expect that they will cease to expound and defend or even discuss in any periodical or other literature which they may publish the views and principles upon which their objectionable practices were founded."[43]

It was not enough to cease the practice of complex marriage and its handmaiden, male continence. Mears wanted to bury the ideas so deep they could never be resurrected. Some notions, Mears believed, were too dangerous even to be imagined. After all, as the *Auburn Weekly* recounted on October 23, 1879, the Mears committee accumulated such a mass of testimony that it would "create in all right-minded people such abhorrence and disgust as would render the institution intolerable."

The Community's immediate neighbors, though, still accepted the Bible communists who were such good businessmen and employers.

Now that the Community had forsaken its unconventional sexual practices, it was both safe and rather poignant. In January 1880, audiences gathered for performances of the Gilbert and Sullivan comic opera *H.M.S. Pinafore*. Something in the story, cloaked with reversals and lighthearted revelations about love's true course, resonated in the moment. The same week in late January that the Oneida Community's version was staged, the Boston Ideal Opera Company brought its own road-show version to Utica. The next month, an Oneida Community traveling troupe introduced the *H.M.S. Pinafore* to nearby towns. The show delighted everyone, prompting talk of a breezy new Pinafore Spirit.[44] Oppressive clouds had shadowed the Community for a long time, and now a light romantic comedy seemed to clear the air.

Soon enough, though, the atmosphere would change yet again.

"Things," *Pinafore*'s Buttercup and the Captain sang, "are seldom what they seem."

14 A PURE AND PIOUS ZEAL

THE ONEIDA COMMUNITY'S SURRENDER did not satiate John Mears. Still, he saw evil and fought on.

On Wednesday, September 3, New York State's temperance advocates convened in Syracuse. They intended serious action. Their Prohibition Party chairman, fifty-two-year-old James J. Bronson, was a Union College graduate and manufacturer who knew how to make things happen. A Presbyterian elder, he had left the Republican Party in 1872 after concluding that neither of the major political parties cared much for temperance.[1]

The Republican, Democrat, and Greenback Parties, the Prohibitionists meeting in Syracuse agreed, all obeyed the power of rum. The reign could only be cracked by abolishing the liquor-licensing system and amending the state's constitution to outlaw the manufacture, importation, and sale of liquor, the advocates believed. Even when opining on suffrage, they stayed tightly focused on this goal: granting women the vote, they calculated, would enhance support for Prohibition candidates.

"We believe woman is generally, with man, the arbiter of domestic peace," the New York conventioneers resolved, "and that her voice for home protection against the assault of liquor should be heard through the ballot at polls."[2]

The Prohibitionists selected Mears to lead the statewide ticket as gubernatorial candidate. The choice made sense, despite his prior poor campaign performance. Mears was known for his temperance fervency, expressed through his essays and lectures. The previous month, he had made an impression as one of the featured speakers during a five-day Gospel Temperance Camp Meeting held in Cazenovia. During the boisterous affair, boys and girls dressed in blue hurled stones at bottles representing corrupt old King Alcohol.[3] Adults came away from the meeting fired up for the cause. The Oneida Community crusade, moreover, had boosted Mears's statewide reputation, and stoked his own appetite as a controversialist. He needed the arena.

Mears readily accepted the gubernatorial nomination, accompanied by a slate of other Prohibitionists running for statewide offices. Mears's teammates included a prominent Poughkeepsie attorney, an undertaker, a Quaker businessman from Skaneateles, and, for good measure, a Rochester-based editor and poet, Alphonso A. Hopkins, whose steadfastness would eventually earn him an honorary doctorate from American Temperance University.[4]

As with Mears's 1878 congressional foray, political pros recognized his biggest potential impact on the gubernatorial race might be indirect. Skeptics said the Prohibition ticket did not amount to anything, except to draw off votes from Republican candidates. Prohibition Party candidates shrugged off the criticism. They considered conventional Republicans and Democrats alike to be morally weak.

"If we are to wait for prohibition for the [Republicans] to give it to us, we will wait a long time," the *Delaware Signal* had warned in January 1879. "This is only a trick of Satan, alias the Republican party."[5]

On Hamilton's campus, students acclaimed Mears for his candidacy. On the evening of Friday, October 3, members of the college's senior class gathered outside the Mears's family home and offered up a song in tribute. Mears came to the door and was greeted by cheers, before senior Charles A. Gardiner stepped forward.

"We all sympathize with you in your work," Gardiner proclaimed. "We would see this evil of intemperance driven from our land."[6]

The earnest Mr. Gardiner was class valedictorian and a prize-winning college orator, who would go on to Columbia Law School, a high-pressure career as a corporate lawyer, and an early death at the age of fifty-three; the victim, it would be said, of exhaustion from overwork.[7] He gave it his all that pre-election night for Mears, invoking the vision of a time "in which Christian, intelligent men shall be called to the forefront, shall hold the reins of government." Mears responded in kind, starting with a recounting of a German legend about a prince who went out, disguised, among his subjects, only to find himself surprised by what he found. Just how, the innocent prince wondered, had this apple gotten into the dumpling?

"So, Doctor Mears said to us," Hamilton graduate Edison E. Dayton recalled, "'I suppose you young gentlemen have come here to find out how your professor in mental and moral philosophy has gotten into politics.'"[8]

While conceding that "I shall not be elected," Mears told the young Hamilton men assembled before him that "the liquor traffic continues to be the most expensive, the most useless and the most damaging of all the evils under which society suffers through the civilized world." Against this dragon, the fight must go on.

"I enjoy few things more than a downright, earnest combat with something that deserves to be combatted," Mears said.

The students cheered.

Mears's second political campaign enjoyed more structural support than his first bid for office. The Prohibition Party funded posters and handbills, and made enough noise to worry Republicans who feared the diversion of votes. In a Tuesday, October 28, rally at New York City's Cooper Union, US Secretary of State William M. Evarts warned that a vote for a minor party candidate was worse than wasted—it threatened dire consequences. The editor of the *Christian Advocate* likewise urged the faithful not to fritter away their voice on small third parties, and rank-and-file Republicans took up the cry.

"Everybody knows that Doctor Mears has no more chance of being Governor of New York than the Sultan of Turkey," the *Lowville Journal and Republican* declared on October 29, adding that a vote for Mears "would be utterly useless to promote prohibition," while it would "nullify our citizenship at a most important crisis in the history of this great nation."

The *St. Lawrence Herald* echoed the warning on November 1, advising New York residents not to "throw away your vote, or vote for phantoms," further observing that "Utopian doctrines promulgated

by visionary enthusiasts are always to be feared and never to be credited til after long and severe tests." Mears, who had fought against
the utopian doctrines espoused by John Humphrey Noyes, was now
damned by the same critique. Mears had become the dangerous
visionary he had warned against.

While Republicans were united behind gubernatorial candidate
Alonzo Cornell, son of the namesake university's founder, Democrats had split. The straight party rallied around incumbent governor
Lucius Robinson, while Tammany Hall operators had broken away
to support the reassuringly titled "Honest John" Kelly. Trickery and
sleight of hand also played their customary role. On October 25, the
Ogdensburg Journal warned that Robinson campaign operatives were
visiting Republican meetings and handing out documents containing Mears's name. "What is really sought," the paper explained, "is
to induce Republican temperance men to help Robinson by pasting
Mears's name upon the head of their tickets."

But Prohibitionists had their legitimate claim on support, as well.

In New York, a sympathetic observer declared just before the election that "quite a number of counties are organized and actively at
work, and a good vote is expected."[9] Oneida County, in particular,
seemed ripe; at least, so Prohibitionists hoped. A newspaper published by a Utica-area temperance organization advised readers that
"if twenty five thousand men would vote" for Mears, the temperance movement would "hold the balance of power."[10] Then, the
theory went, temperance advocates could dictate sobering terms to
the booze-beholden major parties. "A good vote for Professor Mears,
though it might not elect him, would be a fitting rebuke to political
parties for ignoring the temperance cause and nominating unsuitable
candidates," one New Yorker suggested.[11]

About a week before the election, Mears led a rally at Clinton's
Scollard Opera House along with Charles Gardiner, the go-getting
student who had cheerleaded earlier at Mears's house. Gardiner,
though, did not necessarily reflect the dominant sentiment among
Hamilton students. Rather, Mears's reputation for severity made his
candidacy a target for sardonic student barbs.

"Shall our professor of Modern Languages leave us for unknown and untrodden paths?" the jokesters with *The Hamiltonian*, the college yearbook wrote, shedding crocodile tears. "Oh, it cannot be."[12]

Election Day, November 4, was too chilly for last-minute campaigning and, in any event, there were few voters willing to be buttonholed by Mears. Out of more than 930,000 votes cast statewide, Mears received a scant 4,437. Cornell, the Republican who, in theory, had the most to lose from Mears's spoiler candidacy, won handily. In Oneida County, his putative home base, Mears drew fewer votes than the other fringe candidates. Even in Kirkland, the voting jurisdiction that included the village of Clinton and Hamilton College, Mears finished a distant last.

Mears did not surrender; his abstinence campaign would not simply end. The month after the election, Mears took to the stage in Philadelphia, speaking to several hundred poor souls gathered for a free meal and some moral brightening from the Sunday Morning Breakfast Association. Mears was also being urged to take on new causes. One leader with the Presbyterian Church's Board of Home Missions, after praising Mears for his "persistent and successful fight with [the] abominations" of the Oneida Community, suggested he turn his "attention to Utah," and help rouse "public sentiment" against Mormons.[13] Mears was receptive to such a follow-up battle, perhaps alongside his fellow anti-Oneida crusaders.

"If the matter isn't quickly handled," Mears told a Hamilton College colleague, "I will see Bishop Huntington and begin to stir up the church and the country."[14]

In the classroom, too, Mears kept up his attacks against what he called the "sensationalism" of John Stuart Mill as well as the "materialistic teachings and tendencies" of French philosopher Auguste Comte, social Darwinist Herbert Spencer, and Scotland's Alexander Bain.

Bulked up by a large freshman class, Hamilton's enrollment had swelled to 202 for the 1880–81 school year. Mears's son, Henry Haller Mears, was enrolled at the college, listed as a senior that year. He would not, however, graduate from Hamilton. He fell by the wayside, academically, and turned to business, eventually marrying and moving to Philadelphia, where he worked as a broker in oils and paints. Henry's brother Ormsby Mitchell Mears, a Hamilton sophomore, was also living at home that year. Ormsby would go on to graduate from the college and work in a variety of nonscholarly businesses, including service as manager of a Remington Typewriter Co. office in Baltimore. He would never marry.

With the Oneida Community neutered, Mears stayed active on other fronts. He kept writing his "Letter from Central New York" for the *New-York Evangelist*. He used the column to cover pet topics, from Prohibition to penitentiary construction in Oneida County. But all the while, he maintained vigilance over Oneida, on the lookout for backsliding. In the *Independent*'s August 26, 1880, edition, Mears welcomed the fact that the volume of Noyes's history of socialism found in the Community's library "has been mutilated by the removal of all those pages in which the repulsive features of the social life of the Community were described and defended." Evil thoughts were to be erased, the soil salted to prevent their recurrence, even as the successful anti-Oneida campaign stayed on his mind. As he reflected on it, Mears realized that "there was a timeliness to our efforts." While Mears and his allies besieged the Community from outside, even in the face of public ridicule, their seemingly lonely efforts echoed more than they knew.

"Working in the dark as we were, some of us for five or six years, it is an uncommon gratification now to know that, all the time, we had the earnest sympathy of a growing and intelligent minority within," Mears wrote in his August 26 essay.

Mears delighted in the vision of Noyes's late-night flight, in which "his guilty fears drove him hither and thither" until finally, Mears wrote, Noyes "put his polluted feet" on Canadian soil. Even so, Mears sought more. It wasn't enough that Noyes was gone. Mears wanted him brought to justice. We would see, he wrote, whether Canadians would "shut their eyes to the monstrous practices" of a man who "can be defended from the charge of diabolical uncleanness and blasphemy only on the supposition of fanaticism pushed to the very verge of insanity."

Mears concluded by expressing his hope "for the assistance of the Oneida Community in the effort which still lingers to overthrow the polygamy of Utah."

The Oneida Community, though, had better things to do. It was continuing to evolve. Following months of study, the Oneida Community repudiated once and for all its communistic roots and in January 1881 transformed into a joint-stock company. The Community's assets were valued at $600,000, and shares of stock valued at $25 each were divided among 226 Community residents based on a formula that included the length of their residency and the value of their own original investment.[15]

. . .

Outside the college, Mears maintained his temperance zeal and his philosophizing. He kept touting, in particular, Immanuel Kant's *Critique of Pure Reason*, the dense 1781 tome that Mears considered the greatest event in philosophy since the days of Descartes. In homage to his philosophical hero, in July 1881 Mears organized a centennial commemoration of what he sometimes called, simply, the *Kritik*.

With his customary energy, Mears cast a wide net for potential participants; though, as was often the case, not everyone shared his full-throated enthusiasm. Harvard professor Frances Bowen politely cautioned that the public might not be equally attuned to the wonders of Kant. Still, Mears pressed on, and on July 6, several dozen learned men accompanied by a few women materialized in the parlor of Saratoga's Temple Grove. Philosophers and professors represented Johns Hopkins University, the University of California, Amherst College, Yale, and the like.[16] Mears was in his element, orchestrating serious mental gymnastics, preceded by a recitation of the Lord's Prayer.

Mears wanted more. He next helped organize a several-days-long consideration of Kant's work held in Concord, Massachusetts. It was just the place for metaphysicians to reject the false gods of materialism and sensationalism, and it drew a crowd including "Battle Hymn of the Republic" author Julia Ward Howe, who began the proceedings by reading a terribly sincere poem from 1866, "On Leaving for a Time the Study of Kant."[17]

Mears then returned to Hamilton for the start of the 1881–82 school year and the inauguration of the college's new president, Reverend Dr. Henry Darling, on September 15. Mears and the Darling family went way back. It was Henry Darling's father, Judge William Darling, who had religiously inspired Mears as a child in Reading, Pennsylvania. After graduating from Amherst College at the age of nineteen, Henry Darling had, like Mears, spent ministerial time in Philadelphia. There, it was said somewhat ambiguously, "his unsparing labor undermined his health, and he was obliged to give up his charge."[18]

The Hamilton faculty resplendently welcomed Darling, accompanied by the Utica Philharmonic Orchestra, but a dark cast colored the day. President James Garfield, who, on July 2, had been shot by Charles Guiteau, was lingering, prompting the chairman of the Hamilton board of trustees, attorney William J. Bacon, to acknowledge the looming presence of the angel of death.

On September 19, four days after Darling's inauguration, Garfield died. Classes were suspended on Tuesday, September 20, and the chapel bell rang continuously from ten o'clock until noon. Mears spoke at the college's memorial service held on September 26. Garfield's slaying particularly touched Mears—especially, perhaps, in the identity of the assassin. Guiteau's father, Luther, had followed Noyes's teachings, and Charles intermittently belonged to the Community in the 1860s. Guiteau had a hard time of it at Oneida, and after he departed he denounced the Community's moral rot. It was a place, Guiteau wrote with Mears-like flair, where innocent young women were "sacrificed to an experience easier imagined than described."[19]

Mears teared up during his homage to Garfield, which would prove to be his last public speech. At one point, some students thought, the professor came close to sobbing when discussing Plato's *Republic*. Mears always took his philosophy seriously, but he may have been torn by more than the president's death. Mears himself was coming undone. His health had been fraying for more than a year. He was weakening, enough so that in September a student expressed to him some concern. Mears acknowledged he wasn't feeling well. His energy was flagging. He felt offtrack, distracted.

"If I do not get better," Mears told the student, Gilbert Reid, "I will try to go to Europe, and buy some books for the college library."[20]

About the same time, for reasons that are unclear, Mears and his wife sold their house on the hilltop. They had agreed to pay $8,000 for the house in June 1871, buying it from a former Hamilton professor of logic, rhetoric, and elocution named Anson J. Upson. Upson had departed the Hamilton faculty the year before, taking a post at Albany's Second Presbyterian Church. A decade later, on October 6, 1881, Mears filed papers recording the sale of the house back to Upson for the peculiarly exact amount of $7,808. After ten years of residency by the Mears family, the house was reported to have lost precisely $192 in value. The full story behind these transactions is ambiguous, but it might not be pretty. Without elaborating, one Hamilton College historian recounted many years later that Mears "is reputed not to have paid" Upson for the house.[21]

Come Monday, October 24, Mears was guiding his students through the mental maze when his self-control abandoned him. Suddenly, he spasmed. Students, shocked, saw Mears jerk as if bolted from the heavens. Professor Mears, the man of discipline and restraint, fell into disarray. The young men in the recital room took long seconds to recover their wits. Finally, aided by Reverend S. E. Brown from Clinton's Methodist Episcopal Church, students helped Mears to a couch. Once recumbent, Mears suffered four spasmodic episodes between eleven o'clock and noon, before some brawny seniors lifted the couch and carried it to Mears's nearby home. Throughout the afternoon, the seizures continued. By 7 p.m., finally at rest, he could recognize those at his bedside, including Dr. Willis E. Ford, a prominent Utica physician.

Mears's problem, Ford thought, was "blood poisoning," known medically as sepsis. Ford prescribed rest, and for a week or so Mears seemed to be regaining strength. By November 3, the local *Clinton Courier* was reporting that his full recovery was expected. Mears's family was around him. He was conversant. Ever the battler, Mears seemed to have overcome his latest adversary.

"The intervening days," an observer wrote, "have witnessed the uncomplaining struggle of an iron will with physical exhaustion and incurable disease."[22]

Incurable was right; even iron decomposes. Mears began to fail again, and in the early morning of Thursday, November 10, he died.

• • •

Inclement weather shrouded Saturday, November 12, the day of Mears's funeral. A somber sky, cold wind, and a driving rain accentuated the campus gloom and may have kept some mourners away. Nonetheless, Mears's younger brother George had arrived from Philadelphia. The brothers had taken markedly different paths, but they had shared common bonds. As editor of the *American Presbyterian*, John had published what appeared to be George's European travel accounts. George's commercial success as a grain merchant, in turn, had allowed completion of Hamilton's fundraising for the Albert Barnes endowed chair. George would not miss his brother's funeral for the world.

Family members and college faculty attended a private service at Mears's house, where Nicholas Goertner, the indomitable Hamilton College fundraiser, offered a brief prayer. Faculty members then carried the coffin to the church and laid it at the front. On the stage sat President Darling along with former Hamilton president Samuel Gilman Brown, the man who had first noted Mears as a candidate for the endowed Albert Barnes chair. Several other ministers sat alongside them. Reverend Thomas J. Brown of Utica, a friend for some twenty years, alluded to the "toil and troubles . . . difficulties and perplexities that few men are called upon to bear" that had fallen upon Mears's shoulders. He did not elaborate, but he summed up Mears's peculiarly driven personality.

"Inactivity," Brown said, "had no charms for him."[23]

Darling then recounted how he and Mears had been childhood companions back in Reading and, for a time, pastors in neighboring congregations. Darling praised Mears as a minister, as an editor, and as a professor. He spoke of Mears's piety and of his intellect, revealing that "Albert Barnes once said of him that his mind was peculiarly adapted for metaphysics." He meant it as a compliment. After a concluding hymn, the funeral procession led by the Hamilton seniors and trailed by the juniors braved the way to the hilltop college cemetery. The rain and the wind battered the processional, and the mud made walking so treacherous that Mears's family members were urged to stay in the carriages. His mother and brother ignored the advice and stood for a moment by the graveside.

"How the rain poured down as we stood at the grave," Edison E. Dayton, an 1881 Hamilton College graduate, recalled half a century later. "George Mears, the brother, a Philadelphia merchant, weeping, heartbroken!"[24]

Hamilton seniors penned a commemoration, praising Mears's "gentleness, forbearance and self-sacrificing spirit,"[25] and the students draped the senior recitation room in mourning black for thirty days. "The hand no more grasps the pen," the *New-York Evangelist* wrote, "the busy brain no longer evolves the vigorous thought. His sermons, his prayers, his exhortations to holy living are done."[26]

The material world, though, was not yet done with Mears. He left behind some unfinished business, having never prepared a will. His widow, Phebe, subsequently filed papers declaring that the value of the estate did not exceed $1,000. There was no mention of any money gained from the recent sale of their house. Instead, an asset inventory filed with the Oneida County Surrogate Court enumerated the modest domestic possessions accumulated over the years. A looking glass. Chairs. A carpet. Framed photographs.

And books—many, many books. Far and away, the thousand or so volumes in John W. Mears's private library were accounted the most valuable part of his modest estate. They were worth $400 or more if sold. How many of these dealt with the Oneida Community, the inventory did not reveal.

• • •

John W. Mears did not single-handedly shut down the Oneida Community or curtail its sexual communism. The February 1879 Syracuse conference and what followed was a group effort. That was the crusade's strength. Instead of one voice raised against the Oneida

Community, there were many. Certain other men, moreover, prosecuted the cause with a vigor that matched Mears's own. Augustus Beard traveled through Upstate New York in the summer of 1879, consulting with allies and framing strategies. Bishop Frederic Dan Huntington helped originate the conference and hosted a key follow-up. The endorsement by Syracuse University leaders helped elevate the effort beyond the pulpit.

"As the battle waxed hot," one supporter recounted, "and at length such men as Bishop Huntington and Chancellor Haven were seen standing shoulder to shoulder with the professor, things became decidedly interesting."[27]

Nor were massed voices enough; legal proceedings, or the threat of them, reinforced the sermons and editorials. An enduring mystery surrounds the question of what, specifically, led the agitators in the third week of June 1879 to assert so confidently their possession of potent evidence against Noyes. Perhaps they were bluffing. Or, perhaps, an Oneida Community dissident had come forward. Maybe, someone who had closely studied the Community's sexual practices put some clues, quietly, on the table. But whatever information the crusaders may or may not have obtained, the whispers shook a man who thought himself vulnerable. As Huntington recalled later, "Noyes became alarmed at what we were preparing to do by law, and fled."[28]

Mears was also fortunate in his timing. He persisted in an external battle that coincided with the Community's internal disarray. Well after the Community surrendered, Mears himself recognized the role happenstance played in bringing the 1879 fight to a successful completion.

"The movements of individuals, synods, associations and communities without have all the while within been accompanied by a powerful movement within, so that there was a timeliness in our efforts, a kind of providential coincidence, without which victory would not have been won," Mears wrote.[29]

The Community's vulnerabilities started at the top. John Humphrey Noyes was a singular leader, who held his followers together by force of intellect, will, and sexual charisma. A unified belief in Noyes as an inspired leader bound the Community together. As one loyalist put it in 1866, "I see that Mr. Noyes is the source not only of wisdom but of power to this Community."[30] The coming of the new generation undermined this Community cohesion. The religious cords binding members frayed. The spiritual connection among members dissipated. The stirpiculture experiment begun in 1869 bred resentment and tension among those deemed unfit for parenting. Community members, Jessie Catherine Kinsley recounted, began to harbor doubts about Noyes's inspiration and his decision making. There was no one, Kinsley added, who seemed fit to follow Noyes as community leader.

"There was the raid of the ministers upon us," Community member Tirzah Miller mournfully recounted, "but that was nothing compared to the internal dissensions."[31]

Community member Allan Estlake agreed, writing several decades after the Community's demise that "pressure from without could have had no power to break up the Community so long as the true spirit prevailed within."[32] Noyes himself, just days before he fled for Canada, diagnosed the severe ailments weakening the Community.

"A terrible spiritual disease has been upon us," Noyes wrote Abel Easton, "the symptoms of which have been two-partyism, political strife, envies, jealousies . . . unbelief, individual sovereignty, secessions and all sorts of tribulations and calamities."[33]

So Mears happened to strike at an opportune time. In that, he was lucky, but luck does not entirely explain the outcome of Mears's crusade. His spears hit just where the Community's armor was thin and, as importantly, Mears kept striking where others had wearied. The Putney, Vermont, neighbors had driven Noyes and the sexual communists away, but had not extirpated their practices. District Attorney Samuel Garvin could neither convict nor suppress them. Professor Tayler Lewis could not fatally shame them. Hack writers could not sustain public outrage against them.

And then came Mears, again and again. It was Mears, one contemporary said, who had "the talent of inspiring others with his own courage and enlisting them under his banner."[34] Certainly, members of the Oneida Community regarded Mears as their chief antagonist. The Hamilton College professor, Noyes's lieutenant William Hinds conceded mid-fight, "has done all that can be fairly asked of any one man to erase the Oneida Community."[35]

Give him this, then: Mears led what was, at least in his own time, the winning side. He sought the Oneida Community's capitulation and the Community, for many reasons, did surrender. Its sexual practices retreated from radical to conventional. History may now cast Mears as an unsympathetic prude, and the Oneida Community as a possibly cracked but poignant grasp for Eden, but the Presbyterian minister-turned-philosophy professor accomplished his goal and he stayed true to himself. In his own way, he was no less a dedicated idealist than John Humphrey Noyes, his opposite number, the man who roused him to battle. We need not like John W. Mears, but we must reckon with him and his ilk.

"He taught the whole clerical brotherhood," Mears's former student Charles A. Gardiner said, "a lesson in self-respect, and what a pure and pious zeal combined with pluck and persistence can accomplish."[36]

NOTES

BIBLIOGRAPHY

INDEX

NOTES

Prologue

1. John W. Mears, *The Church and Temperance* (New York: National Temperance Society and Publication House, 1872), 15.

2. Mears, *The Church and Temperance*, 11.

3. Helen Lefkowitz Horowitz, *Rereading Sex: Battles over Sexual Knowledge and Suppression in Nineteenth-Century America* (New York: Alfred A. Knopf, 2002), 365.

4. Benjamin Justice, "Thomas Nast and the Public School of the 1870s," *History of Education Quarterly* 45 (Summer 2005): 173.

5. David J. Pivar, *Purity Crusade: Sexual Morality and Social Control, 1868–1900* (Westport, CT: Greenwood Press, 1973), 39.

6. Stephen Eliot Smith, "Barbarians within the Gates: Congressional Debates on Mormon Polygamy, 1850–1879," *Journal of Church and State* 51 (August 2009): 607.

7. Charles E. Rosenberg, "Sexuality, Class and Role in 19th-Century America," *American Quarterly* 25 (May 1973): 136.

8. Kerry Abrams, "Polygamy, Prostitution, and the Federalization of Immigration Law," *Columbia Law Review* 105 (April 2005): 694.

9. Horowitz, *Rereading Sex*, 387.

10. Pivar, *Purity Crusade*, 109.

11. Cristine Talbot, "Turkey Is in Our Midst: Orientalism and Contagion in Nineteenth-Century Anti-Mormonism," *Journal of Law and Family Studies* 8 (2006): 381.

12. Rosenberg, "Sexuality, Class and Role in 19th-Century America," 136.

13. Catherine Lee, "'Where the Danger Lies': Race, Gender, and Chinese and Japanese Exclusion, 1870 to 1924," *Sociological Forum* 25 (June 2010): 257.

14. Abrams, "Polygamy, Prostitution, and the Federalization of Immigration Law," 693.

15. *Brookfield Courier*, September 3, 1879.

16. Anita Newcomb McGee, "An Experiment in Human Stirpiculture," *American Anthropologist* 4 (October 1891): 320.

17. Frank Budlong to John Mears, August 29, 1879, Oneida Community Collection, Special Collections Research Center, Syracuse University Libraries.

18. *New-York Evangelist*, December 8, 1881.

19. Robert Allerton Parker, *A Yankee Saint: John Humphrey Noyes and the Oneida Community* (New York: G. P. Putnam, 1935), 270.

20. Constance Noyes Robertson, *Oneida Community: The Breakup, 1876–1881* (Syracuse, NY: Syracuse Univ. Press, 1972), 79.

21. *Oneida Circular*, April 28, 1873.

22. Allan Estlake, *The Oneida Community: A Record of an Attempt to Carry Out the Principles of Christian Unselfishness and Scientific Race-Improvement* (London: George Redway, 1900), 45.

23. *Oneida Circular*, April 28, 1873.

24. *Utica Morning Herald*, October 25, 1879.

25. *Oneida Circular*, January 15, 1872.

26. *Utica Morning Herald*, October 25, 1879.

27. John W. Mears, *Martyrs of France; Or, The Witness of the Reformed Church of France, From the Reign of Francis First to The Revocation of the Edict of Nantes* (Philadelphia: Presbyterian Publication Committee, 1864), 146.

28. John W. Mears, *The Story of Madagascar* (Philadelphia: Presbyterian Publication Committee, 1873), 309.

1. Sounding the Alarm

1. Leigh Eric Schmidt, "The Fashioning of a Modern Holiday: St. Valentine's Day, 1840–1870," *Winterthur Portfolio* 28 (Winter 1993): 214.

2. Schmidt, "The Fashioning of a Modern Holiday," 236.

3. *New-York Evangelist*, May 11, 1882.

4. *New-York Evangelist*, November 17, 1881.

5. *New-York Evangelist*, November 17, 1881.

6. *Reynolds v. United States*. 90 U.S. 145 (1879).

7. *Christian Advocate*, September 1, 1911.

8. *Syracuse Daily Journal*, February 20, 1879.

9. *American Socialist*, February 20, 1879.

2. Love Thy Neighbor

1. Robert S. Fogarty, *Desire and Duty at Oneida: Tirzah Miller's Intimate Memoir* (Bloomington: Indiana Univ. Press, 2000), 23.

2. George Wallingford Noyes, comp., and Lawrence Foster, ed., *Free Love in Utopia: John Humphrey Noyes and the Origin of the Oneida Community* (Urbana: Univ. of Illinois Press, 2000), 210.

3. Ely Van de Warker, "A Gynecological Study of the Oneida Community," *American Journal of Obstetrics and Diseases of Women and Children* 17 (August 1884): 782.

4. Ellen Wayland-Smith, *Oneida: From Free-Love Utopia to the Well-Set Table* (New York: Picador, 2016), 51.

5. John Humphrey Noyes, *Bible Communism* (Oneida Community, February 1849), 53

6. Fogarty, *Desire and Duty at Oneida*, 48.

7. Allan Estlake, *The Oneida Community: A Record of an Attempt to Carry Out the Principles of Christian Unselfishness and Scientific Race-Improvement* (London: George Redway, 1900), 54.

8. Robert David Thomas, *The Man Who Would Be Perfect: John Humphrey Noyes and the Utopian Impulse* (Philadelphia: Univ. of Pennsylvania Press, 1977), 8.

9. John Humphrey Noyes, *Confessions of John H. Noyes. Part 1. Confession of Religious Experience* (Oneida Reserve: Leonard & Co., 1849), 2.

10. Noyes, *Confessions of John H. Noyes*, 3.

11. Noyes, 4.

12. Thomas, *The Man Who Would Be Perfect*, 26.

13. Thomas, 45.

14. Noyes, *Confessions of John H. Noyes*, 27.

15. William Hepworth Dixon, *New America*, vol. 2 (London: Hurst and Blackett, 1867), 185.

16. William Hepworth Dixon, *Spiritual Wives*, vol. 2 (Leipzig, Germany: Bernard Tauchnitz, 1869), 43.

17. Wayland-Smith, *Oneida*, 32.

18. Wayland-Smith, 33.

19. *Oneida Circular*, October 7, 1872.

20. Thomas, *The Man Who Would Be Perfect*, 92.

21. Robert Allerton Parker, *A Yankee Saint: John Humphrey Noyes and the Oneida Community* (New York: G. P. Putnam, 1935), 59.

22. John Humphrey Noyes, *Dixon and his Copyists* (Wallingford, CT: Oneida Community, 1871), 7.

23. Noyes, *Dixon and his Copyists*, 35.

24. Louis J. Kern, *An Ordered Love: Sex Roles and Sexuality in Victorian Utopias* (Chapel Hill: Univ. of North Carolina Press, 1981), 97.

25. Robert Dale Owen, *Moral Physiology; Or, a Brief and Plain Treatise on the Population Question* (New York: Wright & Owen, 1830–31), 10.

26. Noyes, *Bible Communism*, 49.

27. Kern, *An Ordered Love*, 41.

28. John B. Ellis, *Free Love and Its Votaries: Or, American Socialism Unmasked* (New York: United States Publishing Company, 1870), 201.

29. John Humphrey Noyes, *Male Continence* (Oneida, NY: Office of Oneida Circular, 1872), 18.

30. Richard Demaria, *Communal Love at Oneida: A Perfectionist Vision of Authority, Property, and Sexual Order* (New York: Edward Mellen Press, 1978), 169.

31. Lawrence Foster, *Religion and Sexuality: Three American Communal Experiments in the Nineteenth Century* (New York: Oxford Univ. Press, 1981), 101.

32. Noyes, *Bible Communism*, 30.

33. Spencer Klaw, *Without Sin: The Life and Death of the Oneida Community* (New York: Penguin, 1993), 66.

34. Hubbard Eastman, *Noyesism Unveiled: A History of the Sect Self-styled Perfectionists* (Brattleboro, VT: Hubbard Eastman, 1849), 16.

35. Eastman, *Noyesism Unveiled*, 18.

36. Noyes and Foster, *Free Love in Utopia*, 13.

3. The Oneida Community

1. Whitney R. Cross, "Mormonism in the Burned-Over District," *New York History* 25 (July 1944): 326.

2. Chris Jennings, *Paradise Now: The Story of American Utopianism* (New York: Random House, 2016), 298.

3. Robert Allerton Parker, *A Yankee Saint: John Humphrey Noyes and the Oneida Community* (New York: G. P. Putnam, 1935), 162.

4. *First Annual Report of Oneida Association* (Oneida Reserve, NY: Leonard and Company, 1849), 4.

5. George Wallingford Noyes, comp., and Lawrence Foster, ed., *Free Love in Utopia: John Humphrey Noyes and the Origin of the Oneida Community* (Urbana: Univ. of Illinois Press, 2000), 22.

6. Noyes, *Bible Communism* (Oneida, NY: Oneida Community, 1849), 35.

7. Noyes, *Bible Communism*, 37.

8. Nancy F. Cott, *Public Vows: A History of Marriage and the Nation* (Cambridge, MA: Harvard Univ. Press, 2000), 71.

9. Noyes and Foster, *Free Love in Utopia*, 247.

10. Noyes, *Male Continence* (Oneida, NY: Office of Oneida Circular, 1872), 8.

11. William T. LaMoy, "Two Documents Concerning the Oneida Community's Practice of Complex Marriage," *New England Quarterly* 85 (March 2012): 131.

12. Carl N. Degler, "What Ought to Be and What Was: Women's Sexuality in the Nineteenth Century," *American Historical Review* 79 (December 1974): 1467.

13. Noyes and Foster, *Free Love in Utopia*, 224.

14. *Rock Island Evening Argus*, January 12, 1871.

15. Robertson, *Oneida Community*, 16.

16. John B. Ellis, *Free Love and Its Votaries: Or, American Socialism Unmasked* (New York: United States Publishing Company, 1870), 179.

17. Ellis, *Free Love and Its Votaries*, 143.

18. *O. C. Daily Journal*, January 23, 1866.

19. Maren Lockwood Carden, *Oneida: Utopian Community to Modern Corporation* (Baltimore: Johns Hopkins Univ. Press, 1969), 71.

20. *O. C. Daily Journal*, January 25, 1866.

4. A Vortex of Impurity

1. *Roman Citizen*, April 20, 1888.

2. George Wallingford Noyes, comp., and Lawrence Foster, ed., *Free Love in Utopia: John Humphrey Noyes and the Origin of the Oneida Community* (Urbana: Univ. of Illinois Press, 2000), 260.

3. Noyes and Foster, *Free Love in Utopia*, 260.

4. Noyes and Foster, 137.

5. Daniel Wager, *Our County and Its People, Part II: Biography* (Boston: Boston History Co., 1896), 37.

6. Noyes and Foster, *Free Love in Utopia*, 95.

7. Noyes and Foster, 139.

8. Isaac Bielby, *Sheriffs of Oneida County* (Utica, NY: P. E. Kelly, 1890), 14.

9. *New York Observer*, January 22, 1852.

10. Noyes and Foster, *Free Love in Utopia*, 177.

11. Melanie Zimmer, *Curiosities of Central New York* (Charleston, SC: History Press, 2012), 80.

12. Noyes and Foster, *Free Love in Utopia*, 191.

13. Lawrence Foster, *Religion and Sexuality: Three American Communal Experiments in the Nineteenth Century* (New York: Oxford Univ. Press, 1981), 115.

14. Elizabeth Thompson to John Mears, March 17, 1879, Oneida Community Collection, Special Collections Research Center, Syracuse University Libraries.

15. Lucy Abigail Brainard, *The Genealogy of the Brainerd-Brainard Family in America, 1649–1908* 2 (Hartford, CT: Case, Lockwood and Brainard, 1908), 70.

16. Wager, *Our County and Its People*, 240.

17. D. M. Bennett, *Trial of D. M. Bennett in the United States Circuit Court* (New York: Truth Seeker Office, 1879), 90.

18. John B. Ellis, *Free Love and Its Votaries: Or, American Socialism Unmasked* (New York: United States Publishing Company, 1870), 10.

19. Ellis, *Free Love and Its Votaries*, 13.

20. Ellis, 348.

21. Noyes, *Dixon and his Copyists* (Wallingford, CT: Oneida Community, 1871), 37.

22. Charles Wesley Alexander, *Poor Ellen Stuart's Fate; Or, Victim of the Free Love Institute in Oneida, N.Y.* (Philadelphia: Co-Operative Publishing House, 1868), 36.

23. Alexander, *Poor Ellen Stuart's Fate*, 40.

24. Alexander, 45.

25. Ann Marie Pagliarini, "The Pure American Woman and the Wicked Catholic Priest: An Analysis of Anti-Catholic Literature in Antebellum America," *Religion and American Culture: A Journal of Interpretation* 9 (Winter 1999): 104.

26. *American Socialist*, February 20, 1879.

27. John Seely Hart, *A Manual of American Literature: A Textbook for Schools and Colleges* (Philadelphia: Eldredge & Brother, 1872), 578.

28. *New York Daily Tribune*, November 9, 1848.

29. *Methodist Quarterly Review* 60 (October 1878): 618.

30. *New-York Evangelist*, September 25, 1879.

5. The Virtuous Man

1. *New-York Evangelist*, December 8, 1881.

2. John Mears, *Biographical Notice of Henry Haller Mears, Sr.* (Philadelphia: James B. Rogers Co., 1873), 6.

3. Charles G. Finney, *Charles G. Finney: An Autobiography* (Westwood, NJ: Fleming H. Revell Co., 1908), 266.

4. *New-York Evangelist*, May 17, 1888.

5. Morton L. Montgomery, *History of Berks County in Pennsylvania* (Philadelphia: Everts, Peck and Richards, 1886), 787.

6. Montgomery, *History of Berks County in Pennsylvania*, 550.

7. Mears, *Biographical Notice*, 10.

8. Mears, 11.

9. Ashbel Green, *The Christian Advocate*, vol. 8 (Philadelphia: A. Finley, 1830), 155.

10. *New-York Evangelist*, December 8, 1881.

11. *New-York Evangelist*, December 8, 1881.

12. Lyman P. Powell, *The History of Education in Delaware* (Washington, DC: Government Printing Office, 1893), 105.

13. Powell, *The History of Education in Delaware*, 95.

14. Powell, 104.

15. Powell, 91.

16. *Philadelphian*, July 26, 1844.

17. *The Centennial Celebration of the Yale Divinity School, Held in Connection with the Fourteenth Annual Convocation* (New Haven, CT: Yale University, 1922), 5.

18. *New Englander and Yale Review* 45 (New Haven, CT: William L. Kingsley, 1886), 645.

19. William Boyd, *Fifty Years After, Or, a Half-century of Presbyterianism in Camden, New Jersey* (Philadelphia: Franklin Print, 1890), 27.

20. *New-York Evangelist*, August 1, 1872.

21. *Funeral Services Held in the First Presbyterian Church, Philadelphia, Dec. 28, 1870* (Philadelphia: J. B. Rogers Co., 1871), 12.

22. Robert Doherty, "Social Bases for the Presbyterian Schism of 1837–38: The Philadelphia Case," *Journal of Social History* 2 (Fall 1968): 70.

23. George Junkin, *The Vindication, Containing a History of the Trial of the Rev. Albert Barnes* (Philadelphia: Wm. S. Martien, 1836), xxvi.

24. Boyd, *Fifty Years After*, 27.

25. John Thomas Scharf, *History of Delaware, 1609–1888* (Philadelphia: L. J. Richards, 1888), 489.

26. Boyd, *Fifty Years After*, 29.

27. Boyd, 30.

28. Scharf, *History of Delaware, 1609–1888*, 1198.

29. *Christian Observer*, April 12, 1860.

30. Joseph M. Wilson, *Presbyterian Historical Almanac and Annual Remembrancer of the Church for 1861* (Philadelphia: Joseph M. Wilson, 1861), 160.

31. *Descriptive Catalogue of the Publications of the Presbyterian Board of Publication* (Philadelphia: Presbyterian Board of Publication, 1880), 341.

32. *New-York Evangelist*, May 5, 1870.

33. *Clinton Courier*, March 30, 1871.

34. *American Presbyterian*, November 21, 1867.

35. Isaac Weiner, *Religion Out Loud: Religious Sound, Public Space, and American Pluralism* (New York: New York Univ. Press, 2014), 33.

36. Jon C. Teaford, "Toward a Christian Nation: Religion, Law and Justice Strong," *Journal of Presbyterian History* 54 (Winter 1976): 428.

37. Weiner, *Religion Out Loud*, 33.

38. *American Presbyterian*, March 18, 1869.

39. John L. Smith, comp., *History of the Corn Exchange Regiment, 118th Pennsylvania Volunteers, From Their First Engagement at Antietam to Appomattox* (Philadelphia: J. L. Smith, 1888), 65.

40. *The Courtland Saunders Tract for Soldiers* (Philadelphia: Protestant Episcopal Book Society, 1863), 3.

41. Helen Lefkowitz Horowitz, *Rereading Sex: Battles over Sexual Knowledge and Suppression in Nineteenth-Century America* (New York: Alfred A. Knopf, 2002), 312.

42. Mark J. Dunkelman, *Gettysburg's Unknown Soldier: The Life, Death and Celebrity of Amos Humiston* (Westport, CT: Praeger, 1999), 149.

43. Dunkelman, *Gettysburg's Unknown Soldier*, 151.
44. Dunkelman, 152.
45. Dunkelman, 169.
46. Errol Morris, "Whose Father Was He?" *New York Times*, March 31, 2009.
47. *Daily National Intelligencer*, November 22, 1866.
48. *Philadelphia Evening Telegraph*, July 2, 1867.
49. *Washington Evening Star*, May 14, 1872.
50. Morris, "Whose Father Was He? (Part Four)," *New York Times*, April 1, 2009.

6. Metaphysics and Strife

1. *Annual Report of the Regents of the University of the State of New York*, (Troy, NY: Troy Press Co., 1888), 224.
2. *Annual Report of the Regents of the University of the State of New York*, 226.
3. Walter Pilkington, *Hamilton College: 1812–1962* (Clinton, NY: Hamilton College, 1962), 200.
4. Charles Elmer Allison, *A Historical Sketch of Hamilton College, Clinton, New York* (Yonkers, NY), 62.
5. Minutes, Hamilton College Board of Trustees, December 21, 1870, Hamilton College Archives.
6. *Memorial of Samuel Gilman Brown* (New York: Trow's Printing and Bookbinding Co., 1886), 12.
7. *Philadelphia Evening Telegraph*, December 28, 1870.
8. Henry J. Cookinham, *History of Oneida County, New York From 1700 to the Present Time* (Chicago: S. J. Clark Publishing Co., 1912), 521.
9. *Auburn Daily Bulletin*, May 9, 1877.
10. Minutes, Hamilton College Executive Committee, March 6, 1879, Hamilton College Archives.
11. John Mears to Othniel S. Williams, March 24, 1871, Hamilton College Archives.
12. *Utica Morning Herald*, November 11, 1881.
13. *New-York Evangelist*, April 13, 1871.
14. *New-York Evangelist*, July 27, 1871.
15. John W. Mears, "The Antagonism, Perils and Glory of the Spiritual Philosophy," *American Presbyterian and Theological Review* (October 1871): 602.
16. *New-York Evangelist*, August 10, 1871.
17. *Successful American*, April 1900.
18. John Mears to Othniel S. Williams, August 20, 1871, Hamilton College Archives.

19. Louis Boisot, *Hamilton College Half-Century Annalists Letter*, https://www.hamilton.edu/about/history/half-century-annalists-letters/1877.

20. Pilkington, *Hamilton College*, 206.

21. *New-York Evangelist*, April 13, 1871.

22. *Hamilton Literary Monthly* 6 (February 1872): 233.

23. *New-York Evangelist*, November 17, 1881.

24. *New-York Evangelist*, March 20, 1873.

25. Immanuel Kant, *The Critique of Pure Reason* (Chicago: Encyclopedia Britannica, Inc., 1952), 15.

26. Kant, *The Critique of Pure Reason*, 49.

27. John W. Mears, "The Centennial of Kant's Kritik," *Journal of Speculative Philosophy* 15 (January 1881): 92.

28. *New-York Evangelist*, August 15, 1872.

7. Bridling the Passions

1. *Utica Morning Herald*, November 11, 1881.

2. *New-York Evangelist*, November 17, 1881.

3. John Mears, *The Church and Temperance* (New York: National Temperance Society and Publication House, 1872), 20.

4. John Marsh, *Putnam and the Wolf; Or, the Monster Destroyed* (Hartford: D. F. Robinson and Co., 1829), 17.

5. Ian R. Tyrrell, *Sobering Up: From Temperance to Prohibition in Antebellum America, 1800–1860* (Westport, CT: Greenwood Press, 1979), 87.

6. Tyrrell, *Sobering Up*, 115.

7. *Philadelphia Evening Telegraph*, December 29, 1870.

8. Mears, *The Church and Temperance*, 20.

9. Mears, 14.

10. Wayne E. Fuller, *Morality and the Mail in Nineteenth-Century America* (Urbana: Univ. of Illinois Press, 2003), 102.

11. *Auburn Daily Bulletin*, November 18, 1875.

12. Edward North, "An Address Delivered Before the Sons of Temperance on July 4, 1848," (Utica, NY: H. H. Curtiss, 1848), 4.

13. Charles R. Kingsley, "Hamilton College 1878 Class Annalist's Letter," https://www.hamilton.edu/about/history/half-century-annalists-letters/1878.

14. *Plattsburgh Sentinel*, February 27, 1874.

15. *Lewis County Democrat*, March 4, 1874.

16. Mears, *The Church and Temperance*, 14.

17. *New-York Evangelist*, May 24, 1874.

18. Donna Dennis, *Licentious Gotham: Erotic Publishing and Its Prosecution in Nineteenth-Century America* (Cambridge, MA: Harvard Univ. Press, 2009), 9.

19. Dennis, *Licentious Gotham*, 230.

20. Kate Percival, *The Life and Amours of the Beautiful, Gay and Dashing Kate Percival*, n.d., http://www.gutenberg.org/cache/epub/29827/page29827~images .html.

21. Dennis, *Licentious Gotham*, 230.

22. Donna Dennis, "Obscenity Law and the Conditions of Freedom in Nineteenth-Century America," *Law and Social Inquiry* 27 (2002): 384.

23. Helen Lefkowitz Horowitz, *Rereading Sex: Battles over Sexual Knowledge and Suppression in Nineteenth-Century America* (New York: Alfred A. Knopf, 2002), 309.

24. Dennis, *Licentious Gotham*, 234.

25. Fuller, *Morality and the Mail in Nineteenth-Century America*, 106.

26. Dennis, *Licentious Gotham*, 264.

27. John Humphrey Noyes, *Male Continence* (Oneida, NY: Oneida Community, 1872), 8.

28. Horowitz, *Rereading Sex*, 395.

8. Visiting Oneida

1. *Oneida Circular*, December 7, 1874.

2. *Cazenovia Republican*, August 21, 1873.

3. *Pulaski Democrat*, August 14, 1873.

4. *Delaware Gazette*, August 13, 1873.

5. *Syracuse Daily Journal*, 18 August 1873.

6. *Utica Morning Herald*, October 24, 1873.

7. *New-York Evangelist*, November 6, 1873.

8. N. Emmons Paine, "Hamilton College 1874 Class Annalist's Letter," https://www.hamilton.edu/about/history/half-century-annalists-letters/1874.

9. *Biographical Directory of the United States Congress*, http://bioguide.congress .gov/scripts/biodisplay.pl?index=C000392.

10. Alfred Nevin, ed., *Encyclopedia of the Presbyterian Church in the United States of America* (Philadelphia: Presbyterian Encyclopedia Publishing Co., 1884), 874.

11. M. N. Bagg, *Memorial History of Utica, N.Y.: From Its Settlement to the Present Time* (Syracuse, NY: D. Mason & Co., 1892), 337.

12. *Oneida Circular*, November 17, 1873.

13. Robert Allerton Parker, *A Yankee Saint: John Humphrey Noyes and the Oneida Community* (New York: G. P. Putnam, 1935), 223.

14. Dwight Hall Bruce, *Memorial History of Syracuse, N.Y. From Its Settlement to the Present Time* (Syracuse, NY: H. P. Smith & Co., 1891), 109.

15. *Oneida Circular*, November 3, 1873.

16. Amanda Frisken, "Obscenity, Free Speech and 'Sporting News' in 1870s America," *Journal of American Studies* 42 (December 2008): 545.

17. Frisken, "Obscenity, Free Speech and 'Sporting News' in 1870s America," 546.

18. *New York Herald*, January 18, 1882.

19. *Jackson Weekly Clarion*, June 24, 1869.

20. *Saratogian*, August 7, 1879.

21. *Frank Leslie's Illustrated Newspaper*, April 2, 1870.

22. *Oneida Circular*, November 23, 1874.

23. Spencer Klaw, *Without Sin: The Life and Death of the Oneida Community* (New York: Penguin, 1993), 97.

24. *Oneida Circular*, November 23, 1874.

25. *Chicago Tribune*, January 18, 1879.

26. *Oneida Circular*, December 26, 1870.

27. John B. Ellis, *Free Love and Its Votaries: Or, American Socialism Unmasked* (New York: United States Publishing Company, 1870), 266.

28. *Saratogian*, August 7, 1879.

29. *Malone Palladium*, September 10, 1874.

30. David S. Schaff, *The Life of David S. Schaff, in Part Autobiographical* (New York: Charles Scribner's Sons, 1897), 1.

31. *Oneida Circular*, July 13, 1874.

32. *Plattsburgh Sentinel*, October 30, 1874.

33. *Syracuse Daily Journal*, October 24, 1874.

34. Maren Lockwood Carden, *Oneida: Utopian Community to Modern Corporation* (Baltimore, MD: Johns Hopkins Univ. Press, 1969), 84.

35. A. L. Slawson, *Behind the Scenes; Or, an Exposé of Oneida Community* (Oneida, NY: A. L. Slawson, 1875), 95.

36. *American Socialist*, February 20, 1879.

37. *Oneida Circular*, November 30, 1874.

38. *Oneida Circular*, March 1, 1875.

9. The Utah at Home

1. Alfred Nevin, ed., *Encyclopedia of the Presbyterian Church in the United States of America* (Philadelphia: Presbyterian Encyclopedia Publishing Co., 1884), 659.

2. *Hamilton College Catalogue 1873–74* (Clinton, NY, 1869), 27.

3. Archibald P. Love, "Hamilton College 1876 Class Annalist's Letter," https://www.hamilton.edu/about/history/half-century-annalists-letter/1876.

4. *Roman Citizen*, March 24, 1876.

5. Michael Doyle, *The Forestport Breaks: A Nineteenth-Century Conspiracy Along the Black River Canal* (Syracuse, NY: Syracuse Univ. Press, 2004), 45.

6. Allan Nevins, *The Emergence of Modern America, 1865–1878* (New York: Macmillan and Co., 1928), 311.

7. *The Second Annual Report of the New York Society for the Suppression of Vice* (New York, January 27, 1876), 5.

8. Helen Lefkowitz Horowitz, *Rereading Sex: Battles over Sexual Knowledge and Suppression in Nineteenth-Century America* (New York: Alfred A. Knopf, 2002), 407.

9. Janice Wood, "Prescription for a Periodical: Medicine, Sex and Obscenity as Told in Dr. Foote's Health Monthly," *American Periodicals* 18 (2008): 31.

10. Jane Kinsley Rich, ed., *A Lasting Spring: Jessie Catherine Kinsley, a Daughter of the Oneida Community* (Syracuse, NY: Syracuse Univ. Press, 1983), 44.

11. John Humphrey Noyes, *Male Continence* (Oneida, NY: Office of Oneida Circular, 1872), 30.

12. Ely Van de Warker, "A Gynecological Study of the Oneida Community," *American Journal of Obstetrics and Diseases of Women and Children* 17 (August 1884): 791.

13. *Syracuse Post-Standard*, September 6, 1910.

14. Van de Warker, "A Gynecological Study of the Oneida Community," 789.

15. Van de Warker, 789.

16. Van de Warker, 797.

17. *O. C. Daily Journal*, April 11, 1866.

18. Spencer Klaw, *Without Sin: The Life and Death of the Oneida Community* (New York: Penguin, 1993), 242.

19. Maren Lockwood Carden, *Oneida: Utopian Community to Modern Corporation* (Baltimore, MD: Johns Hopkins Univ. Press, 1969), 99.

20. Robert S. Fogarty, *Desire and Duty at Oneida: Tirzah Miller's Intimate Memoir* (Bloomington: Indiana Univ. Press, 2000), 43.

21. Fogarty, *Desire and Duty at Oneida*, 43.

22. *Ticonderoga Sentinel*, August 3, 1877.

23. *Hamilton Literary Monthly* 6 (January 1871).

24. Reuben Leslie Maynard, *History of the Class of 1884, Hamilton College 1884–1914* (New York, 1914), 35.

25. *Independent*, July 18, 1878.

26. Charles H. Hitchcock, "Hamilton College 1879 Class Annalist's Letter," https://www.hamilton.edu/about/history/half-century-annalists-letters/1879.

27. Archibald P. Love, op. cit.

28. *New York Times*, August 9, 1878.

29. *American Socialist*, August 20, 1878.

30. *Utica Morning Herald*, August 10, 1878.

31. *Mexico Independent*, October 23, 1878.

32. Edwin Hale Abbot, *Apocrypha Concerning the Class of 1855 of Harvard College* (Boston: A. Mudge & Son, 1880), 49.

33. *Westfield Republican*, September 19, 1877.

34. *Congregationalist and Advance*, December 12, 1918.

35. *Mexico Independent*, September 24, 1874.

36. *Independent*, October 31, 1878.

37. *Independent*, October 31, 1878.

38. Horowitz, *Rereading Sex*, 144.

39. James R. Rohrer, "The Origins of the Temperance Movement: A Reinterpretation," *Journal of American Studies* 24 (August 1990): 231.

40. Othniel Pendleton Jr., "Temperance and the Evangelical Churches," *Journal of the Presbyterian Historical Society* 25 (March 1947): 30.

41. Ian R. Tyrrell, *Sobering Up: From Temperance to Prohibition in Antebellum America, 1800–1860* (Westport, CT: Greenwood Press, 1979), 231.

42. Tyrrell, *Sobering Up*, 243.

43. Peter Karsten, "Four 'Cousins-in-Law,'" *Journal of Politics and Law* 8 (2015): 110.

44. Lisa M. F. Andersen, *The Politics of Prohibition: American Governance and the Prohibition Party* (New York: Cambridge Univ. Press, 2013), 26.

45. Amy Kesselman, "The 'Freedom Suit': Feminism and Dress Reform in the United States, 1848–1875," *Gender and Society* 5 (December 1991): 503.

46. Ernest H. Cherrington, *The Evolution of Prohibition in the United States of America* (Westerville, OH: American Issue Press, 1920), 197.

47. Andrew J. Jutkins, *Hand-book of Prohibition: 1885* (Chicago: 87 Washington Street, 1885), 189.

48. *Ogdensburg Journal*, February 2, 1878.

49. *Utica Observer*, October 16, 1878.

10. On Battle's Eve

1. *Independent*, April 11, 1878.

2. Ian R Tyrrell, *Sobering Up: From Temperance to Prohibition in Antebellum America, 1800–1860* (Westport, CT: Greenwood Press, 1979), 261.

3. *Sacramento Union*, January 10, 1879.

4. *Fairport Herald*, February 7, 1879.

5. *Malone Palladium*, February 20, 1879.

6. *Newark Courier*, December 12, 1878.

7. Joseph Cook, *The Boston Monday Lectures* (London: R. D. Dickinson, 1881), 623.

8. *Independent*, March 8, 1878.

9. Augustus Field Beard, *A Crusade of Brotherhood: A History of the American Missionary Association* (Boston: Pilgrim Press, 1909), 35.

10. *Congregationalist and Advance*, May 13, 1920.

11. *Yale Alumni Weekly*, June 9, 1898.

12. Frederic Dan Huntington, *Personal Religious Life in the Ministry and in Ministering Women* (New York: Thomas Whittaker, 1900), 9.

13. *New-York Evangelist*, March 8, 1877.

14. A. L. Byron-Curtiss, "Bishop Frederic Dan Huntington as I Knew Him," *Historical Magazine of the Protestant Episcopal Church* 25 (December 1956): 378.

15. Arria S. Huntington, *Memoirs and Letters of Frederic Dan Huntington* (Boston and New York: Houghton, Mifflin and Co., 1909), 31.

16. Huntington, *Memoirs and Letters of Frederic Dan Huntington*, 326.

17. *Broome Republican*, October 29, 1879.

18. Augustus Beard to John Mears, January 20, 1879, Oneida Community Collection, Special Collections Research Center, Syracuse University Libraries.

19. *American Socialist*, February 20, 1879.

20. *Syracuse Daily Courier*, May 18, 1874.

21. Rev. C. C. Stratton, ed., *Autobiography of Erastus O. Haven* (New York: Phillips and Hunt, 1883), 324.

22. Alexander Winchell, "A Memorial Discourse on the Life and Services of Rev. Erastus O. Haven" (Ann Arbor: University of Michigan, 1882), 37.

23. Stratton, *Autobiography of Erastus O. Haven*, 320.

24. *New York Herald*, November 9, 1874.

25. Spencer Klaw, *Without Sin: The Life and Death of the Oneida Community* (New York: Penguin, 1993), 237.

26. *Utica Morning Herald*, February 13, 1879.

27. *New York Times*, June 16, 1882.

28. Constance Noyes Robertson, *Oneida Community: The Breakup, 1876–1881* (Syracuse, NY: Syracuse Univ. Press, 1972), 79.

11. The Ministers' War

1. *Sixty Years of Saint Lawrence* (Canton, NY: St. Lawrence University, 1916), 56.

2. *The National Cyclopedia of American Biography* II (New York: James T. White & Co., 1882), 141.

3. *Syracuse Standard*, May 8, 1898.

4. *Regents Bulletin of the University of the State of New York* 56 (January 1902), r66.

5. *Utica Morning Herald*, February 15, 1879.

6. *Utica Daily Press*, February 28, 1888.

7. *Christian Advocate*, September 1, 1911.

8. *Western Christian Advocate*, April 26, 1911.

9. Jessie T. Peck, *The True Woman: Or Life and Happiness at Home and Abroad* (New York: Carlton & Porter, 1867), 208.

10. *American Socialist*, February 20, 1879.

11. Henry Reed Stiles, *The History and Genealogies of Ancient Windsor, Connecticut* (Hartford, CT: Case, Lockwood & Brainard Co., 1891), 843.

12. Nancy F. Cott, *Public Vows: A History of Marriage and the Nation* (Cambridge, MA: Harvard Univ. Press, 2000), 30.

13. *American Socialist*, February 20, 1879.

14. L. E. Goulding, *Twenty-Fifth Anniversary of the First Congregational Church, Oswego, N.Y.* (Oswego, NY: B. J. Oliphant, 1882), 15.

15. *American Socialist*, February 20, 1879.

16. Jane Kathryn Riess, "'Heathen in Our Fair Land': Presbyterian Women Missionaries in Utah, 1870–90," *Journal of Mormon History* 26 (Spring 2000): 169.

17. Riess, "'Heathen in Our Fair Land,'" 170.

18. *Syracuse Daily Courier*, February 15, 1879.

19. *Syracuse Daily Courier*, February 15, 1879.

12. Arousing a Sentiment

1. *Independent*, February 20, 1879.

2. *Utica Morning Herald*, February 15, 1879.

3. *New-York Evangelist*, September 25, 1879.

4. *New York Tribune*, March 29, 1879.

5. *American Socialist*, February 20, 1879.

6. *American Socialist*, February 20, 1879.

7. Robert S. Fogarty, *Desire and Duty at Oneida: Tirzah Miller's Intimate Memoir* (Bloomington: Indiana Univ. Press, 2000), 164.

8. Constance Noyes Robertson, *Oneida Community: The Breakup, 1876–1881* (Syracuse, NY: Syracuse Univ. Press, 1972), 96.

9. John E. Smith, *Our County and Its People: A Descriptive and Biographical Record of Madison County, New York* (Boston: Boston History Co., 1890), 70.

10. James H. Smith, *History of Chenango and Madison Counties, New York*, vol. 2 (Syracuse, NY: D. Mason & Co., 1880), 722.

11. Smith, *History of Chenango and Madison Counties, New York*, 722.

12. *Syracuse Daily Courier*, March 10, 1879.

13. *Broome Republican*, October 29, 1879.

14. Ezra Heywood, *Cupid's Yokes: The Binding Forces of Conjugal Life*, (Princeton, MA: Co-operative Publishing Co., 1878), 14.

15. Heywood, *Cupid's Yokes*, 19.

16. Helen Lefkowitz Horowitz, *Rereading Sex: Battles over Sexual Knowledge and Suppression in Nineteenth-Century America* (New York: Alfred A. Knopf, 2002), 425.

17. Horowitz, *Rereading Sex*, 431.

18. Horowitz, 433.

19. Robertson, *Oneida Community: The Breakup, 1876–1881*, 107

20. *Syracuse Morning Standard*, June 20, 1879.

21. *Syracuse Morning Standard*, June 20, 1879.

22. *Broome Republican*, October 29, 1879.

23. *Syracuse Journal*, July 12, 1904.

24. *Syracuse Morning Standard*, June 21, 1879.

25. *Roman Citizen*, June 27, 1879.

26. Augustus Beard to Frederic Dan Huntington, July 26, 1879, Oneida Community Collection, Special Collections Research Center, Syracuse University Libraries.

27. Augustus Beard to Frederic Dan Huntington, July 26, 1879.

28. Wolcott Calkins, "Eating and Drinking Unworthily," *Presbyterian Quarterly and Princeton Review* 2 (October 1873): 739.

29. James O. Putnam, *Addresses, Speeches and Miscellanies* (Buffalo, NY: Peter, Paul and Brother, 1880), 19.

13. Oneida Turns a Page

1. Maren Lockwood Carden, *Oneida: Utopian Community to Modern Corporation* (Baltimore, MD: Johns Hopkins Univ. Press, 1969), 101.

2. Constance Noyes Robertson, *Oneida Community: The Breakup, 1876–1881* (Syracuse, NY: Syracuse Univ. Press, 1972), 110.

3. Pierrepont Noyes, *My Father's House* (New York: Farrar and Rinehart, 1937), 152.

4. Spencer Klaw, *Without Sin: The Life and Death of the Oneida Community* (New York: Penguin, 1993), 245.

5. Jane Kinsley Rich, ed., *A Lasting Spring: Jessie Catherine Kinsley, Daughter of the Oneida Community* (Syracuse, NY: Syracuse Univ. Press, 1983), 51.

6. *Tufts College Register of Officers of Instruction and Government, and Directory of Graduates* (Somerville, MA: Trustees of Tufts College, 1901), 33.

7. *Oswego Daily Times*, July 2, 1879.

8. *Hamilton Literary Monthly*, December 1887, 152.

9. *Oswego Daily Times*, July 2, 1879.

10. Robertson, *Oneida Community: The Breakup, 1876–1881*, 104.

11. Robert S. Fogarty, *Desire and Duty at Oneida: Tirzah Miller's Intimate Memoir* (Bloomington: Indiana Univ. Press, 2000), 60.

12. John Humphrey Noyes, "Essay on Scientific Propagation" (Oneida, NY: Oneida Community, 1872), 12.

13. Lawrence Foster, *Religion and Sexuality: Three American Communal Experiments in the Nineteenth Century* (New York: Oxford Univ. Press, 1981), 76.

14. Fogarty, *Desire and Duty at Oneida*, 21.

15. *Rock Island Daily Argus*, January 12, 1871.

16. Brian Connolly, *Domestic Intimacies: Incest and the Liberal Subject in Nineteenth Century America* (Philadelphia: Univ. of Pennsylvania Press, 2014), 80.

17. Connolly, *Domestic Intimacies*, 91.

18. Connolly, 98.

19. *Albany Law Journal* 22 (1880): 403.

20. Ellen Wayland-Smith, *Oneida: From Free-Love Utopia to the Well-Set Table* (New York: Picador, 2016), 174.

21. *Oswego Daily Times*, July 3, 1879.

22. S. N. D. North, *Old Greek, an Old-Fashioned Professor in an Old-Fashioned College* (New York: McClure, Phillips & Co., 1905), 45.

23. *Utica Morning Herald*, July 26, 1897.

24. Robertson, *Oneida Community: The Breakup, 1876–1881*, 135.

25. *Independent*, September 11, 1879.

26. Wayland-Smith, *Oneida*, 64.

27. Robertson, *Oneida Community: The Breakup, 1876–1881*, 130.

28. Robertson, 132.

29. Robertson, 137.

30. Fogarty, *Desire and Duty at Oneida*, 173.

31. *Broome Republican*, October 29, 1879.

32. *Broome Republican*, October 29, 1879.

33. Fogarty, *Desire and Duty at Oneida*, 179.

34. *Syracuse Morning Standard*, August 30, 1879.

35. *Utica Morning Herald*, August 30, 1879.

36. *Utica Morning Herald*, August 30, 1879.

37. *Utica Morning Herald*, September 1, 1879.

38. Robertson, *Oneida Community: The Breakup, 1876–1881*, 169.

39. Robertson, 185.

40. *Roman Citizen*, October 10, 1879.

41. *Roman Citizen*, October 10, 1879.

42. *Broome Republican*, October 29, 1879.

43. *Utica Morning Herald*, October 23, 1879.

44. Robertson, *Oneida Community: The Breakup, 1876–1881*, 230.

14. A Pure and Pious Zeal

1. Washington Frothingham, *History of Montgomery County* (Syracuse, NY: D. Mason & Co., 1892), 366.

2. *New York Times*, September 4, 1879.

3. *Ithaca Daily Journal*, July 28, 1879.

4. *National Advocate*, November 1918, 144

5. Lisa M. F. Andersen, *The Politics of Prohibition: American Governance and the Prohibition Party* (New York: Cambridge Univ. Press, 2013), 58.

6. *Lowville Times*, October 9, 1879.

7. *Columbia Spectator*, April 29, 1909.

8. Edison E. Dayton, *Brief Sketches of a Few Early Distinguished Graduates of Hamilton College* (Privately printed, 1936), 64.

9. *Newark Union*, November 1, 1879.

10. *Newark Union*, November 1, 1879.

11. *St. Lawrence Herald*, October 4, 1879.

12. *The Hamiltonian* (Clinton, NY: Curtis and Childs, 1881), 93.

13. H. Kendall to John W. Mears, August 31, 1880, Oneida Community Collection, Special Collections Research Center, Syracuse University Libraries.

14. *New-York Evangelist*, November 17, 1881.

15. Maren Lockwood Carden, *Oneida: Utopian Community to Modern Corporation* (Baltimore, MD: Johns Hopkins Univ. Press, 1969), 114.

16. John W. Mears, "The Kant Centennial," *Journal of Speculative Philosophy* 15 (July 1881): 293.

17. Mears, "The Kant Centennial," 303.

18. *Hamilton Literary Monthly*, September 1881, 60.

19. Spencer Klaw, *Without Sin: The Life and Death of the Oneida Community* (New York: Penguin, 1993), 163.

20. *New-York Evangelist*, November 17, 1881.

21. Walter Pilkington, *Hamilton College: 1812–1962* (Clinton, NY: Hamilton College), 167.

22. *Utica Morning Herald*, November 11, 1881.

23. *Clinton Courier*, November 17, 1881.

24. Dayton, *Brief Sketches of a Few Early Distinguished Graduates of Hamilton College*, 62.

25. *Hamilton Literary Monthly*, November 1881, 147.

26. *New-York Evangelist*, November 17, 1881.

27. *New-York Evangelist*, September 25, 1879.

28. Arria S. Huntington, *Memoirs and Letters of Frederic Dan Huntington* (Boston and New York: Houghton, Mifflin and Co., 1906), 326.

29. *New-York Evangelist*, August 26, 1880.

30. *O. C. Daily Journal*, February 7, 1866.

31. Robert S. Fogarty, *Desire and Duty at Oneida: Tirzah Miller's Intimate Memoir* (Bloomington: Indiana Univ. Press, 2000), 164.

32. Allan Estlake, *The Oneida Community: A Record of an Attempt to Carry Out the Principles of Christian Unselfishness and Scientific Race-Improvement* (London: George Redway, 1900), 7.

33. John Humphrey Noyes to Abel Easton, June 18, 1879, Oneida Community Collection, Special Collections Research Center, Syracuse University Libraries.

34. *New-York Evangelist*, September 25, 1879.

35. *American Socialist*, February 10, 1876.

36. *Utica Morning Herald*, November 11, 1881.

BIBLIOGRAPHY

Archives and Special Collections

Hamilton College Archives.

New York Society for the Suppression of Vice records, Manuscript Division, Library of Congress.

Oneida Community Collection, Special Collection Research Center, Syracuse University Libraries.

Oneida County Historical Society.

Presbyterian Historical Society, the National Archives of the Presbyterian Church (USA).

Newspapers

American Socialist
Albany Evening Post
Auburn Daily Bulletin
Brookfield Courier
Broome Republican
Catholic Telegraph
Chicago Tribune
Christian Advocate
Christian Observer
Clinton Courier
Congregationalist and Advance
Fairport Herald
Frank Leslie's Illustrated Newspaper
Fulton Times
Independent
Ithaca Daily Journal

Jackson Weekly Clarion
Lewis County Democrat
Lowville Times
Malone Palladium
Memphis Appeal
Mexico Independent
Newark Courier
New Haven Sunday Register
New York Daily Tribune
New-York Evangelist
New York Herald
New York Observer
The New York Times
New York Tribune
O. C. Daily Journal
Ogdensburg Journal

Oneida Circular
Oswego Daily Palladium
Philadelphia Evening Telegraph
Plattsburgh Sentinel
Rock Island Evening Argus
Roman Citizen
Sacramento Union
Saratogian
St. Lawrence Herald
Syracuse Daily Courier
Syracuse Daily Journal

Syracuse Morning Standard
Syracuse Post-Standard
Ticonderoga Sentinel
Utica Daily Press
Utica Morning Herald
Utica Observer
Vineland Independent
Washington Evening Star
Western Christian Advocate
Westfield Republican

Books and Articles

Abbot, Edwin Hale. *Apocrypha Concerning the Class of 1855 of Harvard College.* Boston: A. Mudge & Son, 1880.

Abrams, Kerry. "Polygamy, Prostitution, and the Federalization of Immigration Law." *Columbia Law Review* 105 (April 2005): 641–716.

Albany Law Journal 22 (1880): 403.

Alewitz, Sam. *Sanitation and Public Health: Philadelphia, 1870–1900.* Case Western Reserve University, 1981.

Alexander, Charles Wesley. *Poor Ellen Stuart's Fate; Or, Victim of the Free Love Institute in Oneida, N.Y.* Philadelphia: Co-Operative Publishing House, 1868

Allison, Charles Elmer. *A Historical Sketch of Hamilton College, Clinton, New York.* Yonkers, New York, 1889.

Alumni Record and General Catalog of Syracuse University. Edited by Frank Smalley. Syracuse: Alumni Association of Syracuse University, 1911.

Andersen, Lisa M. F. *The Politics of Prohibition: American Governance and the Prohibition Party.* New York: Cambridge Univ. Press, 2013.

Annual Report of the Regents of the University of the State of New York 101. Troy: Troy Press Co., 1888.

Anson Judd Upson: A Memorial. Albany: University of the State of New York, 1903.

Armentrout, Don S., and Robert Boak Slocum, eds. *An Episcopal Dictionary of the Church: A User-Friendly Reference for Episcopalians.* New York: Church Publishing, Inc., 1999.

Bagg, M. M., ed. *Memorial History of Utica, N.Y.: From Its Settlement to the Present Time.* Syracuse, NY: D. Mason & Co., 1892.

Barkun, Michael. *Crucible of the Millennium: The Burned-Over District of New York in the 1840s.* Syracuse, NY: Syracuse Univ. Press, 1986.

Beard, Augustus Field. *A Crusade of Brotherhood: A History of the American Missionary Association.* Boston: Pilgrim Press, 1909.

Bell, Alfreda Eva. *Boadicea, the Mormon Wife.* Philadelphia: Arthur R. Orton, 1855.

Bennett, D. M. *Trial of D. M. Bennett in the United States Circuit Court.* New York: Truth Seeker Office, 1879.

Bielby, Isaac. *Sheriffs of Oneida County.* Utica, NY: P. E. Kelly, 1890.

Biographical Directory of the United States Congress. http://bioguide.congress .gov/scripts/biodisplay.pl?index=B000077.

Bowman, Matthew. *The Mormon People and the Making of a Faith.* New York: Random House, 2012.

Boyd, William. *Fifty Years After, Or, a Half-century of Presbyterianism in Camden, New Jersey.* Philadelphia: Franklin Print, 1890.

Brainard, Lucy Abigail. *The Genealogy of the Brainerd-Brainard Family in America, 1649–1908.* Volume 2. Hartford, CT: Case, Lockwood and Brainard, 1908.

Brooks, Elbridge Gerry. *Three Sermons: Suggested by the Death of Rev. Albert Barnes.* Philadelphia: Review Printing House, 1871.

Bruce, Dwight H., ed. *Memorial History of Syracuse, N.Y.* Syracuse: H. P. Smith & Co., 1891.

Byron-Curtiss, A. L. "Bishop Frederic Dan Huntington as I Knew Him." *Historical Magazine of the Protestant Episcopal Church* 25 (December 1956): 378–90.

Calkins, Wolcott. "Eating and Drinking Unworthily." *Presbyterian Quarterly and Princeton Review* 2 (October 1873) 737–41.

Campbell v. Crampton. 2 Fed. Rpt. 417, 1880.

Carden, Maren Lockwood. *Oneida: Utopian Community to Modern Corporation.* Baltimore, MD: Johns Hopkins Univ. Press, 1969.

Channing, Walter. *The Mental Status of Guiteau, the Assassin of President Garfield.* Cambridge: Riverside Press, 1882.

Cherrington, Ernest H. *The Evolution of Prohibition in the United States of America.* Westerville, OH: American Issue Press, 1920.

Connolly, Brian. *Domestic Intimacies: Incest and the Liberal Subject in Nineteenth-Century America*. Philadelphia: Univ. of Pennsylvania Press, 2014.

Cook, Joseph. *The Boston Monday Lectures*. London: R. D. Dickinson, 1881.

Cookinham, Henry J. *History of Oneida County from 1700 to the Present Day*. Chicago: S. J. Clark Publishing Co., 1912.

Cott, Nancy F. *Public Vows: A History of Marriage and the Nation*. Cambridge, MA: Harvard Univ. Press. 2000.

Cross, Whitney R. "Mormonism in the Burned-Over District." *New York History* 25 (July 1944): 326–38.

Darling, Richard W. *Memorial of Henry Darling*. Utica, New York, 1893.

Dayton, Edison E. *Brief Studies of a Few Early Distinguished Graduates of Hamilton College*. Privately printed, 1936.

Degler, Carl N. "What Ought to Be and What Was: Women's Sexuality in the Nineteenth Century." *American Historical Review* 79 (December 1974): 1467–90.

Demaria, Richard. *Communal Love at Oneida: A Perfectionist Vision of Authority, Property, and Sexual Order*. New York: Edward Mellen Press, 1978.

Dennis, Donna. *Licentious Gotham: Erotic Publishing and Its Prosecution in Nineteenth-Century New York*. Cambridge, MA: Harvard Univ. Press, 2009.

———. "Obscenity Law and the Conditions of Freedom in Nineteenth-Century America." *Law and Social Inquiry* 27 (2002): 369–99.

Devoy, John. *Rochester and the Post Express: A History of the City of Rochester from the Earliest Times*. Rochester, NY: Post Express Printing Co., 1895.

Dixon, William Hepworth. *New America*. Volume 2. London: Hurst and Blackett, 1867.

———. *Spiritual Wives*. Volume 2. Leipzig, Germany: Bernard Tauchnitz, 1868.

Doherty, Robert. "Social Bases for the Presbyterian Schism of 1837–38: The Philadelphia Case." *Journal of Social History* 2 (Fall 1968): 69–79.

Doyle, Michael. *The Forestport Breaks: A Nineteenth-Century Conspiracy along the Black River Canal*. Syracuse, NY: Syracuse Univ. Press, 2004.

Dunkelman, Mark J. *Gettysburg's Unknown Soldier: The Life, Death and Celebrity of Amos Humiston*. Westport, CT: Praeger, 1999.

Eastman, Hubbard. *Noyesism Unveiled: A History of the Sect Self-styled Perfectionists*. Brattleboro, VT: Hubbard Eastman, 1849.

Ellis, John B. *Free Love and Its Votaries: Or, American Socialism Unmasked.* New York: United States Publishing Company, 1870.

Estlake, Allan. *The Oneida Community: A Record of an Attempt to Carry Out the Principles of Christian Unselfishness and Scientific Race-Improvement.* London: George Redway, 1900.

Finney, Charles G. *Charles G. Finney; An Autobiography.* Westwood, NJ: Fleming H. Revell Co., 1908.

Fogarty, Robert S. *Desire and Duty at Oneida: Tirzah Miller's Intimate Memoir.* Bloomington: Indiana Univ. Press, 2000.

———. "Religious Inventions in America: New Religious Movements." *OAH Magazine of History* 22 (January 2008): 19–23.

Foster, Lawrence. *Religion and Sexuality: Three American Communal Experiments in the Nineteenth Century.* New York: Oxford Univ. Press, 1981.

———. "The Rise and Fall of Utopia: The Oneida Community Crises of 1852 and 1879." *Communal Societies* 8 (1988): 1–17.

Franklin, C. E., ed. *American Education, From Kindergarten to College.* Albany: New York Education Co., 1902.

Frisken, Amanda. "Obscenity, Free Speech and 'Sporting News' in 1870s America." *Journal of American Studies* 42 (December 2008): 537–77.

Frothingham, Washington. *History of Montgomery County.* Syracuse, NY: D. Mason & Co., 1892.

Fuller, Wayne E. *Morality and the Mail in Nineteenth-Century America.* Urbana: Univ. of Illinois Press, 2003.

Funeral Services Held in the First Presbyterian Church, Philadelphia, Dec. 28, 1870. Philadelphia: J. B. Rogers Co., 1871.

Galpin, W. Freeman. *Syracuse University: The Pioneer Days.* Syracuse, NY: Syracuse Univ. Press, 1952.

Goldsmith, Barbara. *Other Powers: The Age of Suffrage, Spiritualism, and the Scandalous Victoria Woodhull.* New York: Alfred A. Knopf, 1998.

Goulding, L. E. *Twenty-Fifth Anniversary of the First Congregational Church, Oswego, N.Y.* Oswego, NY: B. J. Oliphant, 1882.

Green, Ashbel. *The Christian Advocate.* Volume 8. Philadelphia: A. Finley, 1830.

Guarneri, Carl J. "Reconstructing the Antebellum Communitarian Movement: Oneida and Fourierism." *Journal of the Early Republic* 16 (Autumn 1996): 463–88.

Haines, Michael. "Fertility and Mortality in the United States." http://eh.net/encyclopedia/fertility-and-mortality-in-the-united-states/.

Hamilton College Annual Catalogue, 1870–1871. Clinton, New York, 1870.

Hamilton College Half-Century Annalists' Letters. https://www.hamilton.edu/about/history/half-century-annalists-letters.

Hamilton Literary Monthly, September 1881.

Hamilton Literary Monthly, November 1881.

Hamilton Literary Monthly, December 1887.

Hamiltonian, The. Clinton, NY: Curtis and Childs, 1881.

Hart, John Seely. *A Manual of American Literature: A Textbook for Schools and Colleges*. Philadelphia: Eldredge & Brother, 1872.

Hein, David, and Gardiner H. Shattuck Jr. *The Episcopalians*. New York: Church Publishing, Inc., 2004.

Heywood, Ezra. *Cupid's Yokes: Or, The Binding Forces of Conjugal Life*. Princeton, MA: Co-operative Publishing Co., 1878.

Higginson, Mary Thacher. *Thomas Wentworth Higginson: The Story of His Life*. Boston: Houghton Mifflin Co., 1914.

Hinds, William Alfred. *American Communities and Co-operative Colonies*. Chicago: Charles H. Kerr & Co., 1908.

Horowitz, Helen Lefkowitz. *Rereading Sex: Battles over Sexual Knowledge and Suppression in Nineteenth-Century America*. New York: Alfred A. Knopf, 2002.

Huntington, Arria S. *Memoirs and Letters of Frederic Dan Huntington*. Boston and New York: Houghton, Mifflin and Co., 1906.

Huntington, Frederic Dan. *Personal Religious Life in the Ministry and in Ministering Women*. New York: Thomas Whittaker, 1900.

———. *Home and College*. Boston: Crosby, Nichols, Lee & Co., 1860.

Jennings, Chris. *Paradise Now: The Story of American Utopianism*. New York: Random House, 2016.

Johnson, James E. "Charles G. Finney and Oberlin Perfectionism." *Journal of Presbyterian History* 46 (March 1968): 42–57.

Joy, Arthur F. *The Queen of the Shakers*. Minneapolis: T. S. Denison, 1960.

Junkin, George. *The Vindication, Containing a History of the Trial of the Rev. Albert Barnes*. Philadelphia: Wm. S. Martien, 1836.

Justice, Benjamin. "Thomas Nast and the Public School of the 1870s." *History of Education Quarterly* 45 (Summer 2005): 171–206.

Jutkins, Andrew J. *Hand-book of Prohibition: 1885*. Chicago: 87 Washington Street, 1885.

Kant, Immanuel. *The Critique of Pure Reason*. Chicago: Encyclopedia Britannica, Inc., 1952.

Karsten, Peter. "Four 'Cousins-in-Law.'" *Journal of Politics and Law* 8 (2015): 106–26.

Kern, Louis J. *An Ordered Love: Sex Roles and Sexuality in Victorian Utopias*. Chapel Hill: Univ. of North Carolina Press, 1981.

Kesselman, Amy. "The 'Freedom Suit': Feminism and Dress Reform in the United States, 1848–1875." *Gender and Society* 5 (December 1991): 495–510.

Klaw, Spencer. *Without Sin: The Life and Death of the Oneida Community*. New York: Penguin, 1993.

LaMoy, William T. "Two Documents Concerning the Oneida Community's Practice of Complex Marriage." *New England Quarterly* 85 (March 2012): 119–37.

Lee, Catherine. "'Where the Danger Lies': Race, Gender, and Chinese and Japanese Exclusion, 1870 to 1924." *Sociological Forum* 25 (June 2010): 248–71.

Marsh, John. *Putnam and the Wolf; Or, the Monster Destroyed*. Hartford, CT: D. F. Robinson & Co., 1829.

Marten, James Allen. *Civil War America: Voices from the Home Front*. New York: Fordham Univ. Press, 2007.

Maynard, Reuben Leslie. *History of the Class of 1884, Hamilton College 1884–1914*. New York City, 1914.

Mayo, Louise Abbie. *The Ambivalent Image: Nineteenth-Century America's Perception of the Jew*. Madison, NJ: Fairleigh Dickinson Univ. Press, 1988.

McGee, Anita Newcomb. "An Experiment in Human Stirpiculture." *American Anthropologist* 4 (October 1891): 319–26.

Mears, John. *The Beggars of Holland the Grandees of Spain: A History of the Reformation in the Netherlands, from A.D. 1200 to 1578*. New York: A. D. F. Randolph and Co., 1867.

———. *Biographical Notice of Henry Haller Mears, Sr*. Philadelphia: James B. Rogers Co., 1873.

———. *The Church and Temperance*. New York: National Temperance Society and Publication House, 1872.

———. *From Exile to Overthrow: A History of the Jews from the Babylonian Captivity to the Destruction of the Second Temple*. Philadelphia: Presbyterian Publication Committee, 1881.

———. *Heroes of Bohemia: Huss, Jerome and Zisca*. Philadelphia: Presbyterian Publication Committee, 1879.

———. *Martyrs of France; Or, the Witness of the Reformed Church of France, From the Reign of Francis First to the Revocation of the Edict of Nantes*. Philadelphia: Presbyterian Publication Committee, 1864.

———. *The Story of Madagascar*. Philadelphia: Presbyterian Publication Committee, 1873.

———. "The Antagonisms, Perils and Glory of the Spiritual Philosophy," *American Presbyterian Review* 3 (October 1871): 597–625.

———. "The Centennial of Kant's Kritik." *Journal of Speculative Philosophy* 15 (January 1881): 92–95.

———. "The Kant Centennial." *Journal of Speculative Philosophy* 15 (July 1881): 225—40.

Melton, Julius. *Presbyterian Worship in America: Changing Patterns Since 1787*. Richmond, VA: John Knox Press, 1967.

Memorial of Samuel Gilman Brown. New York: Trow's Printing and Bookbinding Co., 1886.

Miller, Samuel. *Presbyterian Reunion: A Memorial Volume, 1837–1871*. New York: DeWitt C. Lent & Co., 1870.

Mohr, James C. *Abortion in America: The Origins and Evolution of National Policy, 1800–1900*. Oxford: Oxford Univ. Press, 1978.

Montgomery, Morton L. *History of Berks County in Pennsylvania*. Philadelphia: Everts, Peck and Richards, 1886.

Morrison, Howard Alexander. "The Finney Takeover of the Second Great Awakening during the Oneida Revivals of 1825–1827." *New York History* 59 (January 1978): 27–53.

Murlin, Edgar L. *The Red Book*. Albany, NY: James B. Lyon, 1893.

The National Cyclopaedia of American Biography II. New York: James T. White & Co., 1892.

Nevin, Alfred, ed. *Encyclopedia of the Presbyterian Church in the United States of America*. Philadelphia: Presbyterian Encyclopedia Publishing Co., 1884.

Nevins, Allan. *The Emergence of Modern America: 1865–1878*. New York: Macmillan and Co., 1928.

New Englander and Yale Review 45. New Haven, CT: William L. Kingsley. 1886.

New York Society for the Suppression of Vice. *Second Annual Report*. New York, 1876.

———. *Fifth Annual Report*, New York, 1879.

Nordhoff, Charles. *The Communistic Societies of the United States*. New York: Harper and Brothers, 1875.

North, Edward. "An Address Delivered Before the Sons of Temperance on July 4, 1848." Utica, NY: H.H. Curtiss, 1848.

North, S. N. D. *Old Greek, an Old-Fashioned Professor in an Old-Fashioned College*. New York: McClure, Phillips & Co., 1905.

Noyes, George Wallingford, comp., and Lawrence Foster, ed. *Free Love in Utopia: John Humphrey Noyes and the Origin of the Oneida Community*. Urbana: Univ. of Illinois Press, 2000.

Noyes, John Humphrey. *Bible Communism*. Oneida, NY: Oneida Community, 1849.

———. *Confessions of John H. Noyes. Part 1. Confession of Religious Experience*. Oneida Reserve: Leonard & Co., 1849.

———. *Dixon and his Copyists*. Wallingford, CT: Oneida Community, 1871.

———. "Essay on Scientific Propagation." Oneida, NY: Oneida Community, 1872.

———. *History of American Socialisms*. New York: Dover Publications, 1966.

———. *Male Continence*. Oneida, NY: Office of Oneida Circular, 1872.

Noyes, Pierrepont. *My Father's House*. New York: Farrar & Rinehart, 1937.

Olin, Jr., Spencer C. "The Oneida Community and the Instability of Charismatic Authority." *Journal of American History* 67 (September 1980): 285–300.

Oneida Association. *First Annual Report of Oneida Association*. Oneida Reserve, NY: Leonard and Company, 1849.

Ostling, Joan K., and Richard N. *Mormon America: The Power and the Promise*. San Francisco: HarperOne, 1999.

Owen, Robert Dale. *Moral Physiology; Or, a Brief and Plain Treatise on the Population Question*. New York: Wright & Owen, 1830–31.

Pagliarini, Marie Ann. "The Pure American Woman and the Wicked Catholic Priest: An Analysis of Anti-Catholic Literature in Antebellum America." *Religion and American Culture: A Journal of Interpretation* 9 (Winter 1999): 9–128.

Parker, Robert Allerton. *A Yankee Saint: John Humphrey Noyes and the Oneida Community*. New York: G. P. Putnam, 1935.

Paz, D. G. "Monasticism and Social Reform in Late Nineteenth-Century America: The Case of Father Huntington." *Historical Magazine of the Protestant Episcopal Church* 48 (March 1979): 45–66.

Peck, Jesse T. *The True Woman: Or Life and Happiness at Home and Abroad*. New York: Carlton & Porter, 1867.

Pendleton, Jr., Othniel. "Temperance and the Evangelical Churches." *Journal of the Presbyterian Historical Society* 25 (March 1947): 14–45.

Percival, Kate. *The Life and Amours of the Beautiful, Gay and Dashing Kate Percival*. N.d. Electronically republished at http://www.gutenberg.org/cache/epub/29827/pg29827-images.html.

Pilkington, Walter. *Hamilton College: 1812–1962*. Clinton, NY: Hamilton College, 1962.

Pivar, David J. *Purity Crusade: Sexual Morality and Social Control, 1868–1900*. Westport, CT: Greenwood Press, 1973.

Potter, Eliphalet Nott. "Discourses Commemorative of Professor Tayler Lewis, Delivered at Commencement, 1877." Albany, NY: J. Munsell, 1878.

Powell, Lyman P. *The History of Education in Delaware*. Washington, DC: Government Printing Office, 1893.

Putnam, James O. *Addresses, Speeches and Miscellanies*. Buffalo: Peter, Paul and Brother, 1880.

Rich, Jane Kinsley, ed. *A Lasting Spring: Jessie Catherine Kinsley, Daughter of the Oneida Community*. Syracuse, NY: Syracuse Univ. Press, 1983.

Riddle, John M. *Eve's Herbs: A History of Contraception and Abortion in the West*. Cambridge, MA: Harvard Univ. Press, 1997.

Riess, Jana Kathryn. "'Heathen in Our Fair Land': Presbyterian Women Missionaries in Utah, 1870–90." *Journal of Mormon History* 26 (Spring 2000): 225–46.

Robertson, Constance Noyes. *Oneida Community: The Breakup, 1876–1881*. Syracuse, NY: Syracuse Univ. Press, 1972.

———. *Oneida Community Profiles*. Syracuse, NY: Syracuse Univ. Press, 1977.

Rohrer, James R. "The Origins of the Temperance Movement: A Reinterpretation." *Journal of American Studies* 24 (August 1990): 228–35.

Rosenberg, Charles E. "Sexuality, Class and Role in 19th-Century America." *American Quarterly* 25 (May 1973): 131–53.

The Courtland Saunders Tract for Soldiers. Philadelphia: Protestant Episcopal Book Society, 1863.

Schaff, David S. *The Life of Philip Schaff, in part autobiographical.* New York: Charles Scribner's Sons, 1897.

Scharf, John Thomas. *History of Delaware: 1609–1888.* Philadelphia: L. J. Richards, 1888.

Scharf, John Thomas, and Thompson, Westcott. *History of Philadelphia: 1609–1884.* Philadelphia: L. H. Everts, 1884.

Schmidt, Leigh Eric. "The Fashioning of a Modern Holiday: St. Valentine's Day, 1840–1870." *Winterthur Portfolio* 28 (Winter 1993): 209–45.

Sixty Years of Saint Lawrence. Canton, NY: St. Lawrence University, 1916.

Slawson, A. L. *Behind the Scenes; Or, an Exposé of Oneida Community.* Oneida, NY: A. L. Slawson, 1875.

Smalley, Frank, ed. *The Golden Jubilee of Syracuse University, 1870–1920.* Geneva, NY: W. F. Humphrey, 1920.

Smith, John E., ed. *Our County and Its People: A Descriptive and Biographical Record of Madison County, New York.* Boston: Boston History Co., 1890.

Smith, James H. *History of Chenango and Madison Counties, New York.* Vol. 2. Syracuse, NY: D. Mason & Co., 1880.

Smith, John L., comp. *History of the Corn Exchange Regiment, 118th Pennsylvania Volunteers, From Their First Engagement at Antietam to Appomattox.* Philadelphia: J. L. Smith, 1888.

Smith, Stephen Eliot. "Barbarians within the Gates: Congressional Debates on Mormon Polygamy, 1850–1879." *Journal of Church and State* 51 (August 2009): 587–616.

Stiles, Henry Reed. *The History and Genealogies of Ancient Windsor, Connecticut.* Hartford, CT: Case, Lockwood & Brainard Co., 1891.

Stratton, Rev. C. C., ed. *Autobiography of Erastus O. Haven.* New York: Phillips and Hunt, 1883.

Stryker, Peter. *Words of Trust.* Cliftondale, MA: Coates Brothers, 1887.

Survivors' Association, Corn Exchange Regiment. *History of the Corn Exchange Regiment.* Philadelphia: J. L. Smith, 1888.

Taintor, Charles Newhall. *Saratoga Illustrated: The Visitors Guide of Saratoga Springs.* New York: Taintor Brothers & Co., 1876.

Talbot, Christine. "Turkey Is in Our Midst: Orientalism and Contagion in Nineteenth-Century Anti-Mormonism." *Journal of Law and Family Studies* 8 (2006): 363–88.

"Tayler Lewis: In Memoriam." *Methodist Quarterly Review* 60 (October 1878): 604–31.

Teaford, Jon C. "Toward a Christian Nation: Religion, Law and Justice Strong." *Journal of Presbyterian History* 54 (Winter 1976): 422–37.

Thomas, Robert David. *The Man Who Would Be Perfect: John Humphrey Noyes and the Utopian Impulse*. Philadelphia: Univ. of Pennsylvania Press, 1977.

Thwing, Walter Elliot. *Thwing: A Genealogical, Biographical and Historical Account*. Boston: D. Clapp and Son. 1883.

Tufts College Register of Officers of Instruction and Government, and Directory of Graduates. Somerville, MA: Trustees of Tufts College, 1901.

Tyrrell Ian R. *Sobering Up: From Temperance to Prohibition in Antebellum America, 1800–1860*. Westport, CT: Greenwood Press, 1979.

Van de Warker, Ely. "A Gynecological Study of the Oneida Community." *American Journal of Obstetrics and Diseases of Women and Children* 17 (August 1884): 755–810.

Wager, Daniel. *Our County and Its People, Part II: Biography*. Boston: Boston History Co., 1896.

Wayland-Smith, Ellen. *Oneida: From Free-Love Utopia to the Well-Set Table*. New York: Picador, 2016.

Weigley, Russell F., ed. *Philadelphia: A 300-Year History*. New York: W. W. Norton & Co., 1982.

Weiner, Isaac. *Religion Out Loud: Religious Sound, Public Space, and American Pluralism*. New York: New York Univ. Press, 2014.

Weisbrod, Carol, and Sheingorn, Pamela. "Reynolds v. United States: Nineteenth-Century Forms of Marriage and the Status of Women." *Connecticut Law Review* 10 (1978): 828–58.

Weisbrod, Carol. "On the Breakup of Oneida." *Connecticut Law Review* 14 (Summer 1982): 717–32.

Wilson, Joseph M. *Presbyterian Historical Almanac and Annual Remembrancer of the Church for 1861*. Philadelphia: Joseph M. Wilson, 1861.

Winchell, Alexander. "A Memorial Discourse on the Life and Services of Rev. Erastus Otis Haven." Ann Arbor: University of Michigan, 1882.

Wineapple, Brenda. *Ecstatic Nation: Confidence, Crisis and Compromise, 1848–1877*. New York: HarperCollins, 2013.

Wood, Janice. "Prescription for a Periodical: Medicine, Sex, and Obscenity in the Nineteenth Century, as Told in *Dr. Foote's Health Monthly*." *American Periodicals* 18 (2008): 26–44.

Worden, Harriet M. *Old Mansion House Memories*. Oneida, New York, 1950.

Yale University. *The Centennial Celebration of the Founding of the Yale Divinity School, Held in Connection with the Fourteenth Annual Convocation*. New Haven, CT: Yale University, 1922.

Zimmer, Melanie. *Curiosities of Central New York*. Charleston, SC: History Press, 2012.

INDEX

Noyes, John Humphrey (*cont.*)
period of, 21–22; on perfectionism,
4, 21, 22–23, 24, 29; *Perfectionist*
newsletter by, 22; on personal critiques, 33; portrait of, *19*; potential
legal action against, 139–40, 143,
144, 145, 152, 170; on the press,
8–9; on property, 30; "Proposal
for a Modification of our Social
Platform," 152–53; reputation
of, 7; "Salvation from Sin in This
World," 121; on self-control, 17,
20, 76, 137; on sexual intercourse,
16, 22–23, 24, 100; on sexual
practices, 16–18, 22–28, 32–33,
76–77; Skinner's letter to, 152; on
stirpiculture, 77; Syracuse convention of 1879 and, 15, 121, 126;
theological education of, 20–21;
on Turkish baths, 94; Van de
Warker and, 99. *See also* complex
marriage
Noyes, Pierrepont, 143–44
Noyes, Polly (Hayes), 18–19
Noyes, Theodore: on abandonment
of complex marriage, 155; birth
of, 24; Duffield and, 151; on
public sentiment, 153; on regulating sexual practices, 32; sexual
bookkeeping and, 96–97; Van de
Warker and, 97, 99

Obscene Literature Act (New York
State), 74
obscene materials, 73–77; legislation
on, 3, 74–76, 82, 137–38, 145;
mail distribution of, 137, 150;
seizure of, 95–96, 113
O. C. Journal, 7
Ogdensburg Journal, 108, 162

Ohio, 100, 101, 149
older men and women, 17–18, 32, 33
Old School faction, 48, 52
118th Pennsylvania Volunteer Infantry (Corn Exchange Regiment), 55
154th New York Volunteer Infantry
Regiment, 57
162nd New York Volunteer Infantry,
97
Oneida Circular: on ascending fellowship, 17; on John Mears, 88,
89; on "Mills' war," 82; on Oneida
Community doctrine, 38; on
Synod of Presbyterians, 81; on visitors, 84, 88
Oneida Community: abandonment
of complex marriage by, 153–58;
classes of residents in, 153, 154–55;
commercial success of, 78, 146;
community dinner at, 85; community opinion of, 36, 37, 38, 78, 81,
82, 88–89, 90–91, 134, 135–36,
157–58; description of, 4; dissidents in, 140, 144, 164, 170; early
crusades against, 4–7, 14, 34–43;
employment by, 91, 146; establishment of, 4, 29–31; evolution of,
165; facial features of, 151; *First
Annual Report of Oneida Association*, 30, 34, 37; Fourth of July
celebration at, 88, 106; Garvin's
campaign against, 34–38; Luther
Guiteau and, 166; history of, 126;
Frederic Huntington on, 115–16;
informers from, 152; internal
problems of, 103, 104, 134, 138,
152, 164, 170–71; as joint-stock
company, 165; leadership of, 4,
96–100, 103, 134, 170–71; legal
vulnerabilities of, 80, 103–4,

Michael Doyle is the author of *The Forestport Breaks: A Nineteenth-Century Conspiracy along the Black River Canal* and *Radical Chapters: Pacifist Bookseller Roy Kepler and the Paperback Revolution*, both published by Syracuse University Press. A former reporter in the Washington bureau of McClatchy newspapers, he is currently a reporter for E&E News and a professorial lecturer at George Washington University's School of Media and Public Affairs. He graduated from Oberlin College and earned a Master of Studies in Law from Yale Law School and a Master in Government from Johns Hopkins University. He lives with his wife in Arlington, Virginia.